Searching Her Own Mystery

Searching Her Own Mystery

Nostra Aetate, the Jewish People,
and the Identity of the Church

Mark S. Kinzer

FOREWORD BY
Christoph Cardinal Schönborn

CASCADE *Books* • Eugene, Oregon

SEARCHING HER OWN MYSTERY
Nostra Aetate, the Jewish People, and the Identity of the Church

Copyright © 2015 Mark S. Kinzer. All rights reserved. Except for brief quotations in critical publications or reviews, no part of this book may be reproduced in any manner without prior written permission from the publisher. Write: Permissions, Wipf and Stock Publishers, 199 W. 8th Ave., Suite 3, Eugene, OR 97401.

Cascade Books
A Division of Wipf and Stock Publishers
199 W. 8th Ave., Suite 3
Eugene, OR 97401

www.wipfandstock.com

The author and publisher gratefully acknowledge permission to include, as Appendix 3, "The Jewishness of the Apostles and Its Implications for the Apostolic Church," by Jean-Miguel Garrigues, O.P. Originally published in *Nova et Vetera*, English Edition, Vol. 12, No. 1 (2013) 105–21. Also, as Appendix 4, "Finding our Way through Nicaea: The Deity of Jesus, Bilateral Ecclesiology, and Redemptive Encounter with the Living God," by Mark S. Kinzer. Originally published in *Kesher* 24 (2010) 29–52.

All Scripture quotations, unless otherwise indicated, are taken from the Holy Bible, New Revised Standard Version, NRSV, copyright 1989, Division of Christian Education of the National Council of the Churches of Christ in the United States of America. Used by permission. All rights reserved.

All quotations from official Vatican documents, unless otherwise indicated, are taken from the Vatican archive website, http://www.vatican.va/archive/index.htm.

ISBN 13: 978-1-4982-0331-9

Cataloging-in-Publication data:

Kinzer, Mark S.

Searching her own mystery : *Nostra Aetate*, the Jewish people, and the identity of the Church / Mark S. Kinzer, with a foreword by Christoph Cardinal Schönborn, and an appendix by Jean-Miguel Garrigues.

xvi + 262 p. ; 23 cm. Includes bibliographical references and index.

ISBN 13 978-1-4982-0331-9

1. Judaism—Relations—Catholic Church. 2. Catholic Church—Relations—Judaism. 3. Judaism—Relations—Christianity. 4. Christianity and other religions—Judaism. 5. Messianic Judaism. 6. Church. I. Schönborn, Christoph. II. Garrigues, Jean-Miguel, 1944–. III. Title.

BM535 K428 2015

Manufactured in the U.S.A.

For Stephen B. Clark and Fr. Jean-Miguel Garrigues

true guides in my search of the ecclesial mystery

Table of Contents

Foreword by Christoph Cardinal Schönborn | xi
Acknowledgements | xv

CHAPTER 1: The Ecclesiological Challenge of *Nostra Aetate* | 1
A Theological Revolution
Israel-Ecclesiology and Israel-Christology
Israel-Ecclesiology and the *Ecclesia ex Circumcisione*
Mapping the Road Ahead

CHAPTER 2: A Stranger in a Strange (Yet Familiar) Land | 25
From Theological Discourse to Personal Narrative
Family, Friends, Faith
Life in an Almost-Catholic Charismatic Community
From the Charismatic Renewal to Messianic Judaism
Birth of the Roman Catholic—Messianic Jewish Dialogue Group
A Distinctive Perspective
From Personal Narrative to Theological Discourse

CHAPTER 3: *Lumen Gentium*, Gloriam Israel | 40
A Christ-Centered Israel-Ecclesiology
Israel-Ecclesiology and the Jewish People
Eschatological Newness
The Catechism and *Lumen Gentium*
Developing the Teaching of *Lumen Gentium*
Two Complementary Perspectives

TABLE OF CONTENTS

CHAPTER 4: Priesthood, Apostleship, and the People of Israel | 61

The Letter to the Hebrews: Israel's Priesthood and Jesus' Priesthood
The Letter to the Ephesians: Israel's Priesthood and the Apostolic Office
The Letter to the Romans: Israel's Priesthood and the Priestly Remnant
Excursus: Apostolic Succession and Jewish Peoplehood
Conclusion

CHAPTER 5: Israel's Eschatological Renewal in Water and Spirit | 89

The Baptism of Jesus
"The Water of Rebirth"
Conclusion

CHAPTER 6: The Last Supper, the Eucharist, and the Jewish People | 106

The Eucharist, First-Century Judaism, and the Enduring Reality of the
        Jewish People
The Eucharistic Cup: Israel-Ecclesiology Rooted in Israel-Christology
The Eucharistic Bread: Israel-Christology Giving Birth to
        Israel-Ecclesiology
The Twelve: The Last Supper and the Mediation of Jewish Apostles
Conclusion

CHAPTER 7: Praying for Jerusalem, Feasting with the Messiah | 127

Jewish Sacrificial Worship in the Second Temple Period
Israel's Prayer and Israel's Sacrifice
The Eschatological Banquet and the Messianic Sacrifice
The Church and the "Jewish Eucharist"

CHAPTER 8: Jewish Life as Sacrament | 149

Sacrament and *Kedushah*
Judaism's Five Fundamental Sacramental Signs
Jesus, Jewish Sacramental Signs, and the *Ecclesia*
Conclusion

TABLE OF CONTENTS

CHAPTER 9: The Task of Mutual-Indwelling | 172
Ontological Mystery and Sacred Task
Sacramental Sign or Syncretistic Sect?
Steps Forward
A Notre Dame Inscription

APPENDIX 1. *Nostra Aetate* 4 | 191
APPENDIX 2. Documents of the Helsinki Consultation on Jewish Continuity in the Body of Christ | 193
APPENDIX 3. "The Jewishness of the Apostles and Its Implications for the Apostolic Church," by Jean-Miguel Garrigues, O.P. | 198
APPENDIX 4. "Finding our Way through Nicaea: The Deity of Jesus, Bilateral Ecclesiology, and Redemptive Encounter with the Living God," by Mark S. Kinzer | 216

Bibliography | 241
Name Index | 247
Scripture Index | 253

Foreword

It is a pleasure for me to introduce this important book by Mark Kinzer. I have known Mark for several years, during which time I have led a Catholic team in a dialogue group with Messianic Jews. Mark has been a member of this group since its inception in September 2000 when it was assembled by Fr. (and later Cardinal) Georges Cottier, O.P., Theologian of the Pontifical Household under Pope John Paul II. Fr. Cottier took this initiative with the encouragement of both the pope under whom he served and his successor, Benedict XVI. Pope John Paul II, Fr. Cottier, and Cardinal Ratzinger had all met with Messianic Jews in the years of preparation for the pope's act of repentance during his 2000 trip to Israel, and the convening of the dialogue group came within the context of that act.[1]

The group has met annually since its beginning, rotating its location between Jerusalem and Rome (with obvious symbolic import). Over the years the members of this group have come to know and understand one another, and to see each other as fellow believers in Jesus, the Messiah of Israel, the Son of God and Savior of the world. Strong bonds of unity and friendship have developed among us.

Through my experience in the dialogue group I have come to recognize Mark Kinzer as a major theologian whose work deserves serious attention in the Catholic world. I have been particularly struck by Mark's mastery of Catholic theology, which is evident in the current volume. When I first heard Mark speak of his past life, I realized that he had come to this knowledge of Catholicism through personal experience, for he had lived many years as a member of an ecumenical but predominantly Catholic charismatic community, "The Word of God," in Ann Arbor, Michigan.[2]

Mark's theological stature was confirmed for me when I discovered the high regard in which he is held by many in the United States, not only

---

1. For more details on this group and the events leading up to its inception from the perspective of Mark Kinzer, see chapter 2, pages 35–37.

2. Mark provides a vivid description of this community and its impact on his life in chapter 2, pages 29–32.

FOREWORD

among his Messianic Jewish brothers and sisters but also among Christian theologians. Along with Professor William Abraham of Southern Methodist University in Dallas, Mark has organized and led colloquia that have brought together leading Messianic Jewish scholars and a panel of theologians from various Christian Churches.[3] He has been able to assume this role because of the respect shown him by many promising young Messianic Jewish theologians and also by his peers, teachers of Christian theology who seek fidelity to Christ in the midst of an increasingly relativistic culture.[4]

Mark Kinzer became known in the United States through his outstanding books in the field of Messianic Jewish theology. The first is *Postmissionary Messianic Judaism: Redefining Christian Engagement with the Jewish People*, published in 2005. This was followed in 2011 by *Israel's Messiah and the People of God: A Vision for Messianic Jewish Covenant Fidelity*. These volumes have for the first time brought the distinctive voice of Messianic Judaism into discussions concerning the relationship between the Church and the Jewish people. The current volume, which contains much material that was first presented in our dialogue group, continues what Mark began in his earlier books.

Mark is not only a first-rate scholar—he is also a man of action. In addition to the meetings he has organized and led in Dallas with Professor William Abraham, Mark co-founded and co-leads (with Fr. Antoine Levy, O.P.) the Helsinki Consultation on Jewish Continuity in the Body of Christ. This initiative brings together Jews who believe in Jesus, whether from the Messianic Jewish movement or from various Church backgrounds. Meetings have taken place in various cities of Europe, including Helsinki, Paris, Berlin, Oslo, and Ede (in the Netherlands).[5] Mark has also been instrumental in the founding of several notable institutions within the Messianic Jewish world, such as Messianic Jewish Theological Institute, the Messianic Jewish Rabbinical Council, the Hashivenu Theological Forum, and Congregation Zera Avraham (Ann Arbor, Michigan).

---

3. The Christian theologians present have included Catholic scholars such as Bruce Marshall, Fr. Thomas Weinandy, and Fr. Jean-Miguel Garrigues, O.P. Fr. Garrigues has also been a member of the Catholic–Messianic Jewish Dialogue Group from its beginning in 2000. Among the Protestant scholars in attendance have been William Abraham, Kendall Soulen, Gerald McDermott, Fred Aquino, Kurt Anders Richardson, Donald Dayton, and Tommy Givens.

4. The group of young Messianic Jewish scholars includes David Rudolph, who with Joel Willitts has edited the remarkable volume *Introduction to Messianic Judaism*. The group also involves Jennifer Rosner, Jonathan Kaplan, and Akiva Cohen, along with veteran Messianic Jewish scholar Carl Kinbar.

5. For more on the Helsinki Consultation, see chapter 9, pages 182–83, and Appendix 2.

FOREWORD

As the reader will discover in this book, the theological reflections of Mark Kinzer focus upon and are set within the mysterious common reality that brings Judaism and Christianity into a spiritual unity more profound that the diversity of their religious institutions. It can be said that Mark's thinking brings to light the implications of the crucial statement of Pope John Paul II at the synagogue of Rome in 1987: "Your religion is not extrinsic to ours, but is intrinsic to it." Kinzer attempts to think through, in-depth and without syncretism, the meaning of the reciprocal immanence of Israel—the non-rejected People of God—in the Church, and of Messiah Jesus in Judaism. That is what he intends in all his writings, and what he seeks to convey through his concept of "bilateral ecclesiology." This concept presents Messianic Jews as that part of Israel that now houses Jesus as Messiah, Son of God and Savior of the world, just as the apostles and the Jerusalem community of Jewish believers in Jesus welcomed him at the beginning: from inside the people and tradition of Israel. Kinzer's work also draws upon and is paralleled by the writings of contemporary mainstream Jewish thinkers who examine the Jewish roots of faith in Jesus, even to the point of discovering those roots in such doctrines as the Incarnation and the Trinity.[6]

To those within the Christian Churches, and especially to Catholics, Mark Kinzer speaks with respect and appreciation. He tells us that he, a Messianic Jewish rabbi and theologian, is open to receiving the treasures of grace and wisdom deposited by the apostles and developed in the tradition of the Church, provided that we in turn are ready to start breathing with our "two lungs." Pope John Paul II employed this expression to refer to the Christian traditions of East and West. Kinzer uses it to speak of the more original and fundamental ecclesial duality in the one Body of Christ: that between Jews and gentiles. Will we hear the essential question he raises, he and the movement of Messianic Jews in whose name he speaks?

Christoph Cardinal Schönborn, Archbishop of Vienna, Austria

---

6. See, for example, Boyarin, *The Jewish Gospels* and *Border Lines*, and Wyschogrod, *Abraham's Promise*.

Acknowledgements

I would like to thank all the members of the Roman Catholic–Messianic Jewish Dialogue Group, past and present, who together have provided such a fertile environment for the ideas in this book to germinate. Among them, I am especially grateful to Christoph Cardinal Schönborn for contributing such a gracious foreword; to Fr. Peter Hocken, Richard Harvey, and David Rudolph, who gave many helpful suggestions for improving the content; and to Fr. Jean-Miguel Garrigues, who first planted in my mind the thought of writing such a volume. Fr. Jean-Miguel has enriched my life not only with his profound learning and wisdom, but also with his friendship, and for this I dedicate the volume to him. I also dedicate the volume to Stephen B. Clark, whose significant role in my own story I describe in chapter 2. I would never have embarked on this strange path as a Messianic Jew in continual interaction with Catholics if Steve had not taken an interest in me when I was still in my teens. Steve also read an early version of this book, and offered much useful advice. In addition, I thank Daniel Keating, Gerald McDermott, Miklos Vetö, and John Yocum for their perceptive comments on the manuscript, which aided me greatly in the writing process. I am ever grateful for my longtime friends, Fr. Prentice Tipton, Fr. Daniel Jones, and John Keating, who have encouraged me to think that Catholics might be receptive to what I have to share. Last but not least, I acknowledge the patience and support of Roz and Helen, wife and mother-in-law, who stand by me in all my exotic endeavors. For all the above, mentors, colleagues, friends, and family, I never cease to give thanks to the Holy Blessed One who is the ultimate source of every good gift.

1

The Ecclesiological Challenge of *Nostra Aetate*

A Theological Revolution

Two Popes and Four Propositions

On April 27, 2014 the Catholic Church officially recognized Pope John XXIII and Pope John Paul II as saints. Media reports focused on the appeal these two figures held for rival segments of the Church—John XXIII inspired progressives, while John Paul II earned the devotion of traditionalists. Little attention was given to the revolution in Catholic teaching and sensibility that these two Popes *jointly* accomplished—John XXIII as initiator, John Paul II as interpreter, emblematic personality, and implementer.

I refer to the new Catholic teaching concerning the Jewish people and their way of life. Pope John XXIII summoned the Council which would make that teaching an official part of Catholic dogma, and without his personal intervention that Council would have avoided the topic.[1] While he did not live to witness the adoption of *Nostra Aetate* in 1965, this extraordinary breakthrough in Jewish-Catholic relations is rightly credited to his pontificate.

Karol Cardinal Wojtyla was elected pope thirteen years after the adoption of *Nostra Aetate*. The document's teaching concerning the Jewish people had profound personal meaning for this son of Poland. He had grown up in the company of Jews, and had witnessed the tragedy of the Holocaust firsthand. The new pope behaved as though *Nostra Aetate* 4 imposed upon him a sacred obligation to explore its significance theologically and embody its truth in concrete deeds and relationships. With iconic acts such as his visit to the Rome Synagogue in 1986 and his pilgrimage to Jerusalem in

---

1. Connelly, *Enemy to Brother*, 239–40, 49.

2000, and in many public addresses dealing with the relationship between the Catholic Church and the Jewish people, this pope made the fourth chapter of *Nostra Aetate* a tangible and living reality.

The fourth chapter of *Nostra Aetate* inaugurated a revolution in Church teaching.[2] It was adopted only two decades after the fall of Nazi Germany, whose racial ideology was shared in part by many Catholics of that era who questioned whether even baptism could remove the stain upon the Jewish soul resulting from rejection of the Son of God.[3] In 1943 a Catholic theologian as eminent as Karl Adam could argue that the immaculate conception of Mary rendered her virtually a non-Jew: "Through a miracle of God's grace Mary is beyond those characteristics that are passed by blood from Jew to Jew."[4] While the focus on "blood" and "race" was a modern novelty, the belief among Christians that the Jewish people were corporately guilty of the crime of "deicide" (i.e., the murder of God) had a long and tragic history.

This context helps us better appreciate the significance of *Nostra Aetate* 4. This chapter established four propositions as fundamental to the Catholic view of the Jewish people.[5] First, in response to the still recent catastrophe of the Shoah, the document rejected the claim that the Jewish people were corporately culpable for the death of Jesus, and denounced all forms of anti-Semitism. This proposition seems obvious to most Christians in the twenty-first century, and it is difficult for us to conceive of a time when it would be a contentious assertion. The fact that we must now mobilize our historical imagination to understand the controversial nature of this aspect of *Nostra Aetate* is itself a tribute to the document's success.

However, *Nostra Aetate* 4 was not primarily an exercise in combating a false and harmful teaching. The remaining propositions articulated by the document are all positive in character.

The second focuses on the "mutual understanding and respect" that should exist between Christians and Jews owing to their common "spiritual patrimony." The description of this common heritage forms the core of

---

2. The complete text of *Nostra Aetate* 4 is found in Appendix 1.

3. John Connelly shows how widespread such views were among Catholics in this era. Here is one example: "In December 1933, Father Wilhelm Schmidt, the century's leading Catholic anthropologist, told an audience in Vienna that 'a perversion of the Jews' inner being,' was 'punishment' for killing Christ. 'Two thousand years have had a psychological effect on [Jews'] being,' intoned Schmidt, and that could not be 'undone by baptism'" (*Enemy to Brother*, 112).

4. Cited by Connelly, ibid., 21.

5. My numbering of these propositions follows my analysis of the logic of *Nostra Aetate*, rather than the order in which the propositions appear in the document.

Nostra Aetate 4. That heritage includes, of course, the "Old Testament," but it also draws upon the contribution of Jews who cherished and preserved those books after their composition and passed them on to the Church: "The Church, therefore, cannot forget that she received the revelation of the Old Testament through the people with whom God in his inexpressible mercy deigned to establish the ancient covenant." Moreover, Jesus himself and the Virgin Mary come from Jewish stock, as did "the apostles ... as well as most of the early disciples who proclaimed Christ to the world." Based on this "common patrimony," Christians should move beyond the mere renunciation of anti-Semitism and build a new relationship of trust and cooperative endeavor with their Jewish neighbors.

The second proposition of *Nostra Aetate* 4 seeks to foster a positive relationship between Christians and Jews on the basis of a common past. The third proposition goes further and asserts that the Jewish people share with Christians more than a common past: like the Church, the Jewish people have received an irrevocable calling from God and enjoy a special spiritual status in God's presence. Citing Paul's letter to the Romans (11:28–29), the document states that "according to the apostle, the Jews still remain most dear to God because of their fathers, for he does not repent of the gifts he makes nor of the calls he issues." In other words, the Jewish people remain an elect nation, retaining a unique role in the divine plan. The first proposition rejected the view that Jews suffer under a horrific curse. The third proposition declares that, in fact, they live under a singular blessing.

The sharing of ancient treasures should foster a relationship of "mutual understanding and respect" between Christians and Jews, and the Church's recognition of the election of "Abraham's stock" should inspire reverence for the Jewish people and their way of life. However, neither of these propositions requires that her relationship with the Jewish people constitute an essential feature of the Church's ongoing corporate identity. Jesus, his family, and his disciples were all Jews—but that was all in the remote past. Both the Church and the Jewish people enjoy a special status in the sight of God—but it is still possible that the Church's position as "the new people of God" is of such a higher order as to negate any sense of mutual interdependence. The relationship between the two communities may exist purely on an external level—as one might reasonably infer from *Lumen Gentium* 16, adopted almost one year before *Nostra Aetate*. Is there some reason to think that "Christians and Jews" are inextricably linked in God's sight, and that they possess not only a common heritage and two divinely appointed vocations but also an intertwined identity and destiny? The suggestion that such is the case forms the fourth and perhaps most important proposition of *Nostra Aetate* 4. While it is the final assertion in my exposition, in the document itself this proposition appears as the opening statement: "As this sacred synod searches into the mystery of the Church, it recalls the spiritual bond linking the people of the new covenant with Abraham's stock." I have drawn the title of my book from this crucial sentence, and the content of the sentence deserves special attention in my opening chapter.

The Jewish People and Judaism as "Intrinsic" to the Church

Are we justified in placing so much weight on this introductory statement of *Nostra Aetate* 4, which upon initial reading seems no more than a literary transition to a new topic? The history of the document and of its interpretation enable us to answer this question with a resounding "yes." In discussing a draft of the document at a Vatican Council session in September of 1964, the German bishops explained why they thought a Council statement dealing with the Jewish people was essential: "If the Church in Council makes a statement concerning her own nature, she cannot fail to mention her connection with God's people of the Old Covenant. . . ."[6] At that time the Dogmatic Constitution on the Church (*Lumen Gentium*) was in its final stages of development, and its official adoption two months later would constitute one of the greatest achievements of Vatican II.[7] Thus, "the Church in Council" was indeed about to make "a statement concerning her own nature."[8] For these German bishops, such a statement necessarily required reflection on the Church's relationship to the Jewish people.[9] It is this conviction—that the identity of the Church is in some sense inseparable from that of the Jewish people—that is formulated in the introductory sentence of *Nostra Aetate* 4. Rather than a mere literary transition, this sentence provides the fundamental theological rationale for the chapter it introduces.

In 1974 the Vatican Commission for Religious Relations with the Jews issued a document entitled "Guidelines and Suggestions for Implementing the Conciliar Declaration *Nostra Aetate* (n. 4)."[10] The conclusion to the Guidelines includes the following:

6. Norris, "The Jewish People," 259.

7. For more on *Lumen Gentium*, see chapter 3 of this volume.

8. In fact, all the work of the Council—and not just *Lumen Gentium*—could be viewed as part of an effort to speak about the "nature of the Church."

9. In his 1969 commentary on Nostra Aetate, John Osterreicher—one of the document's authors—has this to say about such speeches presented at the Council: "What is new is especially the statement that the Declaration on the Jews belongs essentially to the Church's self-realization, which was the principal task of Vatican II." (Cited by Norris, "The Jewish People," 259.)

10. For the text of this document, see Willebrands, *Church and Jewish People*,

> The Second Vatican Council has pointed out the path to follow in promoting deep fellowship between Jews and Christians. But there is still a long road ahead. *The problem of Jewish-Christian relations concerns the Church as such, since it is when "pondering her own mystery" that she encounters the mystery of Israel.* Therefore, even in areas where no Jewish communities exist, this remains an important problem. There is also an ecumenical aspect of the question: the very return of Christians to the sources and origins of their faith, grafted onto the earlier covenant, helps the search for unity in Christ, the cornerstone.[11]

Nine years after the adoption of *Nostra Aetate*, the Vatican Commission responsible for the implementation of the chapter dealing with the Jewish people singled out its introductory sentence and underlined its unique importance. The "problem" of Jewish-Christian relations does not arise as a result of merely practical and pastoral concerns deriving from the Church's relationship to particular Jewish communities. Instead, it arises as a result of the Church's own essential nature. This means that the "problem" affects the Church as a whole, in all of its parts and manifestations—"even in areas where no Jewish communities exist" and where no immediate pastoral issues present themselves. The issue is of such great importance that addressing it properly offers the hope of healing the Church's own internal divisions.

If any doubt remained concerning the unique importance of the introductory sentence of *Nostra Aetate* 4, it would dissolve in the face of the consistent teaching of Pope John Paul II.[12]

Only five months after being named the Bishop of Rome, the Pope addressed a group of representatives of Jewish organizations:

> As your representative has mentioned, it was the Second Vatican Council with its declaration *Nostra Aetate, No. 4* that provided the starting point for this new and promising phase in the relationship between the Catholic Church and the Jewish religious community. In effect, the Council made very clear that, "while searching into the mystery of the Church," it recalled "the spiritual bond linking the people of the New Covenant with Abraham's stock." Thus it is understood that our two religious

---

211–19.

11. Ibid., 218. Emphasis added.

12. In the collection of his speeches on this topic from 1979 to 1995 found in *Spiritual Pilgrimage*, I have counted at least seven occasions when Pope John Paul II cites and comments on this statement (see 4, 11, 18, 55–56, 63, 126–27, 141–42).

> communities are connected and closely related at the very level of their respective religious identities.[13]

Pope John Paul II articulates the significance of this sentence of *Nostra Aetate* with piercing clarity: the Catholic Church and the Jewish people are bound together not only by a common past but also—and most importantly—"at the very level of their respective religious identities." In his visit to the Rome Synagogue in 1986, the Pope underlined this point by way of another contrast.

> We are all aware that, among the riches of this paragraph number 4 of *Nostra Aetate*, *three points* are especially relevant.... The *first* is that the Church of Christ discovers her "bond" with Judaism by "searching into her own mystery." The Jewish religion is not "extrinsic" to us, but in a certain way is "intrinsic" to our own religion. With Judaism, therefore, we have a relationship which we do not have with any other religion. You are our dearly beloved brothers and, in a certain sense, it could be said that you are our elder brothers.[14]

For John Paul II, the introduction to *Nostra Aetate* 4 means that Jewish religious life is not "extrinsic" but ("in a certain way") "intrinsic" to Christian faith.[15] This extrinsic/intrinsic contrast vividly conveys the significance of the words, "while searching into the mystery of the Church." In the paraphrase offered by Richard John Neuhaus, "The Church does not go outside herself but more deeply within herself to engage Jews and Judaism."[16]

Originally, the Vatican II declaration concerning Judaism and the Jewish people was to appear as an independent document. However, in the course of its deliberations the Council decided to set this teaching in the broader context of "The Relation of the Church to Non-Christian Religions." Thus, section 1 of the final form of *Nostra Aetate* provides a general introduction to "non-Christian religions." Section 2 focuses on "the religions which are found in more advanced civilizations," with Hinduism and Buddhism receiving explicit mention. Section 3 speaks of Islam, and only then does section 4 take up the topic of Judaism and the Jewish people. Whatever the benefits of such an arrangement, the introduction of Judaism as the final member of a series of "non-Christian religions" could be

---

13. Ibid., 4.
14. Ibid., 63.
15. We will say more about the significance of the phrase "in a certain way" in chapter 3. See pages 52–53.
16. Neuhaus, "Salvation," 73.

interpreted as undermining the unique status of the Jewish people and of its relationship to the Church. Pope John Paul II unequivocally rejects such a reading, and does so by leaning once again on his construal of the opening sentence of *Nostra Aetate* 4:

> The universal openness of *Nostra Aetate*, however, is anchored in and takes its orientation from a high sense of *the absolute singularity of God's choice of a particular people*, "His own" people, Israel according to the flesh, already called "God's Church" [*Lumen Gentium* 9]. Thus, the Church's reflection on her mission and on her very nature is intrinsically linked with her reflection on the stock of Abraham and on the nature of the Jewish people (cf. *Nostra Aetate* 4). The Church is fully aware that sacred Scripture bears witness that the Jewish people, this community of faith and custodian of a tradition thousands of years old, is an intimate part of the "mystery" of revelation and of salvation.[17]

For Pope John Paul II, section 4 of *Nostra Aetate* transcends the first three sections and "anchors" and "orients" them. Thus, *Nostra Aetate* does not present Judaism as the noblest member of a general category, "non-Christian religions," but instead views this religious tradition as reflecting the "*absolute singularity of God's choice of a particular people.*" With the Jewish people, we move beyond the realm of natural religion into the sphere of "the 'mystery' of revelation and salvation," in which the Church herself dwells.

The "Spiritual Bond" Linking the Two Communities

Pope John Paul II sees the Jewish people and its religious way of life as in some sense "intrinsic" to the identity of the Church. As the opening sentence of *Nostra Aetate* 4 states, the Church discovers her "bond" to the Jewish people when "searching her own mystery." What precisely is that "bond"? The Pope offered his answer while addressing leaders of the Jewish community in Strasbourg in 1988. He began by acknowledging the irrevocable election of the Jewish people and its vocation to sanctify the divine name and bear witness to God's identity.

> It is then through your prayer, your history, and your experience of faith, that you continue to affirm the fundamental unity of God, his fatherhood and mercy toward every man and woman, the mystery of his plan of universal salvation, and the consequences which come from it according to the principles

---

17. John Paul II, *Spiritual Pilgrimage*, 141–42. Emphasis added.

expressed by the Prophets, in the commitment for justice, peace, and other ethical values.[18]

The Church needs to receive this witness and learn from it, and engagement with the "prayer," "history," and "experience of faith" of the Jewish people will better enable her to understand the "spiritual bond" that links the two communities. However, the deeper meaning of that "spiritual bond" will only be appreciated by the Church when she focuses on "the Good News of salvation" which is central to her own being. The Pope thus continues:

> With the greatest respect for the Jewish religious identity, I would also like to emphasize that for us Christians, the Church, the people of God and Mystical Body of Christ, is called throughout her journey in history to proclaim to all the Good News of salvation in the consolation of the Holy Spirit. According to the teaching of the Second Vatican Council, she could better understand her bond with you, certainly thanks to fraternal dialogue, but also by meditating upon her own mystery. *Now that mystery is rooted in the mystery of the person of Jesus Christ, a Jew, crucified and glorified.*[19]

For Pope John Paul II, *Jesus himself is the bond joining the Church and the Jewish people.* This is because Jesus is the "Christ" (i.e., the Messiah of Israel), and as such lived as a Jew, was crucified as a Jew—or, rather, as the "*King of the Jews*"—and remains a Jew in his resurrected and glorified humanity. The Church's identity is rooted in the person of Jesus, and the identity of Jesus is rooted in his relationship to the Jewish people and its spiritual heritage. Therefore, as the Church ponders her own mystery, she encounters the mystery of Israel.

This truly is a theological revolution. Formerly, perverted expressions of Christian devotion to Jesus had inspired hatred of Jews and Judaism. According to the theological bombshell planted by Pope John XXIII and ignited by Pope John Paul II, this ancient reflex of contempt had been disrupted, and even reversed. Now Christian devotion to Jesus was to become the source of love for the Jewish people and appreciation for Judaism.

This obviously has profound implications for concrete relations between Christians and Jews. But what does this mean for the Church's self-understanding, and for her comprehension of the truth of the "Good News of salvation" which she carries and proclaims?

---

18. Ibid., 126.
19. Ibid., 126–27. Emphasis added.

Israel-Ecclesiology and Israel-Christology

Nostra Aetate and Catholic Theology

While revolutionary in their practical effects, the first and second propositions of *Nostra Aetate* 4—the rejection of anti-Semitism and the acknowledgement of a shared spiritual heritage—could each be embraced without any radical reorientation of the Church's overall theological framework. The third proposition—the affirmation of the irrevocable election in love of the Jewish people—raises questions about the universal salvific mediation of Christ which require attention, but it need not send shock waves through the Church's entire theological system. The fourth proposition, on the other hand, poses a fundamental challenge to the Church's way of understanding herself and the message of grace she proclaims.

If the Jewish people and the Jewish way of life are in any sense "intrinsic" to the very identity of the Church, as Pope John Paul II claimed in interpreting *Nostra Aetate* 4, then the Church's theological vision of herself—in other words, her *ecclesiology*—must account for this reality. Moreover, this accounting cannot be a mere appendix to a pre-existing and self-contained ecclesiological system, but must entail a reconfiguring of the central pillars of the structure.

And if the inner spiritual bond joining the Church to the Jewish people is to be found in "*the person of Jesus Christ, a Jew, crucified and glorified*," then the identity of the one the Church worships and proclaims is likewise formed in part by his enduring relationship to his flesh and blood family. Consequently, the Church's theological vision of the person and work of Jesus—in other words, her *Christology*—must highlight and explore the significance of Jesus' Jewishness.

This means that the Church's theology of the Jewish people cannot exist as a discrete and compartmentalized topic, insulated from the wider framework of Catholic doctrine. The affirmations of *Nostra Aetate* 4 reverberate throughout the entire system of Catholic theology—Christology, ecclesiology, sacramental teaching, and all that remains. In 1985, in an address commemorating the twentieth anniversary of *Nostra Aetate*, Johannes Cardinal Willebrands—then president of the Holy See's Commission for Religious Relations with the Jews—recognized this challenge:

> [O]ur task is to face adequately, study and try to solve, in all fidelity to Catholic normative tradition . . . the questions that a renewed vision of Judaism poses to many aspects of Catholic theology, from Christology to ecclesiology, from the liturgy to

the sacraments, from eschatology to the relation with the world and the witness we are called to offer in it and to it . . . .[20]

The fulfillment of this "task" is still at its preliminary stages. I offer the present volume as a contribution to its ongoing realization.

Israel-Ecclesiology and its Christological Foundation

The ecclesiological challenge posed by *Nostra Aetate* was heightened by the adoption of *Lumen Gentium* (the Dogmatic Constitution on the Church) almost one year earlier. On the one hand, this document anticipates the teaching of *Nostra Aetate* by affirming the enduring election of the Jewish people: "On account of their fathers this people remains most dear to God, for God does not repent of the gifts He makes nor of the calls He issues" (*LG* 16). On the other hand, this affirmation plays no structural role in the document's overall vision of ecclesiology. It is merely one of several statements dealing with those who "have not yet received the Gospel." There is no hint here of an "intrinsic bond" to the Jewish people that the Church discovers by "searching her own mystery."

Nevertheless, *Lumen Gentium* moves ecclesiology decisively in a Jewish direction. It accomplishes this task by highlighting the Church's identity as "the People of God" (*LG* 9–17). *Lumen Gentium* seeks to correct a conventional Catholic view that equated "the Church" with "the Hierarchy." It does so by developing an "Israel-ecclesiology" in which the "Old Testament" picture of the people of God typologically anticipates the Church of Christ. In this way the Council Fathers sought to establish an ecclesial identity that has something in common with that of the Jewish people in its long sojourn through history. *Lumen Gentium* thus both affirms the unique spiritual status of the Jewish people and develops its vision of the Church in a way that makes the Church more like the Jewish people. Yet, it never relates the former proposition to the latter. In so doing (or rather, *not* doing), *Lumen Gentium* left the Church with the heritage of an emphatic question-mark that only became more urgent with the adoption of *Nostra Aetate*.

In its fourth chapter *Nostra Aetate* informs us that the Church's identity as the "new People of God" is bound up with the identity of the Jews as "the people with whom God in His inexpressible mercy concluded the Ancient Covenant." Pope John Paul II teaches that the spiritual link joining the two is "*the person of Jesus Christ, a Jew, crucified and glorified.*" Thus,

---

20. Willebrands, *Church and Jewish People*, 28.

the Israel-ecclesiology of *Lumen Gentium* should be rooted in a particular Christological vision. How can we best articulate that Christological vision?

The Catholic Church now appears to recognize the need to address this question. In the early years of the new century the Vatican Commission for Religious Relations with the Jews suggested that an international group of Christian theologians should gather to study "the specific question of how to relate the universal saving significance of Jesus Christ to Israel's ongoing covenantal life with God."[21] The group began meeting in 2006, and the fruit of its labor was published in 2011 under the title, *Christ Jesus and the Jewish People Today: New Explorations of Theological Interrelationships*. While the question this group addressed is formulated differently than the one I am considering here, their scholarly efforts contribute substantially to the advancement of my own project.

One of the proposals reiterated by several of the articles in this volume draws from the writings of Pope Benedict XVI.[22] Engaging with Jewish concepts in his interpretation of Jesus, Pope Benedict presents Christ as the personal embodiment of the Torah:

> The Torah of the Messiah is the Messiah, Jesus, himself.... In this way the "Law" becomes universal.... In this Torah, which is Jesus himself, the abiding essence of what was inscribed on the stone tablets at Sinai is now written in living flesh, namely, the twofold command of love.... To imitate him, to follow him in discipleship, is therefore to keep the Torah, which has been fulfilled in him once and for all.[23]
>
> Jesus understands himself as the Torah—as the word of God in person. The tremendous prologue of John's Gospel—"in the beginning was the Word, and the Word was with God, and the Word was God" (Jn 1:1)—says nothing different from what the Jesus of the Sermon on the Mount and the Jesus of the Synoptic Gospels says.[24]

The contributors to *Christ Jesus and the Jewish People Today* employ this Torah-Christology in order to demonstrate the ongoing relationship between Jesus and the Jewish people. For them, not only is Jesus the Torah in person—the Torah observed by the Jewish people is also a manifestation of the grace and power of Jesus. Thus, Hans Hermann Henrix writes:

21 Kasper, "Foreword," xiii.

22. See Henrix, "Son of God," 121-22, 131-38; Groppe, "Tri-unity," 175; and Rutishauser, "Old Unrevoked Covenant," 236.

23. Benedict XVI, *Many Religions*, 70.

24. Benedict XVI, *Jesus of Nazareth: Part Two*, 110-11.

> If Christians trust in God's blessing upon Jewish walking in accord with Israel's Torah and if this halakhic "walking" can be considered salvific only when related to the fundamental Christian belief that every salvation is the salvation of Jesus Christ, then saying that Jesus Christ is the living Torah can be understood as denoting such mediation. Then that which for Jews is salvific—life according to the Torah, trust in God's Word, faith in God's promise—would be in contact with Jesus Christ and would be taken up in him in a way that confirms, reaffirms, or reinforces, since Jesus Christ is obedient to the Torah and fulfills it. . . . Whoever obeys the Torah as a Jew and strives toward the goal "to be an incarnation of the Torah," walks on his or her way in a manner that, because of Jesus Christ's link with the Torah, Christians believe to be salvific communion with Christ as the Torah incarnate.[25]

While Pope Benedict did not draw this conclusion from his Torah-Christology, Henrix's proposal deserves serious consideration.

Henrix argues forcefully that the Torah always retains its particular reference to the Jewish people. Therefore, when gentile Christians become disciples of the incarnate Torah, they are thereby brought into relationship to the Jewish people.[26] In this way the Church can discover her link to the Jewish people by searching her own mystery, i.e., Jesus as the living Torah. While this argument has merit, its persuasive power will be lost on most Christians—including those who are theologians. For them, the Torah that Jesus incarnates is generally assumed to be a universal Logos, stripped of its temporally circumscribed ethnic trappings. Pope Benedict himself could be interpreted as saying only this when he states that "the *abiding essence* of what was inscribed on the stone tablets at Sinai is now written in living flesh, namely, the twofold command of love"—the "abiding" and universal "essence" of the Torah, not the Torah as a whole in all its troubling particularity and peculiarity. If Christians are to understand the essential connection between Jesus—and his Church—and the Jewish people, Torah-Christology alone will prove insufficient for the task.

Cardinal Lustiger and Israel-Christology

Henrix appears to recognize the limitations or potential pitfalls of Torah-Christology as an independent christological model. This is evident in the

25. Henrix, "Son of God," 137–38.
26. Ibid., 134–37.

fact that he founds his proposal not only on the Torah-Christology of Pope Benedict XVI but also on the teaching of Pope John Paul II regarding Jesus' Jewish identity. Before raising the topic of Torah-Christology, Henrix quotes the following from the Polish pontiff:

> Jesus' human identity is determined on the basis of his bond with the people of Israel, with the dynasty of David and his descent from Abraham. And this does not mean only a physical belonging. By taking part in the synagogue celebrations where the Old Testament texts were read and commented on, Jesus also came humanly to know these texts.... Thus he became an authentic son of Israel, deeply rooted in his own people's long history....[27]

Henrix thus sets his discussion of Jesus' identity as "Torah in person" within the context of reflections on the significance of Jesus as "an authentic son of Israel." Jesus is rooted in the life of his people both genealogically (through descent from David and Abraham) and culturally (through a spiritual formation dependent on a Jewish religious institution, i.e., the synagogue). Therefore, the Torah he incarnates cannot be abstracted from the life and history of the particular people to whom it was given.

Henrix points us in the right direction, but his exposition of the theological implications of Jesus' identity as an "authentic son of Israel" lacks adequate substance. To remedy this deficiency, we look to the writings of Jean-Marie Cardinal Lustiger. The Cardinal articulates a view of Jesus that may be best termed *Israel-Christology*. According to this perspective, Jesus is the perfect representative and individual embodiment of the Jewish people. He is the Christ—i.e., the Messiah, the King of the Jews. He demonstrates that he is such by obeying the Torah as God always intended it to be obeyed.

In his short but remarkable book, *The Promise*, Cardinal Lustiger offers a set of meditations on the Gospel of Matthew. Commenting on the slaying of the innocents by Herod in Matthew 2, the Cardinal sets forth his basic thesis:

> The most common reading of this chapter assimilates Herod to Israel and sees Jesus only as Jesus himself. Whereas, in fact, the entire logic of the narrative is directed toward showing that Israel is Jesus and that Herod is not the king of Israel.... In this conflict, the figure shown to us of the Son and Messiah sums up the totality of Israel. It is a prophetic text in which the evangelist—as Isaiah and the prophets often do—plays with what the exegetes called the "corporate personality," which refers to both

---

27. Ibid., 116–17.

> a person and a people. The figure of the Messiah is at the same time a figure of Israel; the figure of Jesus is at the same time that of his people, of his Church, and a figure of Israel. What is said of one can sometimes be applied to the other, sometimes to both. Many things can be understood only by recognizing the solidarity of Jesus with those who are his, of the Messiah with his people.[28]

As the messianic King of Israel, Jesus "sums up the totality of Israel." He represents and embodies the people as a whole. Cardinal Lustiger reiterates this theme in his discussion of Jesus' baptism (Matthew 3). When the voice from heaven says, "This is my Son, the Beloved" (Matt 3:17), we are to recognize an allusion to the identity of Israel as God's Son (Exod 4:22–23): "The most obvious level of meaning [in the words of God to Jesus at his baptism] is that Jesus is designated as the Son *par excellence.* He is designated not as a substitute for Israel, but as the very realization of Israel's vocation. He is the one in whom the Promise destined for all of Israel is realized and by whom it can be communicated."[29]

Following his baptism, Jesus goes into the wilderness of Judah for forty days of testing. Just as Jesus recapitulates in himself the people of Israel, so in this act he recapitulates the history of Israel's forty years of testing in the Sinai desert. Cardinal Lustiger draws the appropriate inference: "From that moment, it is made clear that Jesus is able to fulfill the Law of God completely and perfectly, and so he acts as the true Israel should act.... Therefore, his encounter with the Tempter in the desert, just as Israel was tested on coming out of Egypt, will focus on God and on the totality of his Law."[30] Jesus obeys the Torah in its fullness, and so becomes "the very realization of Israel's vocation."

It is possible for non-Catholics to hold such an Israel-Christology without seeing any necessary implications for the Church's ongoing relationship to the Jewish people.[31] It is more difficult for a Catholic to do so, for *Nostra Aetate* 4 affirms both the irrevocable election of the Jewish people and the spiritual bond which links them to the mystery of the Church. If that spiritual bond is found in "*the person of Jesus Christ, a Jew, crucified and glorified,*" as Pope John Paul II asserted, then the Israel-Christology of Cardinal Lustiger offers us a way to explore this bond. The Cardinal himself

---

28. Lustiger, *The Promise*, 33, 39.
29. Ibid., 64.
30. Ibid., 28.
31. A prime example of an eminent scholar who adopts such a position is N. T. Wright.

takes the first steps on this path. Reflecting on Jewish suffering through the generations, and especially in the Shoah, he writes:

> We must believe that all the suffering of Israel, persecuted by pagans because of its Election, is a part of the Messiah's suffering, just as the killing of the children in Bethlehem makes up a part of Christ's passion. Otherwise, God himself would appear incoherent regarding his promise to Israel. If Christian theology is unable to inscribe in its vision of the Redemption, of the mystery of the Cross, that Auschwitz also makes up a part of Christ's suffering, then we have reached the summit of absurdity.[32]

Jesus' identity as the individual embodiment of the Jewish people thus affects not only the Jews of his own day but also all Jews of future generations. It is not only the martyrs of the Church whose suffering is linked to the atoning work of Jesus, but also the martyrs of the Jewish people.

As those joined inextricably to their Messiah, the Jewish people become a test of whether the Church has truly received Jesus as her Lord. Cardinal Lustiger has this to say about the title, "King of the Jews," which was placed by the Romans over the cross: "This title designates, from the pagans' point of view, not the king 'of Israel,' but the king 'of the Jews,' to emphasize that which was the most ethnic and contemptible aspect in the Romans' eyes. He whom the disciples recognize as universal Lord is so only to the extent that his disciples, Jew and non-Jews alike, accept that he is the king of the Jews."[33] If Christians treat the Jewish people as just another ethnicity, without any special connection to Jesus and the Church, they show that they are not yet worthy to be called Christians.

> To make of Israel only a particular case, and, ultimately, an ethnic case—which it is also in certain respects—is a temptation for the Christian. We yield to this temptation if we consider the Jewish population as we would any other. . . . But the mystery of Israel remains at the center of the Christian faith. If we consider it unessential, we expose just how far we are from being Christians.[34]

For Cardinal Lustiger, Israel-Christology has profound implications which Christians ignore at their own peril.

When set in the context of Israel-Christology, Torah-Christology also proves immensely valuable. The two become complementary ways of

---

32. Lustiger, *Promise*, 50.
33. Ibid., 85.
34. Ibid., 93.

looking at the humanity and divinity of Jesus through a Jewish lens. We are less tempted to detach the Torah which Jesus incarnates from the integral reality of the Jewish people and their way of life if we first grasp the intimate bond between Jesus and his flesh and blood family.

"The mystery of Israel remains at the center of the Christian faith." Cardinal Lustiger here articulates a principle implicit in *Nostra Aetate* 4. Once the Church fully recognizes this principle, the new consciousness will send shock waves through her understanding of Christology, ecclesiology, sacramental theology, and the entire framework of Christian truth.

Israel-Ecclesiology and the *Ecclesia ex Circumcisione*

Nostra Aetate and Jewish Disciples of Jesus

Cardinal Lustiger's seminal contribution to the Christological unpacking of *Nostra Aetate* 4 cannot be divorced from his own identity as a Jew. He was proud to be a Jew, and he considered his faith in Jesus to be a realization of that identity rather than its nullification: "in becoming a Christian, I did not intend to cease being the Jew I was then. I was not running away from the Jewish condition. I have that from my parents, and I can never lose it. I have it from God, and he will never let me lose it."[35]

> For me at the time, the contents of Judaism were no different from what I was discovering in Christianity. I saw Judaism then as a historical condition marked by persecution. I did not think for one moment of leaving it. But it found its fulfillment in welcoming the person of Jesus, the Messiah of Israel; it was in recognizing him, and only in recognizing him, that Judaism found its meaning.[36]

Cardinal Lustiger always saw himself as a Jewish disciple of Jesus, and his insight into "the mystery of Israel" derived from his personal experience of encountering "Christ as Messiah and image of the Jewish people."[37]

In a recent volume chronicling the thirty years of theological controversy which prepared the way for the composition and adoption of *Nostra Aetate* 4, John Connelly underlines the essential role played in the drama by Catholics from a Jewish background. He focuses most of his attention on John Oesterreicher, but also credits the efforts of Dietrich von Hildebrand,

---

35. Lustiger, *On Christians and Jews*, 6.
36. Ibid., 11.
37. Ibid., 10.

Paul Demaan, Annie Kraus, Bruno Hussar, Renee Bloch, Geza Vermes, Gregory Baum, Leo Rudloff, and Raissa Maritain. These Jewish Catholics affirmed the enduring theological significance of the Jewish people, but they also believed that their own identity as Jews was fulfilled in Christ.

While acknowledging their indispensable role in making *Nostra Aetate* 4 possible, Connelly also argues that the truths enunciated by that document led ultimately to the Church's renunciation of any missionary agenda in relation to the Jewish people. A major reason for this development was the insight gained in late 1948 by one of the pioneers of a Catholic theology of the Jewish people, Karl Thieme:

> The new reading of Paul's letter to the Romans opened his mind to the revolutionary idea that God had meant Jews to continue as a people after the time of Christ. Suddenly he was projecting the Jewish decision not to follow Christ as perfectly understandable. Not only that, but the Jews' refusal seemed justified, because *for Jews to accept Christ would have meant the end of the Jewish people*.[38]

Individual Jews (such as Monsignor Oesterreicher or Cardinal Lustiger) who become Catholics may continue to identify as Jews. However, it is rare for those of them who marry to have children or grandchildren who identify as Jews. If all Jews were to become Catholics, then indeed this would seem to entail the *end of the Jewish people*.

Does this mean that, despite the past contributions of Jewish disciples of Jesus such as the Monsignor and the Cardinal, we are now in an era when Jews should be discouraged from believing in Jesus and when those who find their way to such faith no longer have a distinctive part to play in the unfolding drama of Jewish-Christian relations? In the present volume I will argue against such a proposition. I do so not as a Jewish Catholic but as a Messianic Jew—a Jewish disciple of Jesus who lives a traditional Jewish way of life and seeks to be a loyal member of the Jewish people. The Messianic Jewish voice has not previously been heard in this discussion. I believe that we are now ready to speak, and that what we have to say can enable Catholics to better appreciate the implications of their own authoritative decisions.

Recovering the *Ecclesia ex Circumcisione*

Increasingly in the post-*Nostra Aetate* environment one hears Catholic scholars speak of the *ecclesia ex gentibus* (the Church from the gentiles) and

---

38. Connelly, *Enemy to Brother*, 204. Emphasis added.

the *ecclesia ex circumcisione* (the Church from the circumcision) in reference to the early centuries of Church history.[39] Thus, in its 1985 document, "Notes on the Correct Way to Present the Jews and Judaism in Preaching and Catechesis in the Catholic Church," the Holy See's Commission for Religious Relations with the Jews speaks of the particular and universal dimensions of the incarnation and the Church:

> Thus the Son of God is incarnate in a people and a human family. This takes away nothing, quite the contrary, from the fact that he was born for all men . . . and died for all men. . . . Thus he made two people one in his flesh (cf. Eph 2:14–17). This explains why with the *ecclesia ex gentibus* we have, in Palestine and elsewhere, an *ecclesia ex cirumcisione*, of which Eusebius for example speaks (H.E., IV, 5).[40]

The text from Eusebius mentioned here describes the community of Jewish disciples of Jesus which had its origins in Jerusalem, and which was governed by Jewish bishops until the Bar Kochba revolt of 132 C.E. This Jewish *ecclesia* receives similar attention from Christian Rutishauser, S.J., in his article for *Christ Jesus and the Jewish People Today*:

> The *ecclesia ex gentibus* ("Church from the Gentiles") takes its position in difference but in proximity to Judaism as God's people. In this process, the *ecclesia ex Judaeis*—the community of the "Church from the Jewish people" gathered by Christ (see Romans 9–11)—is the bond between the Church out of the nations and nascent rabbinic Judaism, which was further interpreting and living out the Sinai Covenant.[41]

In light of the language of *Nostra Aetate* 4, Rutishauser's use of the word "bond" in this context has particular significance. Jesus himself—the Messiah of Israel and the individual embodiment of the Jewish people—is the fundamental spiritual bond linking the Church to the Jewish people. However, at her beginnings the linking-role of Jesus was mediated by Jewish apostles and a Jewish Mother Church in Jerusalem.

For a host of reasons, the *ecclesia ex Judaeis* (an expression equivalent to *ecclesia ex circumcisione*) disappeared early in the Church's first millennium.

---

39. These Latin terms are found in a mosaic of the fifth-century Church of St. Sabina in Rome. For a volume from a Catholic scholar which uses this terminology in its title, and which was published only a few years after the adoption of *Nostra Aetate*, see Bagatti, *Church from the Circumcision*. The book has a photograph of the St. Sabina mosaic on its cover.

40. Section III, paragraph 23. See Willebrands, *Church and Jewish People*, 233.

41. Rutishauser, "Old Unrevoked Covenant," 239.

Rutishauser suggests that the loss of this communal Jewish setting for life in Jesus had radical consequences for the validity of the Christian "mission to the Jews." Rutishauser recognizes that the "claim of Jesus Christ" was "truly a claim for Jews and also for other people," but in a "differentiated way" that would enable Jewish disciples of Jesus to continue to live as faithful Jews in loyalty to the Jewish people as a whole (i.e., as part of the *ecclesia ex Judaeis*) while empowering gentiles to worship the God of Israel without becoming Jews.[42] The breakdown of this differentiated mission and differentiated community posed a dilemma for the Church which she has never adequately confronted or resolved: "If the classical Christian 'mission to the Jews' with the purpose of integrating them through baptism into the Church—i.e., into the *ecclesia ex gentibus*, the Church out of the nations as she is in fact—cannot really be an option, it is also true that the universal importance of Jesus to Christian eyes cannot be questioned."[43] Rutishauser acknowledges that the empirical Church as presently constituted—"as she is in fact"—is only "the *ecclesia ex gentibus*, the Church out of the nations."[44] She is unable to offer prospective Jewish disciples of Jesus an environment in which they can fulfill their distinctive covenantal responsibilities as Jews, and so any deliberate "mission to the Jews" from the Church "cannot really be an option." Yet, the Church still cannot be true to herself if she denies "the universal importance of Jesus." This is a dilemma indeed.

Cardinal Lustiger likewise refers to the two-fold character of the Church at its foundation, and employs the ancient Latin terms to capture this dimension of her identity. He makes explicit what is only implicit in the assertions of Rutishauser—namely, that the Church's claim to *catholicity* hinges on her adequately expressing this two-fold reality:

> The Church appears as "catholic" . . . meaning "according to the whole." She is "according to the whole" because she is composed of both Jews and pagans. In order to remain "Catholic" in the original sense—that is, "according to the whole"—recognizes, in a single gift of God's grace, both the *Ecclesia ex circumcisione*

---

42. Ibid., 242.

43. Ibid., 243.

44. As Rutishauser perceives, in normal use the English word "Church" connotes what has become de facto the "*ecclesia ex gentibus*, the Church out of the nations." Because of this, I will in this volume avoid using the word "Church" to refer to the fully catholic reality of the Body of Christ and instead employ the Greco-Latin term *ecclesia* to speak of that reality which always remains in essence a communion of Jews and gentiles.

(the Church born from circumcision) and the *Ecclesia ex gentibus* (the Church born from the pagan nations).[45]

Thus, like Rutishauser, the Cardinal sees the disappearance of the *ecclesia ex circumcisione* as highly problematic. Unlike Rutishauser, however, the Cardinal does not accept the situation as historically inevitable—or even as divinely ordained—but instead considers gentile Christians of the Byzantine era to be culpable for this disappearance. He also asserts that the result was a situation which became a "cause of unfaithfulness to Christ":

> The Jerusalem Church, destroyed under Byzantine pressure, was undoubtedly a major loss for the Christian conscience. The memory of the grace bestowed was thus practically erased—not by the Church, as the bride of Christ, but by Christians. This became for them a source of temptation and a spiritual trial, a cause for unfaithfulness to Christ. Herein lies one of the major problems of Christianity.[46]

Elsewhere he describes the dissolution of the "Jewish Church" as "both a sin and tragedy."[47] While grieving over the loss of the Church's two-fold catholic form, Cardinal Lustiger retains a hope that this form could one day be restored. He pins this hope not on Messianic Jews, but on the Jewish Catholics of the new State of Israel: "Contemporary history has placed before us another paradoxical event: the rebirth of the State of Israel.... In this situation, a 'Church,' an *Ecclesia ex circumcisione*, as it is designated in a mosaic at Saint Sabina in Rome, once again becomes conceivable."[48] Cardinal Lustiger thus shows himself unwilling to regard the *ecclesia ex circumcisione* as irrecoverable. He sees her loss as tragic, and her restoration as possible and desirable.

Writing as a Messianic Jew in conversation with Roman Catholics, I will make a version of Cardinal Lustiger's thesis my own, exploring its meaning and supporting its validity through biblical exegesis. If the Church is to uphold an Israel-ecclesiology of the sort expounded in *Lumen Gentium* (as she should), she must root that ecclesiology in both Israel-Christology and in a recovery of the foundational character of the *ecclesia ex circumcisione*. In Jesus the Messiah of Israel, and in the *ecclesia ex circumcisione*, we discover the double "spiritual bond" between the Church and the Jewish people which the Church encounters when she "searches her own mystery."

---

45. Lustiger, *Promise*, 6, 125. See also Lustiger, *On Christians and Jews*, 15.
46. Lustiger, *Promise*, 7.
47. Lustiger, *On Christians and Jews*, 70.
48. Lustiger, *Promise*, 126.

Mapping the Road Ahead

This book takes the documents of the Second Vatican Council as its starting point, and its proposal can be understood only in the context of the theological efforts undertaken by Catholics since the Council to reflect on the "mystery of Israel" and its relationship to the "mystery of the Church." This volume also originates in my own personal experience as a Messianic Jew whose entire adult life has been spent in friendship, community, and theological engagement with Catholics. To understand what I am saying and why I am saying it, the reader needs to know something about that experience. Therefore, in the next chapter I will shift from a discursive to a narrative mode, and tell something of my own story.

My focus in the present chapter has been on the meaning and implications of *Nostra Aetate* 4, but I have also commented briefly on the Vatican II Dogmatic Constitution on the Church (*Lumen Gentium*) which was adopted almost one year before *Nostra Aetate*. This foundational document presents a type of Israel-ecclesiology and, in passing, anticipates *Nostra Aetate*'s affirmation of the irrevocable election of the Jewish people. Yet, in leaving the connection between these two truths unexamined, and in speaking of the Church in terms that suggested discontinuity with the genealogical-Israel that was her antecedent, *Lumen Gentium* raised as many questions as it answered. Therefore, before entering into the heart of my argument, I will devote the third chapter of this book to a study of *Lumen Gentium* and the Jewish people.

With discussion of *Nostra Aetate* and *Lumen Gentium* in the background, and having informed the reader of the personal experience which has brought me to the point of writing this book, I will proceed in the following five chapters to elaborate on and argue for my thesis—namely, that Jesus as "King of the Jews," and the *ecclesia ex circumcisione* as his appointed mediator, together constitute the "spiritual bond" linking the Church to the Jewish people. My argument will consist of a series of biblical studies dealing with the sacramental life of the Church. Chapter 4 will look at holy orders, chapter 5 will focus on baptism, and chapters 6 and 7 will discuss the Eucharist. In chapter 8 I will employ the Catholic concept of sacrament to reflect on Jewish religious life in light of the material presented in the previous chapters. The book will conclude with a chapter considering the practical implications of what I am proposing.

The majority of this book will consist of biblical exegesis. In part, this is because I was trained as an exegete, and I am doing what I do best. However, I also believe that this is what is most required in our current situation. Catholics need a way to understand the implications of *Nostra Aetate* 4 and

Lumen Gentium (as interpreted by means of *Nostra Aetate*) for the entire range of Catholic doctrine and theology. To accomplish this task, Catholic theologians cannot follow their usual method and draw upon a rich storehouse of pre-Vatican II Church teaching. As regards the Jewish people and Judaism, that storehouse is rather bare. Just as *Nostra Aetate* itself focused on interpretation of the biblical text, so we who stand in its debt must go back to the basic sources of the Church's faith and rethink their meaning.[49]

Throughout the chapters that follow I focus intently on the theological significance of Jesus' identity as a Jew, and its implications for our understanding of the Church's identity and her sacramental life. As a result, I devote far less attention to Jesus' identity as the eternal Son of God, the Second Person of the Trinity, who opens the way for human beings and the created order to share in his divine life. This means that my treatment of Christology, the Church's identity, and the sacraments falls far short of comprehensiveness and perfect balance. This would be a deficiency if I were aiming to present a comprehensive or perfectly balanced Christology, ecclesiology, or sacramental theology. However, that is not my purpose. I am only attempting to fill some gaping holes in the Catholic Church's teaching on these subjects.

To remove any doubts, let me state from the outset that I concur wholeheartedly with Thomas Torrance and his commitment to a dual Christological orientation:

> So far as our knowledge of Jesus Christ is concerned . . . we should adopt a two-fold approach. On the one hand, we should seek to understand Christ within the actual matrix of interrelations from which he sprang as Son of David and Son of Mary, that is, in terms of his intimate bond with Israel in its covenant relationship with God throughout history. On the other hand, however, we should seek to understand Christ . . . in the light of what he is in himself in his internal relations with God . . . .[50]

In other words, thorough and balanced Christological reflection requires attentiveness to both Israel-Christology and the doctrine of the Trinity. In this current volume I focus on the former. I am examining a topic that has received little theological attention, and so I am limiting the scope of my

---

49. As Gerhart Riegner notes, "of all the documents promulgated by the Second Vatican Council, it [i.e., Nostra Aetate] is the only one which contains no reference whatsoever to any of the Church's teachings—patristic, conciliar or pontifical" (Preface to Willebrands, xi). John Connelly emphasizes the fact that Nostra Aetate 4 "ignored many centuries of tradition" and "centered its understanding of the Jews on three chapters in one of Paul's epistles" (Connelly, *From Enemy to Brother*, 4).

50. Torrance, *Mediation*, 3.

discussion in order to give it the space it deserves. I ask the reader to judge the volume on what it seeks to accomplish, and not on what it leaves for the moment unsaid.[51]

While I attend more to the Israel-context than the trinitarian context of Jesus' person and mission, the latter actually constitutes an essential presupposition of the type of Israel-Christology set forth here. Israel-Christology can only aid the Church in understanding her relationship to the Jewish people when it is set within a broader framework of convictions that includes both *Nostra Aetate*'s affirmation of Jewish covenantal identity and the Church's ancient creedal heritage. Without the former, Israel-Christology goes the way of N. T. Wright, a path in which Jesus so fulfills Israel's destiny that those Jews who do not accept him as Messiah are excluded from Israel's covenantal identity.[52] Without the latter, Israel-Christology can easily become a form of dual-covenant theology. In fact, already in 1952 the Jewish theologian Will Herberg proposed just such an Israel-Christology:

> As the one by whom and through whom the covenant of Israel is opened to mankind, Christ appears in early Christian thinking as, quite literally, an incarnate or one-man Israel, the Remnant-Man. Through union in faith with him, the gentile believer becomes part of Israel; he therefore comes under the covenant and thereby becomes heir to the promises of God in Israel.[53]

For Herberg, this means that Jesus has covenantal significance for gentiles but not for Jews, who are already in covenant with God. To his credit, Herberg recognizes that this form of Christology will be considered inadequate by traditional Christians: "I know that what I say here will not satisfy those who are Christians, although they will, I hope, recognize its truth so far as it goes."[54] For a mainstream Jewish theologian, this type of Israel-Christology represents a noteworthy theological advance. For a Christian theologian, on the other hand, it lacks the universal soteriological implications which necessarily derive from Jesus' divine identity. The Israel-Christology of Cardinal Lustiger presupposes both *Nostra Aetate* and the Nicene Creed, and

---

51. In my writing and teaching for the Messianic Jewish world I have argued that Messianic Jews should receive Nicene orthodoxy as a gift bequeathed to the entire *ecclesia*—Jewish and gentile—by the early *ecclesia ex gentibus*. To better understand my view of this topic, see my article "Finding our Way through Nicaea," reprinted in Appendix 4.

52. The following comment from Wright illustrates his thinking: "throughout the letter [to the Romans] as well as elsewhere ... [Paul] has systematically transferred the privileges and attributes of 'Israel' to the Messiah and his people" (Wright, *Climax*, 250).

53. Herberg, "Judaism and Christianity," 244–45.

54. Herberg, "A Jew Looks at Jesus," 261.

the Israel-Christology of the following chapters functions within the same theological framework.

Before concluding this chapter, I would like to comment on a term that will at times be employed in this book. When I speak of "genealogical-Israel," I am referring to the Jewish people as a community that traces its descent back to the biblical patriarchs and matriarchs. The term is thus equivalent to Paul's "Israel according to the flesh (*kata sarka*)" (1 Cor 10:18). The context of the argument in 1 Corinthians demonstrates that the phrase *kata sarka* has no pejorative connotation in this verse, but, as in Romans 1:3, merely refers to physical descent. However, Paul's pejorative use of the phrase elsewhere in his writings (e.g., Rom 8:5) makes its English equivalent problematic as a description of the Jewish people.

"Genealogical-Israel" has four advantages as an English rendering of "Israel *kata sarka*": (1) the phrase has biblical resonance, since genealogies are a central component in the way the biblical narrative establishes membership in familial groupings; (2) the phrase emphasizes physical descent, as is also the case in Paul's use of *kata sarka*; (3) at the same time, the phrase allows for the inclusion of individuals who enter the family from outside the genealogical grouping (as with Tamar, Ruth, and Bathsheba in Matthew's genealogy of Jesus—see Matt 1:3, 5, 6); and (4) the phrase also permits the inference that membership in the family is socially as well as biologically constructed, since not every biological descendant is mentioned in a biblical genealogy (e.g., only as an exception are women included).

In this study, I stand on the shoulders of several giants—most notably, Pope Saint John XXIII, Pope Saint John Paul II, and Jean-Marie Cardinal Lustiger. With their help, and the wisdom of Scripture, we may be able to behold an ecclesiological landscape unperceived by our forbears. May we be obedient to the vision in our days, so that the Church may fully express her catholic identity, and discover that her mystery and the mystery of Israel are wrapped together, each within the other.

2

A Stranger in a Strange (Yet Familiar) Land

From Theological Discourse to Personal Narrative

All have heard of Pope Saint John XXIII and Pope Saint John Paul II, and many know of Cardinal Lustiger. These are teachers who command attention by their proven wisdom and courage as much as by their positions of eminence. But who is Mark Kinzer, and why should Catholics listen to what he has to say about their Church and her relationship to Judaism and the Jewish people?

I have already stated that I am a Messianic Jew—a Jewish disciple of Jesus who seeks to live a traditional Jewish way of life. I serve as Rabbi of a small Messianic Jewish congregation in Ann Arbor, Michigan. I am also a theologian and biblical scholar, and founder of a theological institute established to educate the next generation of Messianic Jewish leaders.

But what is my connection to the Roman Catholic world? Why does that world elicit from me such passionate concern and insatiable curiosity? To answer these questions, I must temporarily veer from the path of theological discourse and tell something of my personal story. While acknowledging the distinction in literary genre, we should not exaggerate the difference between theology and personal narrative. The God of Israel, the God and Father of Jesus Christ, acts in history. When I reflect upon the events of my own life, I cannot but believe that I have seen God act in the midst of and through those events.

Let me begin with a short episode from the middle of the story. It is the fall of 1977—twelve years after the conclusion of the Second Vatican Council, and three years after my graduation from college. I sit in the backseat of a car driving from Rome to Florence. Behind the wheel sits the man who many expect to be the next Pope. His name is Giovanni Cardinal Benelli, and he has recently become the Archbishop of Florence after serving for ten years at the right hand of Pope Paul VI.[1] Next to him sits my mentor, Steve Clark, a leader in the Catholic Charismatic Renewal. I am working this year as Steve's assistant, and am only along for the ride.

We have just made our way out of Rome's congested traffic when Steve mentions to the Cardinal that I am Jewish. His Eminence immediately becomes quite animated (he is, after all, Italian), and asks me to tell him my story. We have an abundance of time, and my audience is as attentive as it is captive. So, I launch into the extended version of my autobiography. The Cardinal asks many questions about my family background, my religious upbringing, my encounter with Jesus at the age of nineteen, and the importance of my identity as a Jew. My story does not reach its conclusion until we have nearly arrived in Florence.

As Steve and I say goodbye to our driver in front of his episcopal residence in Florence, I am astonished and bewildered. Cardinal Benelli is an exalted figure in the hierarchical world of Catholicism, and Steve Clark is one of the most influential intellectual and pastoral voices in a noteworthy movement for spiritual renewal in the Catholic Church. There were a multitude of issues of importance they could have discussed during their hours together on the road. Yet, they wasted much of their precious time together listening to the story of a young Jewish man who had found in Jesus the fulfillment of his Judaism.

I learned personally on this day how much had changed in the Catholic approach to Jews and Judaism in the wake of the Second Vatican Council. Jews and Judaism are now respected by many, and are seen to possess enormous importance in the divine plan. I also learned that some of the highest placed Catholic officials are spiritual men seeking to discern the work of God, even among people who are lowly and apparently insignificant.

I am writing this book in 2014, one year before the fiftieth anniversary of the adoption of *Nostra Aetate* and the conclusion of the Second Vatican Council. I am now sixty-two years of age—six years older than Cardinal Benelli was on that autumn day in 1977. Much has happened in my relationship to Catholics and the Catholic Church in the decades that have passed since we drove together from Rome to Florence. If the remainder of this

---

1. In 1969 *Time Magazine* had described his role in this way: "When Pope Paul VI sits down at breakfast, the newspaper clippings and reports in front of him have been prepared and organized by Archbishop Giovanni Benelli. When there is a sudden crisis in the Roman Catholic Church, the man who rushes to the papal chambers with the message is Archbishop Benelli. When a cardinal prefect of a curial congregation wishes to see the Pope, his appointment is arranged—or postponed—by the same Benelli. And when President Richard Nixon helicoptered into St. Peter's Square two weeks ago, who was there to greet him officially but Giovanni Benelli." ("The Pope's Powerful No. 2").

A STRANGER IN A STRANGE (YET FAMILIAR) LAND

book is to make any sense, I must take you with me on a journey somewhat like the one I traveled that day with Cardinal Benelli. Hopefully, you will find the tale as intriguing as he did.

Family, Friends, Faith

I grew up in the last Jewish neighborhood within the city limits of Detroit. My father and mother were first-generation Americans whose parents had immigrated to the United States from Eastern Europe early in the twentieth century. Like most Jews of that era, they had each felt the personal impact of Christian-inflected anti-Semitism. My mother recounted her shame and confusion when, as a child, other children accused her of being a Christ-killer. My father told of being passed over by a potential employer because he was Jewish. Despite such experiences, my parents were remarkably free of anti-Christian prejudice, and my mother was just as quick to tell how Catholic neighbors had arranged for Mass to be said on her behalf when she, a prematurely-born infant, was clinging to life by a tenuous thread.

My father had special affection and respect for Catholics and their Church. He admired Pope John XXIII, and spoke with intense emotion of how this man had saved the lives of thousands of Jews during the Second World War. On a more personal level, my father had attended a Catholic law school (the University of Detroit), which had admitted him to its program after he had finished only two years of undergraduate classes upon returning from military service. Many of his instructors were priests, and his stories of them always depicted them as generous, fair, and wise. My father loved being a lawyer, and he was forever grateful to his alma mater for welcoming him and preparing him for his profession. Upon graduation, he was taken under the wing of a wise and accomplished Irish Catholic attorney by the name of Leo Sullivan. In my father's eyes, his mentor could do no wrong. When Leo died of a heart attack in middle age, my father grieved as though for an elder brother. In memory of his friend, he began donating money to a Catholic charity that Leo had favored, and he continued the practice for the rest of his life.

In keeping with my family environment, I grew up without any notable religious prejudices—but also without any notable religious knowledge. Most of my friends before high school were either Jewish or Catholic, and in the settings that were important to me—such as the classroom, the basketball court, or the baseball field—it did not seem to make much difference whether they were one or the other. On one occasion, however, the difference surfaced in a disturbing manner. I was twelve or thirteen years old at the time, and one of my Catholic friends told me that I would go to hell after I died because I was Jewish and did not believe in Jesus. I found such views repellent, and thought he needed some physical education to clarify his thinking. The incident holds some prominence in my memory, for I did not often express myself with my fists. Unfortunately, my angry response probably confirmed his opinion of my hopeless spiritual condition.

My first glimpse of the substance of the Catholic faith—or, at least, of its rich cultural expression—came as a result of a freshman history class in college. The course focused on medieval Europe, and I was introduced for the first time to monasticism, Romanesque and Gothic architecture, Francis of Assisi, and Thomas Aquinas. The professor was sympathetic to the values and virtues of the period, and the material had a powerful effect on my imagination. I now saw the beauty of that civilization in which faith, piety, learning, rational discourse, and artistic expression were all integrated as expressions of a coherent vision of the meaning of human life. I was aware of medieval anti-Judaism, but that did not disturb me greatly, since I had little affection for Jewish life myself. Of course, I was still convinced that the Catholic religious beliefs of that bygone era were illusory. But my imagination had been awakened to an ideal that had previously been unrecognized, and—in retrospect—I can see that I had turned a decisive corner in my spiritual life.

The moment of illumination was slow to come, but it is surely no accident that the defining event consisted of a seven-week backpacking expedition to Western Europe. In England, Scotland, France, Italy, Austria, and the Netherlands I saw with my own eyes the remnants of the civilization I had read about in my freshman history class. Many other factors contributed to my forsaking agnosticism and embracing faith in God and in Jesus, but I cannot discount the role played by my visits to Saint Peter's Basilica, the Sistine Chapel, Notre Dame de Paris, and Westminster Abbey.

It was only after I had received the gift of faith that my identity as a Jew became a pressing issue for me. In an ironic twist, Jesus kindled in me for the first time a love for Judaism and a commitment to the Jewish people. The details of that story have little relevance in this context, and I have written of them elsewhere.[2] The key point to note here is that my renewed sense of Jewish identity added a layer of complication to my thinking about Catholicism. I could no longer minimize the history of Catholic anti-Judaism as a minor blemish on the achievements of the High Middle Ages.

---

2. Mark S. Kinzer, "Messianic Fulfillment." See also the autobiographical comments in my *Postmissionary*, 17–21.

A STRANGER IN A STRANGE (YET FAMILIAR) LAND

I returned to school in the fall of 1971 a changed person. I had come to believe in God, to acknowledge Jesus as the Messiah, and to realize that my identity as a Jew was important. However, I still lacked a clear sense of how I was to live this out. Little did I know at the time, but more changes were on the horizon.

Life in an Almost-Catholic Charismatic Community

In the first week of my sophomore year at the University of Michigan I attended a charismatic prayer meeting of an ecumenical Christian community called "The Word of God." These prayer meetings had begun four years earlier, but the community itself had only formed one year before I first walked into the St. Thomas Parish social hall. Yet, to me—nineteen years old, with little experience and less knowledge of Christian institutions—this group of over 500 appeared to be as solidly established as the turn-of-the-century Catholic sanctuary to which the social hall was attached.

The group had been founded by four Catholic laymen—Steve Clark, Ralph Martin, Jim Cavnar, and Gerry Rauch—who had met as students at Notre Dame, and who had moved to Ann Arbor in 1967 to launch an evangelistic outreach to students. In that same year they were among the first group of Catholics to experience a Pentecostal awakening (which they called "being baptized in the Spirit"). Energized by this transformative encounter with God, their prayer meetings grew from just ten participants to over one hundred in four months. The Catholic Charismatic Renewal, born among them and their network of friends across the country, grew nationally and internationally at a similar pace. Ann Arbor became the Jerusalem of this movement, the symbol and institutional center for its diverse and widespread constituency.

It is difficult to imagine that either the Word of God in Ann Arbor or the Catholic Charismatic Renewal around the world would have emerged in the late 1960s apart from the Second Vatican Council which had concluded only a couple of years earlier. In many Catholic settings the years immediately following the Council brought chaos, confusion, and bizarre forms of experimentation. While the Catholic Charismatic Renewal was not totally immune to such phenomena, to a great extent it embodied and manifested the love of Scripture, creative engagement with tradition, and Christ-centered openness to the Spirit, which were hallmarks of the Council. The Word of God in Ann Arbor had all of this, along with a renewed consciousness of what it meant to be part of the Body of Christ and the people of God—a consciousness central to the ecclesiology enunciated so powerfully in *Lumen Gentium*. Here one could find capable lay leadership, a commitment to ecumenical engagement, and a fervent dedication to living and proclaiming the good news. In Ann Arbor, at least, and in the international movement that looked to this city as its capital, the Second Vatican Council was alive and well.

I felt much ambivalence in my first two years of participation in The Word of God. On the one hand, I could not deny the vivid sense of the presence of God when the community gathered for worship. I respected its leaders, and drew much personal support from the other student members who lived in my university residence hall. It was also exciting to live in the hub of an international movement, with a sense that the world was watching. On the other hand, as a Jew and a non-Catholic, I felt like a stranger in a strange land. Two-thirds of the community membership, and virtually all of its leaders, were Roman Catholic. Our main community meetings were held in Catholic buildings; priests in clerical garb and nuns in habits were often present, and sometimes addressed the group; weekly folk-Masses were held in the lounge of our residence hall, and the midnight Mass at the Catholic student center was an unofficial community event. We hosted Catholic visitors—or, perhaps more accurately, pilgrims—from all over the world, and organized and staffed Catholic Charismatic conferences which were held in Ann Arbor and elsewhere. I appreciated much of what I was learning about Catholicism, but this seemed to be too much of a good thing. I was overwhelmed, and as a Jew I felt near to cultural suffocation.

I survived the shock—and then began to flourish. After graduation from the University of Michigan in 1974, I joined one of the two households of a celibate brotherhood led by Steve Clark. Steve had taken interest in me in my first year of involvement with The Word of God, and quickly became a trusted mentor. He had a Jewish father, but had been raised without any religious identity. Steve had come to faith in Christ as an undergraduate at Yale, and there had become a Roman Catholic. He was just what I needed at that moment—brilliant, learned, sympathetic, attuned to the distinctive traits of a Jewish temperament, and respectful of my concerns and Jewish commitments. Steve never attempted to persuade me to become a Catholic, but he did provide me with a winsome model of what Catholic thought and life could be at its best.

At the ripe age of twenty-four I became a member of the governing body of The Word of God. There were approximately twenty of us in leadership, and the community itself now numbered close to two thousand members. In that same year our community entered into a partnership with Leo Joseph Cardinal Suenens, Archbishop of Malines-Brussels and primate of Belgium. Cardinal Suenens had been a prominent architect of Vatican II, serving as one of its four moderators, and giving shape to its key documents. In the early 1970s he discerned the significance of the Catholic Charismatic Renewal as a fruit of the Council and a potential instrument of its aims, and he took the bold step of becoming its episcopal patron and champion. He visited Ann Arbor (as our most distinguished pilgrim), and invited Steve Clark and Ralph Martin to relocate to Brussels to work with him in integrating the Charismatic Renewal into the life of the Catholic Church. Steve and Ralph accepted the invitation, and moved to Belgium in the fall of 1976.

One year later I joined Steve in Brussels to work as his assistant and travel companion. I soon became familiar with the episcopal residence of the Cardinal, and joined Steve as he visited some of the dynamic Catholic Charismatic communities that had emerged in France. That year Steve was also guiding my personal study to help me think through two major topics: how I should live as a Jewish disciple of Jesus, and how Jewish life related to the Eucharist. Two texts were especially helpful for me that year—Jean Cardinal Daniélou's *The Theology of Jewish Christianity* and Louis Bouyer's *The Eucharist* (the second of these volumes will play an important role in the later chapters of this book). In this way I was introduced to the Nouvelle Théologie which had played such a constructive role at Vatican II. In this way I also came to see more clearly the profound connection between Judaism and Catholicism.

A Synod of Catholic Bishops was gathering in Rome in the fall of 1977 to discuss the topic of catechesis, and Cardinal Suenens would of course be among them. The real subject of discussion in Rome that month, however, was of more burning interest: who would be the next Pope? The health of Pope Paul VI was failing, and it was evident to all that a conclave was imminent. With this at the forefront of his mind, Cardinal Suenens invited Steve, Ralph, and others of us who had accompanied them from Ann Arbor to join him in Rome and to hold daily prayer meetings there. He would attend those meetings, and bring along other Cardinals whom he thought were likely candidates to be the next successor to Peter. Our group would pray with and for each of these guests, encouraging them in their work and preparing them for what might lay in store for them. It was thus that I met Cardinal Benelli, and on the following day came to have him as my chauffeur on the road to Florence.

I returned to Ann Arbor in 1978, and for the next eleven years devoted myself to pastoral work in the Word of God, including the development of a Messianic Jewish neighborhood group. I was also engaged in service beyond the boundaries of our local community life—writing articles and books for our publishing operation and teaching Scripture to leaders of related communities from around the world.³ Through these latter activities I came to know two men who would eventually play an important role in my engagement with Catholicism—Fr. Peter Hocken and Johannes Fichtenbauer.

Fr. Peter was an English priest who at that time lived as part of the Mother of God Community, a Catholic Charismatic body in Washington, DC.⁴ Fr. Peter specialized in the history of renewal movements in the Church, with a particular focus on Pentecostalism. I met Fr. Peter in 1980 at a theological conference organized by our community in which we were both presenters.⁵ We immediately sensed an intellectual and spiritual affinity. Fr. Peter displayed a keen interest in the Messianic Jewish movement, which had begun at much the same time as the Catholic Charismatic Renewal. He believed that these two movements were central to God's purposes for the Church and the world in the remainder of the twentieth century and beyond.⁶ After our first interaction in 1980, Fr. Peter and I would always find time to meet and talk at any event that we both attended.

Johannes Fichtenbauer founded and led a Charismatic community in Vienna, Austria. I met him when he visited Ann Arbor for an extended stay in the late 1970s, but we became better acquainted in the 1980s when I travelled to Europe each summer to teach Scripture to leaders of various Charismatic communities. Johannes was outspoken, outgoing, dedicated, and abounding in vision for the future. In coming years our paths would converge in a manner that neither of us anticipated in the 1980s.

From the Charismatic Renewal to Messianic Judaism

While my primary communal sphere in the 1970s and 80s was the world of Catholic and ecumenical Charismatic communities, in the late 1970s I also began to develop close ties to the Messianic Jewish movement. As noted above, this movement began in the same period as the Catholic Charismatic Renewal. It developed initially as a dynamic youth revival within an existing movement known as Hebrew Christianity. Hebrew Christians were Jews who, while believing in Jesus and participating in various Protestant

---

3. The journal for which I wrote was *Pastoral Renewal*, and the publishing house was Servant Publications.

4. The Mother of God Community included among its members two other significant Catholic theologians—Fr. Francis Martin and Fr. Thomas Weinandy.

5. The papers from that conference were later published in Williamson and Perotta, *Christianity Confronts Modernity*.

6. Fr. Peter has articulated these convictions clearly in several of his books. For example, see *Glory* and *Challenges*.

Churches, continued to call themselves Jews and to see a theological significance to their Jewish identity. They had their own conferences, organizations, and publications, and were especially active in missionary activity to their Jewish neighbors. While expressing loyalty to the Jewish people and (after 1948) support for the Jewish state, their theology and piety differed little from that of their fellow congregants in the Protestant Churches they attended. They worshipped on Sunday, and viewed the ritual laws of the Torah as obsolete.[7]

In the late 1960s the youth of the Hebrew Christian movement became dissatisfied with this bifurcation of their identities—Jewish in ethnicity, Christian in religion. They—and those older leaders who resonated with their vision—sought a more integrated life as Jewish disciples of Jesus. To make this a reality, they established their own Messianic Jewish congregations, which worshipped on Saturday and adopted certain elements of traditional Jewish liturgy. Many of them were also affected by the charismatic awakening that was spreading within the Christian world, and were looking for new forms of community. Out of the new congregations that emerged, the Messianic Jewish movement was born.

After coming to believe in Jesus in 1971, my first mentor was a Jewish man who had participated actively in the Hebrew-Christian movement but who had left it because of what he considered its lack of Jewish integrity. His name was Haskell Stone, and in some ways he was a forerunner of what became the Messianic Jewish movement. However, Haskell never connected with the new movement, and was unable to introduce me to its leaders or institutions. While I attended a Conservative synagogue in Ann Arbor and observed Jewish holidays with other Jewish members of the Word of God, I had no direct ties to the Messianic Jewish movement until 1977.

In an odd yet providential ordering of events, my initial exposure to the new movement came through my role within the Word of God and the Catholic Charismatic Renewal. In 1977 our community took a leading role in organizing and staffing a conference in Kansas City that Pentecostal historian Vincent Synan has called the "climax" of the twentieth-century Charismatic movement.[8] Fifty thousand people from a variety of denominational traditions gathered together for worship and preaching in a Kansas City stadium. In addition, the denominational groups each had their own conference sessions. The committee overseeing the general conference (which

---

7. On Hebrew Christianity and the emergence of Messianic Judaism, see Kinzer, *Postmissionary*, 263–302.

8. Bailey, "Witness."

included Steve Clark and Ralph Martin) decided that one of the groups to be represented would be the Messianic Jews.

The Word of God in Ann Arbor took responsibility for providing administrators for each of the denominational conferences. Our community was ecumenical, and so we could staff each conference with an administrator who was part of that particular tradition. There was not much debate as to who would be the administrator for the Messianic Jewish conference.

The chair of the Messianic Jewish conference was Dr. David Stern, and I was to function as his assistant. At this time David was not yet a well-known figure in the Messianic Jewish world. He was then preparing to immigrate to Israel to begin what he rightly considered his life-work. Within a decade he would become one of the most recognized spokesmen for Messianic Judaism in the world—furnishing the movement with its own interpretative translation of the New Testament into English, a New Testament commentary for lay readers based on his translation, and a widely read programmatic statement of the movement's meaning and purpose.[9] Our close working relationship in Kansas City established a foundation for a lasting friendship.

As the conference administrator, I participated in the leadership team meetings, which included all of the Messianic Jewish conference speakers. It was a colorful cast of characters, and the experience gave me a speedy education in the nature of the new movement.[10]

A major Messianic Jewish leader whom I did not meet at the Kansas City conference was Daniel Juster. Dan was the chief architect in the formation of the first Messianic Jewish congregational organization, the Union of Messianic Jewish Congregations (UMJC). Well educated, well read, and a capable thinker, Dan added another seminal theological voice to Messianic Judaism.[11] In the early 1980s I visited Dan at his home in Gaithersburg, Maryland. I had become suspicious of what I saw as divisive sectarian tendencies in the Messianic Jewish movement at large, but my time with Dan reassured me. Here was a man with a broad vision of the Church and the Jewish people, who—like Fr. Peter Hocken in a different context—combined respect for tradition with sensitivity to the renewing activity of the Holy Spirit. As it turned out, in the 1990s Dan's congregation would rent

---

9. See Stern, *New Testament*; Stern, *New Testament Commentary*; and Stern, *Messianic Jewish Manifesto*.

10. Speakers included Moishe Rosen, Manny Brotman, Art Katz, David Chernoff, Paul Liberman, Ray Gannon, Phil Goble, and Mike Evans.

11. His major work of popular theology, *Jewish Roots*, was published in the early 1980s. A revised fourth edition is now available.

space from the Mother of God Community, and Dan would develop a close friendship with Fr. Peter.

At the end of the 1980s The Word of God in Ann Arbor experienced a leadership crisis resulting from disagreements within the broader international community to which it belonged.[12] The crisis produced a split in the Ann Arbor community, with the majority of community members deciding to refrain from participation in either group. The crisis also led to a parting of the ways between Steve Clark and co-founder Ralph Martin. All the Messianic Jewish members were part of the majority that did not participate in either body, and I joined with them in 1993 to form Congregation Zera Avraham (Offspring of Abraham). I also returned to school, and in 1995 completed my PhD in Second Temple Judaism and the New Testament.[13]

I was now ready and eager to contribute theologically to the Messianic Jewish movement. However, the Messianic Jewish movement was not quite ready for me. The religious world of Messianic Judaism had been shaped heavily by conservative evangelical Protestant models of thought and piety. While I understood and respected this expression of Christian faith, my own intellectual and spiritual formation owed far more to Jewish and Catholic sources. My theological framework and idiom appeared strange to my new community, and many suspected that I was not quite "orthodox" in my doctrine. I leaned too much on tradition—Jewish and Christian—in my interpretation of Scripture; embraced ritual as an integral expression of a life of faith; and highlighted the significance of community as a check on unfettered American individualism. It would take a while for many in the movement to understand my way of thinking and expressing myself.

Birth of the Roman Catholic—Messianic Jewish Dialogue Group

But the Messianic Jewish movement was changing. In the summer of 1995 a group from our congregation drove to Chicago to attend the national conference of the Union of Messianic Jewish Congregations, and to begin the process of joining the UMJC. At this conference the President of the UMJC, Marty Waldman, announced the launching of a new initiative, to be called Jerusalem Council II (later, the name was modified to "Toward Jerusalem Council II"). The long-term goal of this project was to inspire leaders from

---

12. The international community is called "The Sword of the Spirit," and it remains to this day a vibrant Christian presence in many countries.

13. My University of Michigan dissertation was entitled *"All Things Under His Feet": Psalm 8 in the New Testament and in Other Jewish Literature of Late Antiquity.*

the full spectrum of the Christian world to gather for an ecumenical council which would do for Jewish disciples of Jesus what the first Jerusalem Council did for gentile disciples—namely, acknowledge their distinctive vocation and eliminate cultural expectations inappropriate to that vocation. However, this second Jerusalem Council would have the additional burden of reckoning with an extended history in which the Church had actively suppressed Jewish life among baptized Jews.

Dan Juster joined with Marty Waldman in advancing this initiative. They quickly realized that their goal was unlikely to be attained in the near future, and thus adopted a more modest agenda—but their long-term aims remained the same. To my surprise, Dan and Marty involved Catholics in the project from its inception—and two of the earliest Catholic participants were my old acquaintances, Fr. Peter Hocken and Johannes Fichtenbauer. Johannes was now a Catholic deacon, and his prominence in Catholic circles increased in 1995 when his long-time friend Fr. Christoph Schönborn was named Archbishop of Vienna. Johannes soon took a new position as the head deacon of the Archdiocese of Vienna. Eventually, Fr. Peter would move to Vienna, making that city the center of Catholic concern for relationship with the Messianic Jewish world.

Fr. Peter's efforts to facilitate a relationship between the Catholic Church and Messianic Jews extended beyond his work in Toward Jerusalem Council II. In 1997 he met Fr. Georges Cottier, Theologian of the Papal Household, who had taken an interest in the Messianic Jewish movement.[14] Their interaction eventually led in September 2000 to the convening of an informal, unofficial, and confidential dialogue at a secluded monastery in Camaldoli, Italy. Seven Messianic Jews and eight Catholics participated in this initial gathering. Fr. Peter, Fr. Cottier, and Johannes Fichtenbauer were among the eight Catholics. Dan Juster and I were among the seven Messianic Jews (the other five were all from the land of Israel).

The timing of this original meeting was momentous. In March of that year Pope John Paul II had made his historic pilgrimage to Jerusalem, in which he had prayed for forgiveness for "the behavior of those who in the course of history have caused these children of yours [i.e., the Jewish people] to suffer." On the Sunday immediately before the beginning of our dialogue, a statement signed by over 220 eminent Jewish leaders appeared in the *New York Times*. Called *Dabru Emet* (Speak Truth), the document recognized the marked improvement that had occurred in the Christian Church's view of Judaism, and called upon Jews to become informed of these developments

---

14. In 2003 Fr. Cottier was named a Cardinal by Pope John Paul II, whom he served so ably as Papal Theologian.

and to reconsider their critical attitudes toward the Church. In comparison to these two milestones in Jewish-Christian relations, our small private meeting in a remote region of Italy might seem insignificant. Only time will tell if that is in fact the case.

Over these past fourteen years our Dialogue Group has remained informal and unofficial, though no longer confidential. It is the personal initiative of some prominent Catholics and Messianic Jews, rather than a Vatican sponsored ecumenical conversation. Still, from the Catholic side we have always operated under the oversight of a bishop (for the past several years that role has fallen to Cardinal Schönborn). I have never ceased to marvel that such highly placed figures as Cardinals Cottier and Schönborn would see the importance of the Messianic Jewish movement. Of course, I think they are right to do so—but I also realize that our movement is small, fractious, immature, and still highly influenced by evangelical Protestant forms of thought and piety. From these two Cardinals, princes of the Catholic Church, I have experienced the same discerning openness that I encountered on the road to Florence with another Cardinal decades before.

For me personally, one of the greatest fruits of the Roman Catholic–Messianic Jewish Dialogue Group has been my friendship with Fr. Jean-Miguel Garrigues of Toulouse, France. Fr. Jean-Miguel is one of the most respected Catholic theologians in France. In particular, he has written extensively on the Catholic theology of the Jewish people.[15] Fr. Jean-Miguel had worked with his longtime friend, Christoph Cardinal Schönborn, in the composition of the new *Catechism of the Catholic Church*, taking special concern for the sections of the Catechism dealing with Judaism.[16] He has been the leading Catholic theologian in our dialogue group, and he and I have often found ourselves as the main presenters in our meetings. Our discussions and debates have enlarged and refined my thinking, and I hope that they have had the same salutary effect for him.

Fr. Jean-Miguel, Cardinal Schönborn, Cardinal Cottier, Fr. Peter, and Johannes Fichtenbauer—all had experienced the impact of the Catholic Charismatic Renewal in its early years, in the wake of the Second Vatican Council. Is it merely a coincidence that these were the Catholics who sensed most vividly the historical significance of the Messianic Jewish movement?

---

15. See Garrigues, *L'unique Israël* and *Le people*.

16. The Catechism was officially approved in 1992. Its Latin edition was published in 1994, and its English translation appeared in 1995.

A Distinctive Perspective

As should be clear at this point, I write this book from a distinctive perspective. I have experienced Catholic life as closely as is possible without actually becoming a Catholic. After an early session in the Roman Catholic–Messianic Jewish Dialogue Group, one of the Catholic participants approached me and said, "You know us in the way we know ourselves." I recognized the truth in his statement without taking it as a compliment to my intellectual acumen. My inside knowledge of Catholicism derived not from special abilities but from a providentially peculiar life-experience. I have had the privilege of living and working among dedicated, theologically-informed, and spiritually-vibrant Catholics, and this has imparted both knowledge and appreciation. In continuity with my youthful response to my freshman history class at the University of Michigan, I see the beauty in Catholicism. Yet, I remain a non-Catholic.

My primary reason for doing so is not because I deny certain central points of Catholic doctrine (though there are such points that I do not affirm), but because I see no way to fulfill what I understand to be my religious obligations as a Jew within a Roman Catholic context. As I have argued in an earlier volume, I believe that all Jews—including those that are baptized—are assigned the responsibility of living a Torah-observant life, in accordance with the basic pattern transmitted by Jewish tradition.[17] This requires serious engagement with the wider Jewish community and adherence to the Jewish calendar. For Jewish disciples of Jesus, this also requires a distinctive ecclesial environment that supports faith in Jesus along with Jewish religious observance and Jewish communal involvement. As a result, I have contended that the *ecclesia* should be conceived of as inherently twofold in character: it is a body of Jews and gentiles, with the Jewish disciples of Jesus remaining a visible communal presence within the one *ecclesia*, joining her to the Jewish people as a whole. I have called this model *bilateral ecclesiology*; it resembles closely the framework suggested by Cardinal Lustiger, which envisions the one catholic *ecclesia* as consisting of both an *ecclesia ex circumcisione* and an *ecclesia ex gentibus*.

The emergence of the Messianic Jewish movement at the end of the twentieth century amounts to an attempt to recapture this crucial bilateral dimension of the Church's life. This movement provides a concrete expression of the truth which Pope John Paul II saw in the introductory sentence of *Nostra Aetate* 4: "The Jewish religion is not 'extrinsic' to us, but in a certain way is 'intrinsic' to our own religion."

---

17. Kinzer, *Postmissionary*.

Thus, I write as a "non-Catholic" (i.e., one who has not been admitted to the Roman Catholic communion) because I believe that the Catholic Church is not yet sufficiently "catholic"—according to the definition of that word offered by Cardinal Lustiger: the Church is catholic (i.e., "according to the whole") because "she is composed of both Jews and pagans," of "both the *ecclesia ex circumcisione* (the Church born from circumcision) and *the ecclesia ex gentibus* (the Church born from pagan nations)."[18] Like this Jewish Cardinal, I do not seek to purge the Church of its dross but to widen its tent-pegs.

From Personal Narrative to Theological Discourse

I will now turn off the side path of autobiography and make my way back to the main road on which we must journey in the coming pages. At this point the reader should be able to understand why I write this book, and hopefully also desires to continue the journey with me.

More can be gained from this chapter-long digression than mere insight into the motives and concerns of the author. In both its substance and intent, this book is not only a theological reflection on a historical ecclesiological drama. The theological ideas found in these pages have emerged from more than forty years of participation in the drama itself. The purpose of the book goes beyond the desire to improve existing theoretical paradigms. It is written as an attempt to discern how all concerned actors—gentile Christians, Jewish disciples of Jesus, mainstream Jews—should perform their next scenes. Thus, while returning to the main road of theological discourse, my ultimate concern remains with the ostensible side path; the overarching goal in view is to participate in shaping the future of the story.

Our next station is a place we have never really left—the ecclesiological vision of the Second Vatican Council. Having spoken of some of the historical and personal results of that vision, we must now reflect on the vision itself and its development and interpretation in light of *Nostra Aetate* 4.

---

18. Lustiger, *Promise*, 6, 125.

3

Lumen Gentium, Gloriam Israel[1]

"The Church's self-realization . . . was the principal task of Vatican II."[2] So wrote Monsignor John Oesterreicher, one of the authors of *Nostra Aetate*. From this perspective, ecclesiology was ever front and center in the mind of the Council Fathers. If that is indeed the case, then the Council's 1964 Dogmatic Constitution on the Church known as *Lumen Gentium* has pride of place as the most fundamental theological document produced by Vatican II.

Viewed in its own historical context, *Lumen Gentium* must be regarded as a theological achievement of the highest order. Writing less than a decade after the conclusion of the Council, Thomas Torrance—one of the greatest Protestant theologians of the second half of the twentieth century—had this to say about the document:

> *Lumen Gentium* is the first fully authoritative formal declaration of the *doctrine* of the Church ever made by Rome in its long history. . . . Here at last the Roman Catholic Church has produced a doctrine of the Church as the Body of Christ which, in its careful theological formulation, goes far to meet the Reformed criticism of the ways in which it had traditionally been conceived.[3]

---

1. This chapter draws heavily on a paper I presented to the Roman Catholic–Messianic Jewish Dialogue Group in 2008. The initial document was prepared in consultation with the Messianic Jewish team, and was ultimately endorsed by the entire Messianic Jewish contingent An abbreviated version of the paper appeared ("Messianic Gentiles") in *First Things* with a response from Matthew Levering. A more complete version is found in Kinzer, *Israel's Messiah*, 156–74.

2. Cited by Norris, in "The Jewish People," 259.

3. Torrance, *Reconciliation*, 59–60.

As noted in chapter 1, the ecclesiology of *Lumen Gentium* gave new prominence to a vision of the Church as the people of God, akin to the people of Israel. Torrance also underlined the significance of this feature of the document:

> Another outstanding aspect of the new orientation in the Roman Catholic doctrine of the Church is its development of the Biblical concept of the Church as the covenanted people of God destined to spread out all over the world, that is the one messianic people which in living continuity with historical Israel was reborn in Christ and universalized through the coming and indwelling of the Spirit at Pentecost.[4]

In the terms we have been employing, *Lumen Gentium* explored the meaning and implications of Israel-ecclesiology. This immediately raised the question of the Church's relationship to genealogical-Israel, i.e., the Jewish people. While *Lumen Gentium* touches upon this question in passing, the document does not aim to offer a direct and full response to it. Happily, one would need to wait less than a year in order to see that question addressed with the seriousness it deserved.

That would come to pass with the adoption of *Nostra Aetate* in 1965. From one angle, *Nostra Aetate* 4 merely develops the teaching of *Lumen Gentium* in a manner that one might have expected. From another angle, however, *Nostra Aetate* 4 presents a challenge unanticipated in *Lumen Gentium*, a challenge that requires new developments in the ecclesiological paradigm of the earlier document. In this chapter I will examine the Israel-ecclesiology of *Lumen Gentium* in light of *Nostra Aetate* and propose a way forward for the doctrinal development of that ecclesiology.

A Christ-Centered Israel-Ecclesiology

As Torrance perceived, *Lumen Gentium* treats two biblical concepts as central to the identity of the Church: the Body of Christ and the people of God. The first concept highlights the Church's union with the crucified and risen Jesus and her identity as the continuing earthly embodiment of his presence (*LG* 7). Because the Church is the Body of Christ, she serves as a sacrament in the midst of the world, mediating to the world the reality of the risen Lord (*LG* 48). The second concept highlights the Church's identity

---

4. Ibid., 61. As we will note later in this chapter, Torrance may have exaggerated the extent to which *Lumen Gentium* describes the Church as "in living continuity with historical Israel."

as an ordered society with continuity through time (*LG* 9–17). Because the Church is the people of God, she lives as a community that is fully in the world, though not of it. The first concept emphasizes the Church's union with God through Christ in the Spirit; the second emphasizes the Church's role as the communal expression in this world of a humanity renewed and transformed through the redemptive work of the Messiah. By linking the two concepts, *Lumen Gentium* asserts that the Church is both a mystical reality and a fully human community, and that neither may be emphasized legitimately at the expense of the other.[5]

In line with this dual identity, the document describes the functions of the Church in terms of the traditional threefold office of Christ as priest, prophet, and king (*LG* 10–13, 21, 25–27, 34–36).[6] Characterizing the Church in this way implies her union with Christ as his Body, since she corporately assumes the same functions that properly belong to him as her Head. On the other hand, the three offices refer originally to established roles of leadership within the people of Israel, and their prominence in the document therefore implies a likeness to the communal and institutional reality of Israel's life. The reiterated motif of the threefold office thus confirms and reinforces the central importance of the Church's dual identity as the Body of Christ and the people of God.

Perhaps the greatest strength of *Lumen Gentium* is its overall design, which gives such prominence to this dual identity. The document addresses some of the most distinctive and controversial teachings of Roman Catholicism—such as the infallibility and universal jurisdiction of the Pope, the immaculate conception and bodily assumption of Mary, and the seven sacraments—but it contextualizes these teachings in a spiritual and communal framework that gives new perspective on their meaning. Beginning with trinitarian reflection on the Church's mystery as the Body of Christ (*LG*

---

5. "But, the society structured with hierarchical organs and the Mystical Body of Christ, are not to be considered as two realities, nor are the visible assembly and the spiritual community, nor the earthly Church and the Church enriched with heavenly things; rather they form one complex reality which coalesces from a divine and a human element. For this reason, by no weak analogy, it is compared to the mystery of the incarnate Word. As the assumed nature, inseparably united to Him, serves the divine Word as a living organ of salvation, so, in a similar way, does the visible social structure of the Church serve the Spirit of Christ, who vivifies it, in the building up of the body" (*LG* 8).

6. The threefold office of priest/prophet/king provides a key structural motif for the entire document. Thus, the Church as the people of God is described in its priestly (*LG* 10–11), prophetic (*LG* 12), and royal roles (*LG* 13–16). The next unit shows how the episcopal office (with its subordinate clergy) embodies and represents these three roles (*LG* 21, 25–27). Finally, the document portrays the laity as participating in its own distinctive manner in the threefold office (*LG* 34–36).

2–4), *Lumen Gentium* makes clear that the spiritual reality of the Church takes precedence over her juridical structure. The document then proceeds to discuss the Church as a human society, but it does so by characterizing the Church as the people of God (*LG* 9–17). The Church's nature as an ordered community, a people, with continuity through time, involves all her members and not just her official leaders. Thus, the communal reality of the Church also takes precedence over her juridical structure. Of course, *Lumen Gentium* sees the Church's hierarchical structure as of immense importance, and devotes much of its space to explaining its role (*LG* 18–29). At the same time, by setting the discussion of the hierarchy within the context of the Church's nature as the Body of Christ and the people of God, the document indicates that the hierarchical structure exists to serve ends greater than itself.[7] Similarly, by presenting the Council teaching on Mary as an appendix to its teaching on the Church (*LG* 52–69), rather than devoting a special document to her, the Council indicates that Mary's primary role is to serve as a model, type, and mother for the Church, rather than to function as an independent object of devotion.

Israel-Ecclesiology and the Jewish People

In ascribing such importance to the Church's identity as the people of God, *Lumen Gentium* raises the ecclesiological question that is our primary concern here: what is the relationship between the Church and the Jewish people?

The document first speaks of "the people of Israel" at the beginning of its trinitarian introduction (*LG* 2), which considers the divine plan conceived "before time began":

> All the elect, before time began, the Father "foreknew and predestined to become conformed to the image of His Son, that he should be the firstborn among many brethren." He planned to assemble in the holy Church all those who would believe in Christ. Already from the beginning of the world the foreshadowing of the Church took place. It was prepared in a remarkable way throughout the history of the people of Israel and by means of the Old Covenant. In the present era of time the Church

---

7. It should also be noted that *Lumen Gentium* sets its teaching on the Papacy (*LG* 22) in the broader context of the episcopate and apostolic succession (*LG* 19–21). The bishop of Rome exercises "full, supreme and universal power over the Church" (*LG* 22), but he does so as the head of an episcopal college—though he does not need the explicit approval of the other bishops to exercise his authority.

was constituted and, by the outpouring of the Spirit, was made manifest.

God's purpose—"to raise men to a participation in the divine life"—is realized in his plan "to assemble in the holy Church all those who would believe in Christ." The history of the people of Israel "foreshadows" and "prepares" for the establishment of the Church, which is "constituted" through Christ's person, life, and work, and "manifested" by the outpouring of the Spirit. Thus, the Church appears to be an essentially new reality in the world. She shares some features in common with the people of Israel in the old covenant, but she is fundamentally discontinuous with it.[8] The goal of the divine plan, conceived "before time began," is the establishment of the Church, and God's dealings with the people of Israel in the Old Covenant were all ordered to prepare for that goal.

This view of "old covenant Israel" is reiterated and developed in *LG* 9— the document's primary treatment of this theme. The paragraph introduces the motif of the Church as the people of God. It begins by describing God's corporate purpose for humanity, and how that purpose leads to the election of the people of Israel and the establishment of God's covenant with them:

> At all times and in every race God has given welcome to whosoever fears Him and does what is right. God, however, does not make men holy and save them merely as individuals, without bond or link between one another. Rather has it pleased Him to bring men together as one people, a people which acknowledges Him in truth and serves Him in holiness. He therefore chose the race of Israel as a people unto Himself. With it He set up a covenant. Step by step He taught and prepared this people, making known in its history both Himself and the decree of His will and making it holy unto Himself.

The ultimate purpose of this election, however, does not have to do with Israel itself as a particular community, but with the new universal reality that is the Church:

> All these things, however, were done by way of preparation and as a figure of that new and perfect covenant, which was to be ratified in Christ, and of that fuller revelation which was to be given through the Word of God Himself made flesh. "Behold

---

8. Thus, Torrance goes too far in characterizing *Lumen Gentium*'s Israel-ecclesiology as portraying the Church as "the one messianic people which in living continuity with historical Israel was reborn in Christ." I will propose that the ecclesiology of *Lumen Gentium* can be strengthened by bringing it into line with what Torrance thought it was already saying.

the days shall come saith the Lord, and I will make a new covenant with the House of Israel, and with the house of Judah.... I will give my law in their bowels, and I will write it in their heart, and I will be their God, and they shall be my people.... For all of them shall know Me, from the least of them even to the greatest, saith the Lord." Christ instituted this new covenant, the new testament, that is to say, in His Blood, calling together a people made up of Jew and gentile, making them one, not according to the flesh but in the Spirit. This was to be the new People of God. For those who believe in Christ, who are reborn not from a perishable but from an imperishable seed through the word of the living God, not from the flesh but from water and the Holy Spirit, are finally established as "a chosen race, a royal priesthood, a holy nation, a purchased people . . .who in times past were not a people, but are now the people of God."

The covenant with Israel, which establishes Israel as a nation, is but a "preparation" and "figure" of a new and better covenant that will establish "the new people of God." This new people—whose membership is determined not by physical but spiritual birth—is the Israel mentioned by Jeremiah 31 as the recipient of the "new covenant." Thus, *Lumen Gentium* implies that the Church is a new reality, patterned in some ways on the people of Israel and marvelously prepared for by it, but essentially discontinuous with it. One might infer from this characterization of the Church that "the race of Israel" no longer has a particular divine vocation in the world (beyond that of other ethnic groups), and that Jews who enter the Church have no particular divine vocation—specifically as Jews—within the ecclesial sphere.

After further description of the Church as a "messianic people" called to be "an instrument for the redemption of all," *LG* 9 proceeds to speak of it as a true people possessing all "those means which befit it as a visible and social union."

> Israel according to the flesh, which wandered as an exile in the desert, was already called the Church of God. So likewise the new Israel which while living in this present age goes in search of a future and abiding city is called the Church of Christ. . . . While it transcends all limits of time and confines of race, the Church is destined to extend to all regions of the earth and so enters into the history of mankind . . . .

The document here draws language from the Apostle Paul, who refers to "Israel according to the flesh" (1 Cor 10:18). It then goes beyond the language of Paul and the New Testament, by referring to the Church as "the new

Israel." Such terminology, combined with the preparatory nature of Israel's calling, could suggest that fleshly Israel no longer retains a unique and positive vocation in the world. At the same time, by noting that "Israel according to the flesh ... was already called the Church of God," *Lumen Gentium* hints that the historical discontinuity between the two Israels—the one in the old covenant, the other in the new—might not be as radical as first appeared.

Only one paragraph of *Lumen Gentium* (*LG* 16) explicitly addresses the relationship between the Church and the Jewish people after the coming of Christ.

> Finally, those who have not yet received the Gospel are related in various ways to the people of God. In the first place we must recall the people to whom the testament and the promises were given and from whom Christ was born according to the flesh. On account of their fathers this people remains most dear to God, for God does not repent of the gifts He makes nor of the calls He issues.

By citing Romans 11:28–29 *Lumen Gentium* decisively rejects the notion that genealogical-Israel has forfeited its election and no longer holds a distinctive divine vocation in the world beyond that of other ethnicities. This unambiguous affirmation of the special status of the Jewish people anticipates what I have referred to as the "third proposition" of *Nostra Aetate*. *Lumen Gentium* thus explicitly counters the supersessionist inferences one might make on the basis of other statements in the same document.

However, to a certain extent the context of this rejection of supersessionism undermines its positive message. The Jewish people are presented as the first of many groups "who have not yet received the Gospel"—they are part of a broader category of adherents of "non-Christian religions." Such adherents, we learn, "are related in various ways to the people of God." The Jewish people, therefore, are not *part of* the people of God, i.e., the Church, but are—like all human beings—*related to it* because of the Church's universal vocation. Thus, at the very point at which *Lumen Gentium* issues an unequivocal positive statement about the Jewish people, it implicitly distances Israel from its own original status as the people of God, and implicitly treats Israel's religious tradition, rooted in divine revelation, as merely the first among many non-Christian traditions.[9]

9. Of course, this also is an issue in *Nostra Aetate*, which has as its formal title "Declaration on Relation of the Church to non-Christian Religions," and which deals with Judaism in the same context as it deals with Islam, Buddhism, and Hinduism. To see how Pope John Paul II interprets this feature of *Nostra Aetate*, see chapter 1, pages 6–7. The relationship between Judaism and Christian faith is better captured by John Howard Yoder in his assertion that Judaism is a "non-non-Christian religion" (*Schism*,

Lumen Gentium thus presents an Israel-ecclesiology that leaves room for the Jewish people. The Church is a "new Israel" which resembles the people of the old covenant in many ways, and therefore one must learn from old covenant Israel in order to discover the mystery that is the Church. At the same time, genealogical-Israel retains a special status in the plan of God as the heir of promises and gifts that have not been recalled. *Lumen Gentium* affirms both propositions, while offering little insight into how the two statements are related. A gap remains between the two "Israels," and it is unclear how or whether it can be filled.

Eschatological Newness

In contrast to the view of Thomas Torrance, I would argue that *Lumen Gentium's* overall perspective on the Jewish people—both before and after the coming of Christ—displays an inadequate appreciation for the Church's "living continuity with historical Israel."[10] This is demonstrated by the "gap" in *Lumen Gentium* between the "two Israels," as noted above. It is further displayed in the document's use of the term "new." *Lumen Gentium* speaks of the "New People of God" and the "New Israel." It likewise speaks of the Church as first "constituted" in our era, apparently by the death and resurrection of Christ. This suggests that the adjective "new" should be understood as referring to the appearance of a reality that did not in any sense exist before. The new people, the new Israel, was *foreshadowed* by the old, and thus shares certain of its features by way of analogy, but the two realities are not intrinsically interconnected.

In many biblical texts the underlying Hebrew and Greek words rendered here as "new" would be more suitably translated as "eschatologically renewed." One is dealing with an "old" or existing reality that is eschatologically transformed by the sovereign action of God. Thus, the new heavens and new earth of Isaiah (65:17; 66:22) and Revelation (21:1) are glorified forms of what existed before. The "new human" that is "put on" in baptism

---

147, 156). This relationship is also expressed practically in the Vatican decision to relate to Judaism through an organ concerned with intra-Christian dialogue, as noted by Richard John Neuhaus: "From the Jewish side, when after the council the Catholic Church was formalizing its conversations with non-Christians, the Jewish interlocutors insisted that they not be grouped with the Vatican dycastery designed to deal with other religions but be included under the secretariat for promoting Christian unity. There were political reasons for that insistence, not least having to do with the politics of the Middle East, but that arrangement has, I believe, much more profound implications than were perhaps realized at the time" (Neuhaus, "Salvation," 68).

10. See the second paragraph of this chapter.

(Eph 4:24; Col 3:10)—i.e., Jesus—is but the old human (i.e., a true descendant of Adam and Eve), raised from the dead and eschatologically transformed. The continuity—and discontinuity—of Jesus' own life serves as the basic paradigm of eschatological newness. The risen Jesus is new, different, yet also the same human being as the one who was born of Mary. He is unrecognized by his disciples until he makes himself known (Luke 24:13-32), yet his hands and feet still show the marks of his violent death (Luke 24:40; see John 20:24-28).

In keeping with this pattern, the Church should be viewed as a *renewed* Israel, a renewed people of God. It is an eschatological form of Israel, anticipating the life of the world to come through the gift of the Spirit. As an eschatological reality, it is also an expanded and reconfigured Israel, including within its ranks people from all the nations of the world. However, in the apostolic period it still maintained continuity with genealogical-Israel—founded and led by Torah-observant Jews (i.e., the apostles and elders), centered in the holy city of Jerusalem, and containing at its heart a visible corporate expression of Jewish life (i.e., the Jerusalem congregation of disciples of Jesus). This continuity also found expression in the early Church's relationship to the wider Jewish world, which had not accepted her claim to be an expanded eschatological Israel. For Peter, Paul, and James, the leaders of the Jewish people were still *their* leaders, and the Jewish people were still *their* people—the people of God (e.g., Acts 23:1-5).

Likewise, Jeremiah 31 directs the eschatological promise of the "new covenant" to genealogical-Israel itself and not to the Church as a separate reality only prefigured by genealogical-Israel. According to Jeremiah, God promises *Israel* the renewal of the covenant made with them when they came out of Egypt. Wolfhart Pannenberg describes this dimension of the new covenant with admirable precision:

> Jeremiah 31:31-32 and Isaiah in 59:21 promise the new covenant not to another people but to Israel as the eschatological renewal and fulfillment of its covenant relationship with its God. When at the Last Supper that he held with his disciples on the night of his arrest Jesus related the promise of the new covenant to the table fellowship with his disciples that he sealed with his self-offering, he was not snapping the link of this promise to the people of Israel. Instead, he was showing that fellowship with himself is for the whole Jewish people the future of salvation that breaks in already in the fellowship of the band of disciples. The later inclusion of non-Jews in the Christian community on

the basis of the confession of Jesus that is sealed by their baptism does nothing to change this.[11]

To this point in time, only a small portion of genealogical-Israel has entered fully into this renewed covenant, but the promise extends to Israel as a whole, and the promise will be fulfilled. In this sense, genealogical-Israel remains the people to whom that new or renewed covenant uniquely belongs as a heritage.

The Catechism and *Lumen Gentium*

The revised *Catechism of the Catholic Church* (*CCC*), officially approved in 1992, interprets the material in *Lumen Gentium* related to the Jewish people in light of *Nostra Aetate* and the teaching of Pope John Paul II. In the process, it clarifies certain expressions whose meaning could have been construed in a supersessionist manner. Thus, when speaking of genealogical-Israel's priestly status, the Catechism employs the present rather than the past tense: "Israel is the priestly people of God, 'called by the name of the Lord,' and 'the first to hear the word of God,' the people of 'elder brethren' in the faith of Abraham" (*CCC* 63). The Catechism leaves no ambiguity as to the referent of these words—it is the Jewish people. This is shown by the phrase "the first to hear the word of God," which derives from the Good Friday prayer for the Jewish people introduced in the 1970 edition of the Roman Missal:

> Let us pray for the Jewish people, *the first to hear the word of God*, that they may continue to grow in the love of his name and in faithfulness to his covenant. Almighty and eternal God, long ago you gave your promise to Abraham and his posterity. Listen to your Church as we pray that the people you first made your own may arrive at the fullness of redemption.[12]

Furthermore, the phrase "elder brethren" derives from the words of Pope John Paul II addressed to the Jewish community of Rome when he visited their synagogue in 1986. Thus, the Catechism affirms the enduring priestly status of the Jewish people while also following *Lumen Gentium* in emphasizing the priestly identity of the Church.

The Catechism later affirms explicitly the irrevocable character of God's gifts to genealogical-Israel. The form which this affirmation takes is

---

11. Pannenberg, *Systematic Theology*, 477.

12. Emphasis added. The phrase, "the first to hear the word of God," also appears as a title for the Jewish people in *CCC* 839.

itself instructive: it appears as a commentary on the problematic opening line of *Lumen Gentium* 16—"Those who have not yet received the Gospel are related to the People of God in various ways." The commentary proceeds to interpret this line—and the teaching concerning the Jewish people that follows it—in light of the all-important introductory sentence of *Nostra Aetate* 4:

> *The relationship of the Church with the Jewish People.* When she delves into her own mystery, the Church, the People of God in the New Covenant, discovers her link with the Jewish People, "the first to hear the Word of God." The Jewish faith, unlike other non-Christian religions, is already a response to God's revelation in the Old Covenant. To the Jews "belong the sonship, the glory, the covenants, the giving of the law, the worship, and the promises; to them belong the patriarchs, and of their race, according to the flesh, is the Christ," "for the gifts and the call of God are irrevocable." (CCC 839)
>
> And when one considers the future, God's People of the Old Covenant and the new People of God tend toward similar goals: expectation of the coming (or the return) of the Messiah. (CCC 840)

While the opening line of *Lumen Gentium* 16 might be taken to imply a merely external relationship between the Church and the Jewish people, the Catechism makes clear on the basis of *Nostra Aetate* that the relationship is actually an internal one. While the opening line of *Lumen Gentium* 16 might be taken to imply a difference *in kind* between the Christian faith and all other religions and merely a difference *in degree* between Judaism and those other religions, the Catechism makes clear that "The Jewish faith" is "unlike other non-Christian religions," for it "is already a response to God's revelation." While the opening line of *Lumen Gentium* 16 might be taken to imply that genealogical-Israel was no longer "the People of God" but only "related to the People of God," the Catechism makes clear that the Jews remain "God's People of the Old Covenant." The use of this phrase by the Catechism accords with Pope John Paul II's 1980 gloss: "the people of God of the Old Covenant, *never revoked by God*."[13]

While *Lumen Gentium* identifies the Church as the "New Israel," in that document her assumption of this title requires and involves no intrinsic connection to the Jewish people. The *Catechism*, on the other hand, makes

---

13. John Paul II, *Spiritual Pilgrimage*, 15. Emphasis added. The Pope's gloss was then taken by Norbert Lohfink as the starting point for his book, *The Covenant Never Revoked*.

clear that the entry of gentiles into the Church—and their new identity as participants in the life of Israel—involves a "turning toward the Jews":

> The magi's coming to Jerusalem in order to pay homage to the king of the Jews shows that they seek in Israel, in the messianic light of the star of David, the one who will be king of the nations. Their coming means that pagans can discover Jesus and worship him as Son of God and Savior of the world only by turning toward the Jews and receiving from them the messianic promise as contained in the Old Testament. The Epiphany shows that "the full number of the nations" now takes its "place in the family of the patriarchs," and acquires *Israelitica dignitas* (is made "worthy of the heritage of Israel"). (*CCC* 528)

The coming of the magi to Jerusalem prefigures the response of the gentiles to the message of the Jewish apostles of the Jewish Messiah, and the latter enables gentiles to take their "place in the family of the patriarchs"—but only through a new bond that is established between them and the flesh and blood "family of the patriarchs."

The Catechism thus provides an authoritative commentary on those ambiguous sections of *Lumen Gentium* that relate to the Jewish people. There is now no danger that the two propositions of *Lumen Gentium*—the identity of the Church as the People of God and the identity of genealogical-Israel as the recipient of irrevocable gifts—might be seen as in conflict with one another. Moreover, by stressing the opening line of *Nostra Aetate* 4 the Catechism asserts that these two propositions are in fact closely intertwined. However, the Catechism makes no attempt to explain the nature of the link, nor does it give any prominence to the Jewish people when presenting its teaching about the Church (*CCC* 748–975). The Catechism makes much progress, but it leaves for another day the task of articulating the full implications of *Nostra Aetate* for ecclesiology.

Developing the Teaching of *Lumen Gentium*

While *Lumen Gentium* fails to establish a connection between the identity of the Church and the identity of the Jewish people, it does provide us with some of the conceptual tools required to fulfill that task. Reading *Lumen Gentium* in the light of *Nostra Aetate*, the Catechism, and the teaching of Pope John Paul II and of Cardinal Lustiger, I would highlight four major points from the document which, with some development, have the potential to open new doors in our understanding of the relationship between the Church and the Jewish people.

People of God, Body of Christ

The first concerns the relationship between the two primary biblical concepts employed by *Lumen Gentium*: the people of God and the Body of Christ. While *Lumen Gentium* emphasizes these two ecclesiological concepts, it nowhere discusses the connection between them. Happily, the Catechism sheds new light on this connection: "The images taken from the Old Testament [to speak of the Church] are variations on a profound theme: the People of God. In the New Testament, all these images find a new center because Christ has become the head of this people, which henceforth is his Body" (*CCC* 753). Here we find hints of what I have called Israel-Christology. Jesus "has become the head of this people"—he sums up the people of Israel in himself and fulfills (now and in the eschaton) Israel's mission in the world. As he becomes Israel's head, so Israel becomes his Body. This means that Jesus effects an eschatological renewal of covenantal identity for those Jews who are united to him in baptism, while enabling gentiles who believe in him to participate for the first time in Israel's blessings. But what does this mean for those who are already members of "the people of God" but who remain unbaptized? Cardinal Lustiger points us in the right direction:

> As messianic subject, Christ is composed of all those who belong to him through baptism and faith. And *in a certain way*—I repeat, *in a certain way*—the Jewish people are a part of him . . . . In their particularity, the Jewish people carry the heart of the revelation. And *in a certain way*, they also bear the image of the Messiah, of Christ.[14]

Drawing upon a phrase from an oft-quoted statement in the Vatican II Pastoral Constitution on the Church in the Modern World (*Gaudium et spes*), Cardinal Lustiger implies that "*in a certain way*" all those who are part of genealogical-Israel receive a new status as members of his Body.[15] Those Jews who receive the good news affirm their new status as members of his Body, and enter into the eschatologically renewed and expanded Israel. Those who do not receive the good news are put in an anomalous and precarious situation—yet Jesus remains their sovereign and head, whether

---

14. Lustiger, *On Christians and Jews*, 74, 66. Emphasis added.

15. "For, by his incarnation, he, the Son of God, has *in a certain way* united himself with each man" (*Gaudium et Spes* 22; emphasis added). Through this allusion, Cardinal Lustiger implicitly distinguishes between three modes of union with "the Son of God": (1) his union with humanity and every human being by virtue of his incarnation as a human being; (2) his union with the Jewish people and individual Jews by virtue of his incarnation as the Messiah of Israel; (3) his union with those who confess him in faith, are baptized into his death, and receive the gift of the Holy Spirit.

they acknowledge the fact or not. He was born "the King of the Jews" (Matt 2:2), he was crucified under the same title (Matt 27:11, 29, 37), and he will bear it for all eternity. Thus, for Jews, participation in the life of the people points them toward membership in the Body of their appointed messianic king. For gentiles, on the other hand, the situation is reversed. All gentiles who are joined to the Body of Christ through faith and baptism thereby become part of an expanded people of Israel. For them, membership in the Body leads to citizenship in the commonwealth of Israel.

As for how membership in Messiah's Body leads to citizenship in Israel, we must reflect on the fact that Jesus was born a Jew, was circumcised on the eighth day, and lived as a faithful Jew throughout the course of his earthly life. When he was raised from the dead, his Jewish identity carried over into his glorified existence, just as did his masculine gender. To say that Jesus *was* a Jew is a fact of history. To say that Jesus *is* a Jew is a fact of explosive theological consequence. The Son of God does not assume a generic human nature, but the humanity descended from Abraham, Isaac, and Jacob, Sarah, Rebecca, Rachel, and Leah. When gentiles become part of that body, they become part of a Jewish body. They do not themselves become Jews, but they become part of the Jewish commonwealth. In this way Israel-Christology fills the "gap" separating genealogical-Israel from the people of God of the renewed covenant. Israel-Christology gives birth to an Israel-ecclesiology that confirms rather than undermines the enduring election of genealogical-Israel, and that clarifies the bond joining the *ekklesia* to the original heir of the promises.

Priest, Prophet, and King

A second central motif of *Lumen Gentium* likewise takes on new significance when viewed in the context of Israel-Christology. This motif is the threefold office of priest/prophet/king that Christ shares with his Body. While *Lumen Gentium* introduces the threefold office of Christ in its section on the Church as the people of God (*LG* 10–16), it nowhere relates this theme to the life of genealogical-Israel. Yet that is its source.[16] The Torah

---

16. According to Matthew Levering, Thomas Aquinas describes the salvific work of Jesus in terms of the threefold office in a way that properly situates the Savior within the life and history of the people of Israel: "Christ's life uniquely engages the central roles of the divinely constituted society of ancient Israel. By this means, Aquinas shows how each aspect of Jesus' ministry has an intelligible place in God's plan for human salvation through the words and deeds of Christ Jesus, who fulfills the purposes of divine Wisdom for Israel, as these purposes have been revealed in Israel's Torah" (Levering, *Fulfillment*, 50).

defines Israel's institutions of leadership according to the offices of priest, prophet, and king (Deut 16:18—18:22). The English theologian Colin Gunton renders explicit the relationship that *Lumen Gentium* leaves implicit:

> Like all societies, Israel had religious, moral and political dimensions to her life, and it can be said that the offices corresponding to them were those of priest, prophet and king. . . . All of them . . . are equally oriented at once to Israel's relation to God and to the social order consequent upon that. They were called in order to maintain Israel's faithfulness to the covenant.[17]

To describe Jesus as priest, prophet, and king is to affirm that God has appointed him the definitive ruler of Israel, the one called "to maintain Israel's faithfulness to the covenant," and that the entire line of Israel's national leadership is summed up in him.

> In what he does and teaches, this Spirit-inspired prophet concentrates in himself the work of the lawgivers, prophets, kings, priests, and indeed wisdom teachers of Israel. Their work comes to a head in him. . . . In his person, and through the various acts and phases of his historic career, Jesus fills the offices and institutions of Israel with distinctive and definitive meaning . . . .[18]

In this way, the life of the people of Israel goes beyond preparing for and foreshadowing the Church; even more, Israel "provides the logic of Christology."[19]

What are the practical consequences of this connection between the threefold office of Christ and the national life of the people of Israel? It leads to the same conclusions as those suggested above in discussing the relationship between the people of God and the Body of Christ. Jesus' divine appointment to these national offices puts him in relationship with the Jewish people as a whole, and with every Jew. He is the priest, prophet, and king from whom the priestly, prophetic, and royal aspects of Jewish life derive. Jews enter into a relationship with him by virtue of being part of the people—whether they know it or not, whether they like it or not. This relationship does not guarantee all Jews a place in the world to come—but, in a mysterious way, it founds and constitutes their covenantal identity in this world.[20] When Jews acknowledge Jesus as Israel's priest, prophet, and king,

---

17. Gunton, *Christian Faith*, 69.
18. Ibid., 106, 72.
19. Ibid., 80.
20. Catholic teaching recognizes that baptism likewise provides no guarantee to Christians that they will receive a place of blessedness in the world to come.

they confirm their own identity as members of the eschatologically renewed people of Israel. Thus, participation in the people of God orients Jews to a relationship with Christ (though most Jews do not yet discern the meaning of the signs). For gentiles, on the other hand, the process takes place in reverse order: relationship with Christ initiates them into the people of God. Israel-Christology again gives birth to an Israel-ecclesiology that affirms the covenantal status of genealogical-Israel.

These two central motifs of *Lumen Gentium*—the Church as the people of God and Body of Christ, and as participant in Christ's threefold office—can thus be seen as variations on a common theme of Israel-Christology. Jesus sums up not only the line of Israel's leaders, but Israel's life as a whole. He is the one-man Israel, who carries the entire people in himself even more than did his ancestor Jacob. If the elect status of genealogical-Israel endures, as asserted by *Lumen Gentium* and *Nostra Aetate*, that election must be rooted in the elect Son of God who became the Son of David. We should not resist the natural conclusion: all Jewish identity "comes to a head in him." *Lumen Gentium* recognizes that this is true for Christ's relationship with the Church. We should take this further, and affirm it also of his relationship with the Jewish people.

Mary, Daughter of Zion

What we have found in these two themes has an exact parallel in a third central theme of *Lumen Gentium*: the Virgin Mary as "type" of the Church. The document concludes with teaching on Mary because it seeks to properly contextualize her important role. Rather than viewing her as an independent object of devotion, Catholics are encouraged to see her as an individual embodiment of what the Church should be as a whole:

> Wherefore she is hailed as a pre-eminent and singular member of the Church, and as its type and excellent exemplar in faith and charity. (*LG* 53)

> By reason of the gift and role of divine maternity, by which she is united with her Son . . . , the Blessed Virgin is also intimately united with the Church. As St. Ambrose taught, the Mother of God is a type of the Church in the order of faith, charity, and perfect union with Christ. For in the mystery of the Church, which is itself rightly called mother and virgin, the Blessed Virgin stands out in eminent and singular fashion as exemplar both of virgin and mother. (*LG* 63)

> Seeking after the glory of Christ, the Church becomes more like her exalted Type, and continually progresses in faith, hope and charity, seeking and doing the will of God in all things. Hence the Church, in her apostolic work also, justly looks to her, who, conceived of the Holy Spirit, brought forth Christ, who was born of the Virgin that through the Church He may be born and may increase in the hearts of the faithful also. The Virgin in her own life lived an example of that maternal love, by which it behooves that all should be animated who cooperate in the apostolic mission of the Church for the regeneration of men. (*LG* 65)

The Virgin becomes a model for individual Catholics in her virtue, and for the Church as a whole in her maternal love. In that love the Church gives birth to her children through the waters of baptism, and nurtures them in the teaching of Christ.

But what of Mary's relationship to the people of Israel? Only once does *Lumen Gentium* allude to that relationship, calling her "the exalted Daughter of Zion" (55). This singular reference deserves far more attention than it receives. When Scripture presents the people of Israel as a corporate reality, it normally speaks of the community using masculine language. The community is Jacob, God's son and representative in the world. However, when it speaks of the capital city of Jerusalem, the language is feminine. The city represents the corporate reality of the community in relationship to God, her spouse, and the people themselves are her children. Just as Jesus embodies Israel as priest, prophet, and king, so Mary embodies Zion, mother of all the faithful.

Mary is a type of the Church, but she becomes that type through her role as the individual personal representation of the holy city, and of the Temple that resided at its center. By neglecting this dimension of Mary's identity, *Lumen Gentium* again accentuates discontinuity at the expense of continuity. As the Church is seen as a radically new reality, prefigured by, but discontinuous with, the old, so the imagery of Zion appears as merely figurative prophetic foreshadowing of a new multinational community in which Jews are but another redeemed ethnicity.

But is not Mary still a Jewish mother, just as Jesus is still a Jewish Messiah? In giving birth to the Messiah, was she not an expression of Israel's entire history and life, the sum of humble and faithful Jews through the centuries—a history that was as necessary to Jesus' conception as Mary's own fiat? If indeed Mary has a special place in the heavenly courts and if indeed she watches over her children on earth—do not her people according to the flesh have a special place in her heart among those beloved children?

The *Ecclesia ex Circumcisione*

The fourth and final element of *Lumen Gentium* to be noted here is of a different order. It is not a theme of the document, but a fragment of a paragraph within it; and the development of this paragraph that I am offering may not express the conscious intentions of those who framed the original document. But, like the authors of Scripture, the authors of conciliar documents do not always understand the full meaning of what they write. The unit to which I refer is drawn from *LG* 9:

> Christ instituted this new covenant, the new testament, that is to say, in His Blood, calling together *a people made up of Jew and gentile*, making them one, not according to the flesh but in the Spirit. This was to be the new People of God. For those who believe in Christ, who are reborn not from a perishable but from an imperishable seed through the word of the living God, not from the flesh but from water and the Holy Spirit, are finally established as "a chosen race, a royal priesthood, a holy nation, a purchased people ... who in times past were not a people, but are now the people of God."[21]

This text recognizes that the Church is "a people made up of Jew and gentile," united according to the Spirit. In its immediate context—apart from *Nostra Aetate* 4, the teaching of Pope John Paul II, and the revised Catechism—this expression could mean simply that membership in the Church is independent of restrictions based on ethnicity. The unity of this people is "not according to the flesh," and membership within her does not originate with birth "from the flesh." In this regard, the "new People of God" differs from the "Israel according to the flesh" which preceded her, even though she inherits many of its privileges (e.g., the new covenant) and titles (e.g., chosen race, royal priesthood, holy nation, people of God).

However, once we take account of the fact that "Israel according to the flesh" not only remains "the priestly people of God" (*CCC* 63) but is encountered within the Church's own mystery (*Nostra Aetate* 4), this text appears in a different light. Its potential meaning becomes even more distinct when we consider Cardinal Lustiger's teaching that the Church's catholicity refers specifically to her being "composed of both Jews and pagans," and that this originally meant that she consisted of two corporate environments— "the *Ecclesia ex circumcisione* (the Church born from circumcision) and the *Ecclesia ex gentibus* (the Church born from the pagan nations)."[22] If

---

21. Emphasis added.
22. Lustiger, *Promise*, 6, 125.

the Body of Christ is an eschatologically renewed and expanded form of genealogical-Israel, rather than a separate entity created by God *ex nihilo* and only prefigured by the Israel of the old covenant, then one would expect that the presence of Jews in her midst would be *an essential component of her identity*. Along with Mary the daughter of Zion, and the apostles, these Jews would serve as an extension of the Jewish identity of the risen Jesus in the heart of the Church, assuring her legitimacy as a partaker of the divine promises (such as that of the new covenant itself) given to genealogical-Israel. The Jewish members of the Church are a prophetic sign of the Church's historical continuity with "the people of God of the Old Covenant, never revoked by God."

The presence of genealogical-Israel within the Body of Christ also constitutes a prophetic sign pointing *forward* to the eschatological fullness of the people of God. Interpreting Paul's teaching on the eschaton in Romans 11, the Catechism asserts that corporate recognition of Jesus as Messiah by the Jewish people will precede his return in glory:

> The glorious Messiah's coming is suspended at every moment of history until his recognition by "all Israel," for "a hardening has come upon part of Israel" in their "unbelief" toward Jesus [Rom 11:20–26]. St. Peter says to the Jews of Jerusalem after Pentecost: "Repent therefore, and turn again, that your sins may be blotted out, that times of refreshing may come from the presence of the Lord, and that he may send the Christ appointed for you, Jesus, whom heaven must receive until the time for establishing all that God spoke by the mouth of his holy prophets from of old" [Acts 3:19–21]. St. Paul echoes him: "For if their rejection means the reconciliation of the world, what will their acceptance mean but life from the dead?" [Rom 11:15] The "full inclusion" of the Jews in the Messiah's salvation, in the wake of "the full number of the Gentiles" [Rom 11:12, 25], will enable the People of God to achieve "the measure of the stature of the fullness of Christ" [Eph 4:13], in which "God may be all in all" [1 Cor 15:28]. (*CCC* 674)

The "people of God" will not reach their destined fullness till the Jewish people—as a corporate reality—and the *ecclesia* come together as one flock with one Shepherd, to celebrate the glory of God through Israel's Messiah in the power of the Holy Spirit. Before that day arrives, is the Church of Jesus Christ only an *ecclesia ex gentibus*? Or, to the contrary, are the Jews in her midst called to be an essential sign of the catholic fullness yet to come?

In light of the developments in Catholic teaching after 1964, *Lumen Gentium* 9 assumes a different visage: "Christ instituted this new covenant

... calling together a people made up of Jew and gentile." The presence of gentiles in this people is essential to its universal vocation; however, the presence of Jews is just as essential to its claim to be a transformed and renewed expression of Israel, anticipating in its corporate life the eschatological "measure of the stature of the fullness of Christ." This conclusion leads to even more challenging questions. Is it sufficient for these Jewish members of the Church to be hidden like leaven in her universally expanding dough? Should their identity as Jews not be treasured, celebrated, and visibly expressed? And is it sufficient for these Jewish members of the Church to live dispersed among their gentile brothers and sisters, isolated from one another and without any distinctive corporate identity among themselves? Is the *ecclesia ex circumcisione* an invisible community of unrelated individuals, or is it called to be a manifest social reality, like the universal *ecclesia* of which it is part? These are questions that must be addressed in any twenty-first-century interpretation of *Lumen Gentium* in light of *Nostra Aetate*.

Two Complementary Perspectives

Comparing *Lumen Gentium* 16 with *Nostra Aetate* 4, Johannes Cardinal Willebrands has suggested that they offer two complementary perspectives on one reality.[23] The first takes the Church as its point of reference, and speaks of the way the Jewish people are related to her. The second takes the Jewish people as its point of reference, and speaks of the way the Church is related to them. Using the language we have explored in this chapter, we might say that *Lumen Gentium* focuses on the Church as the Body of Christ to which the Jewish people are oriented through their messianic king, whereas *Nostra Aetate* focuses on genealogical-Israel as the people of God within whose expanded tent-pegs Christians now also reside through baptism into Christ.

This reading of *Lumen Gentium* 16 adheres to a hermeneutic of continuity, and there is a long and venerable Catholic tradition of employing such a hermeneutic in the interpretation of official documents. In this case, reading one document in light of another yields genuine insight. We see how these two documents belong together and need each other. Catholics cannot adequately approach the mystery of their own identity if they treat genealogical-Israel and its religious way of life only as a non-Christian religion related externally to the Church. However, Catholics also cannot adequately approach the mystery of Jewish identity if they treat it as something unrelated to the mystery of Christ.

---

23. Willebrands, *Church and Jewish People*, 43.

My fundamental thesis should now be clear. I am proposing that Israel-ecclesiology derives from Israel-Christology and the mediation of the *ecclesia ex circumcisione*, and that the Church is joined to the mystery of genealogical-Israel through these same realities. I am also proposing that Christ is as much the inner mystery of the Jewish people as he is the mystery of the Church. In this way the links between *Lumen Gentium* and *Nostra Aetate* which were formerly shrouded in darkness enter into the light of day.

It now remains for us to test this thesis by examining the biblical basis for the central sacraments of the Church's life. If we are on the right track, we should discover a connection to the Jewish people where it was never expected—in holy orders, in baptism, and in the Eucharist. Moreover, if in fact the risen Christ rightly holds the title "King of the Jews," then we should also expect to find a sacramental dimension in the midst of the religious life of the Jewish people by means of which his hidden presence imparts grace to his flesh and blood family. For Christ is not only the "light of the gentiles"—he is also the "glory of Israel" (Luke 2:32).

4

Priesthood, Apostleship, and the People of Israel

In the previous chapter I proposed new directions for the development of Catholic ecclesiology. Those new directions all entail a reconsideration of the way the Church's identity is related both to biblical Israel and to the post-biblical reality of the Jewish people. I have proposed an Israel-ecclesiology rooted in Israel-Christology that affirms the enduring election of the Jewish people and that recognizes the theological significance of Jewish identity within the Body of Christ. Such an ecclesiology has the potential to reconfigure our understanding of the *ecclesia* and its relationship to genealogical-Israel.

If this thesis has merit, it should shed light on the sacramental life of the *ecclesia* and bear fruit in new insights regarding the meaning of New Testament texts. In the remainder of this book I will test my thesis according to these two criteria: Does it expand and deepen—without contradicting—a traditional Catholic understanding of the sacraments? Does it open up new dimensions of meaning in key New Testament passages, without undermining authoritative readings of the past?

In the present chapter I will consider the implications of such an Israel-ecclesiology for the sacrament of holy orders. The Catechism defines the sacrament of holy orders as follows: "Holy Orders is the sacrament through which the mission entrusted by Christ to his apostles continues to be exercised in the Church until the end of time: thus it is the sacrament of apostolic ministry" (*CCC* 1536). After explaining the term "Orders" (*CCC* 1537–38), the Catechism focuses attention on the priestly character of "apostolic ministry" (*CCC* 1539–53). Priestly ministry and apostolic ministry are thus bound together, and both are founded on the priestly ministry of Jesus (*CCC* 1544–45). In this chapter I will contend that the offices of priest and apostle are both integrally connected to the corporate vocation of the

Jewish people. Furthermore, I will propose that Jewish followers of Jesus fulfill a particular priestly—and thus sacramental—role that derives from that corporate vocation and from its foundation and realization in the Messiah.

I will begin by examining the Letter to the Hebrews in order to ascertain the relationship between the priesthood of Jesus and the priesthood of Israel. I will then turn attention to the Letter to the Ephesians in order to understand the apostolic ministry and its relationship to the election and vocation of genealogical-Israel. Finally, I will consider several texts from the Letter to the Romans and from the early Church in order to clarify the priestly calling of Jewish disciples of Jesus.

The Letter to the Hebrews: Israel's Priesthood and Jesus' Priesthood

According to Catholic teaching, ordained priesthood derives directly from the priesthood of Christ. It is related to the priesthood of the entire Church, but not derived from it (*CCC* 1547). The ministerial priest acts "in the name of the whole Church," but Catholic teaching emphasizes that this "does not mean that priests are the delegates of the community. . . . It is because the ministerial priesthood represents Christ that it can represent the Church" (*CCC* 1552-3). The priest participates—in union with his bishop—in the apostolic *diakonia*, which derives directly from the calling of Christ and which is itself instrumental in establishing the Church as a catholic reality.

This pattern differs from the way the Torah construes the relationship between the national priesthood of Israel and the ministerial priesthood of the sons of Aaron. Israel's priestly election as a people is prior to, independent of, and a condition for the priestly election of one of its families. This is evident from the chronological order of these discrete elections (Israel, Exod 19:6; Aaron and his sons, Exod 28:1). The quasi-priestly role of Aaron's Levitical tribe arises even later in the narrative (Exod 32:29), and the Torah explains that the Levites are chosen as a substitute for the first-born sons of all the tribes (Num 3:11-13). This further reinforces the secondary nature of the Levitical priesthood, and its dependence on Israel's antecedent priestly calling as a nation.

The subordination of the Aaronic priesthood to Israel's national priesthood takes even more radical forms in some streams of the Jewish exegetical tradition.[1] According to the sixteenth-century Italian commentator Sforno,

---

1. I cite these rabbinic exegetical traditions to underline the point already asserted, namely, the secondary and derivative character of the Levitical priesthood. My intention here is not to affirm their conclusion or argue their case.

God's original purpose for Israel at Sinai involved neither a circumscribed tabernacle nor a priestly caste. Instead, God intended initially that all Israel would have immediate access to the divine presence. However, Israel sinned by worshipping the golden calf, and as a consequence they could no longer benefit from such intimate proximity to God. From this point forward they would require priestly mediation.[2] Sforno's reading drew support from Rashi's contention that the instructions to Moses regarding the building of the tabernacle and the ordination of the priests (Exod 25–31) were delivered *after* the incident of the golden calf (Exod 32) rather than before.[3]

I do not present this dis-analogy as a critique of the Catholic theology of ministerial priesthood. Catholic teaching on priesthood is not founded on a direct correspondence between the Church's ministry and the Aaronic office, and that teaching remains firmly intact when such a correspondence is weakened.[4] Instead, I seek to underline the central importance of the priestly vocation of the people of Israel for understanding the priesthood of Jesus—an importance that Catholics might overlook by focusing exclusively on Israel's *ministerial* priesthood. While the Torah's depiction of the Aaronic priesthood and its sacrificial duties contains a wealth of material which may be read typologically and applied to the priestly work of the Messiah, Jesus was not a descendant of Aaron and he never served in the Jerusalem Temple. But he *was* an Israelite—indeed, as the proleptic messianic king, he summed up all Israel in his own person. As the one-man Israel, Jesus enacted and perfected Israel's priestly calling, offering himself to God in whole-hearted love and obedience. In doing so he carried his people in himself, along with the nations of the world whom Israel was called to represent (Exod 19:5–6), and the entire creation.

This claim may appear dubious in light of the letter to the Hebrews, which is the only text in the New Testament that speaks explicitly of the priesthood of Jesus. Hebrews points out that Jesus lacked Aaronic descent and never served at the altar of the earthly temple (Heb 7:13–14), but the letter does not then associate his priesthood with that of Israel as a whole. Instead, it describes Jesus as a priest "according to the order of Melchizedek"—i.e., after the pattern of a non-Israelite priest-king to whom Abram showed special deference (7:4–10). Hebrews appears to decouple priesthood from

---

2. See Sforno on Exod 24:18; 31:18 (*Commentary*, 416–17, 450–51).

3. See Rashi on Exod 31:18 (*Shemos/Exodus*, 444).

4. The Catechism, in line with Church tradition, emphasizes the typological connection between the Aaronic priesthood and the priesthood of Christ (*CCC* 1544; 1541). Nevertheless, such a typological relationship does not necessarily entail a precise correspondence between the two. Moreover, the priesthood of Jesus is not *founded on* this typology.

physical descent (7:16), and this could imply a nullification of the priestly significance not only of the Aaronic genealogy but also of Israelite descent in general. Is this letter suggesting, through the figure of Melchizedek, that Jesus' priesthood transcends not only that of Aaron but also that of Israel?

A careful reading of Hebrews, and of the biblical texts that the letter interprets, leads to a different conclusion. Hebrews bases its theology of Jesus' priesthood primarily on Psalm 110, and only secondarily on Genesis 14. The psalm, which bears the superscription *leDavid Mizmor* ("A psalm of David"), addresses the Davidic king who reigns in Jerusalem: "The Lord sends out from Zion your mighty scepter; rule in the midst of your foes" (v. 2). The psalm asserts that this anointed son of David receives the divine promise, confirmed by an oath: "The Lord has sworn and will not change his mind: 'You are a priest forever according to the order of Melchizedek'" (v. 4). Just as Melchizedek ruled over Jerusalem as a priest-king, so this triumphant descendant of David will rule from Zion as a priest-king.[5] The point of the psalm is not to glorify Melchizedek, but instead to exalt the honor of the Davidic king.

In this light, the verses in Hebrews that emphasize Jesus' non-Levitical descent deserve careful attention: "For the one of whom these things are spoken [in Psalm 110] belonged to another tribe, from which no one has ever served at the altar. For it is obvious that our Lord was descended from Judah, and in regard to that tribe Moses said nothing about priests" (Heb 7:13–14). Hebrews does not merely point out Jesus' lack of a Levitical pedigree, which would have been sufficient if its primary purpose were to challenge the relevance of fleshly genealogy in the new messianic context. In fact, Hebrews *underlines* Jesus' *actual* genealogical descent—from the tribe of Judah, to which David belonged. While Moses did not speak about a Judahite priesthood, the divine oracle in Psalm 110 does exactly that when it anticipates a future son of David who will reign as a priest forever.

Jesus' Davidic descent is thus a necessary condition for him to qualify as the eternal priest of Psalm 110—but it is not sufficient. Generations of David's sons had come and gone, but none before Jesus were worthy of this honor. According to Hebrews, what distinguished Jesus from all other sons of David was the indestructible life within him which was manifest in his resurrection from the dead: "And it is even more obvious when another priest arises, in the likeness of Melchizedek, who has become a priest, not according to a commandment in the Torah concerning fleshly descent, but according to the power of an indestructible life" (Heb 7:15–16). It is Jesus'

---

5. According to the synoptic tradition, Jesus finds significance in the paradoxical connection between David, as the putative author of the psalm, and David's descendant whom David calls "Lord" (see Mark 12:35–37).

fulfillment of the first verse of Psalm 110, when he was raised from the dead and seated at the right hand of God on high (see Heb 1:13; 10:12–14), which enables him to function as an "eternal priest, according to the order of Melchizedek." The same pattern is found in Romans 1:3–4, but there the issue is Jesus' messianic rather than priestly credentials: "the gospel concerning his Son, who was descended from David according to the flesh and was declared to be Son of God with power according to the spirit of holiness by resurrection from the dead, Jesus Christ our Lord...." Just as a particular fleshly genealogy was necessary but not sufficient for messiahship, so a particular fleshly genealogy was necessary but not sufficient for the role of eternal priest. According to the New Testament, both roles also required resurrection. The pattern is identical because Hebrews recognizes, in accordance with Psalm 110, that Jesus' eternal priesthood is an aspect of his role as Israel's messianic king. His identity as Messiah is primary; his role as priest derives from and is dependent upon that primary identity.[6]

This conclusion supports our contention that Israel's national priesthood provides the essential background for Jesus' priesthood. This is the case because Israel's Messiah is inherently a representative and corporate figure, who bears his people in his own person. If Jesus' priesthood is a function of his messiahship, then his priesthood is brought into direct relation to Israel's priestly role as a people. Israel-Christology lays the foundation for the priestly ministry of Jesus, and thus also for the priestly ministry of the *ecclesia*.

The Letter to the Ephesians: Israel's Priesthood and the Apostolic Office

As the Catechism states, "Holy Orders is the sacrament of apostolic ministry" (*CCC* 1536). Apostolic ministry has a priestly character because it involves participation in Christ's own ministry. If the priestly office of Jesus constitutes an eschatological realization of Israel's national holiness and priestly vocation, as implied by the Letter to the Hebrews, then this should also be true for the apostolic office. A careful reading of Ephesians

---

6. The relationship between Jesus' kingship and priesthood also has implications for how Catholics understand holy orders. The apostolic ministry involves not only priesthood, but also pastoral government (i.e., kingship) and authoritative teaching (i.e., the function of the prophet and the sage). This widening of the concept of holy orders is reflected in the Vatican II Decree on the Pastoral Office of Bishops in the Church. That document also made clear that "It is the bishops who enjoy the fullness of the sacrament of orders, and both priests and deacons are dependent on them in the exercise of their power" (chapter II, paragraph 15).

1–3 in light of recent scholarship confirms that this is indeed the case. These chapters also illustrate vividly the meaning and importance of an Israel-ecclesiology that highlights the messianic dimension of the Jewish people, both before and after his coming in the flesh, and that likewise expresses the enduring theological significance of the Jew-gentile distinction, even within the one Body of Christ.

The Hermeneutical Significance of Ephesians 2:11–22

All readers of Ephesians recognize that verses 11–22 of its second chapter speak of the new relationship between Jews and gentiles established by the redemptive work of Christ. Many who study the letter consider these to be the only verses of the book that take up this subject. Moreover, the unit is seen as eliminating all distinction between Jews and gentiles and abolishing the commandments of the Torah that inscribe this distinction in Jewish flesh and in the Jewish way of life. The one new universal humanity of the Christian Church has now replaced the obsolete ethnic particularity of genealogical-Israel.[7] When the author later marvels at the miracle of what God has done for gentiles through the coming of Christ (Eph 3:5–6), he is but celebrating the universal scope of the divine plan which has now made the Jewish people an irrelevant anachronism.[8]

Several exegetes of recent decades have challenged this conventional reading of Ephesians.[9] These scholars interpret Ephesians 2:11–22 as an acknowledgement of the unique dignity of genealogical-Israel which continues to be expressed in the united *ecclesia* of the Messiah—an *ecclesia* in which the enmity between Jews and gentiles is overcome while the differentiation between them remains. Furthermore, these commentators consider this unit to be central to the letter as a whole, and by reading other units with this one in mind they show how the theme of Jew-gentile communion

---

7. Thomas Slater articulates this position with admirable clarity and concision: "Ephesians 2:11–22 states that the ethnic boundaries that segregated gentiles and nongentiles have been destroyed by Christ. In place of those socioethnic demarcations is the name 'Christians.' Thus, Eph 2:11–22 does not argue that the gentiles remain gentiles or that they must remember their pasts but that they have been transformed and given a new ethnicity that replaces the old one, and this new identity is the same identity for both Jews and gentiles" (Slater, "Review").

8. For an erudite commentary which espouses such a reading of the letter, see Lincoln, *Ephesians*.

9. See Barth, *Israel*, 79–117, and *Ephesians 1–3*; Johnson, *Writings*, 407–21; Yoder Neufeld, *Ephesians*; McRay, *Paul*, 334–51; and Yee, *Ethnic Reconciliation*.

in the Messiah pervades the kerygma proclaimed throughout Ephesians 1–3.

Markus Barth and John McRay each assert the prime importance of Ephesians 2:11-22 for the letter as a whole based on the content of those verses.[10] Thomas R. Yoder Neufeld adds an illuminating structural argument in support of this thesis. Yoder Neufeld proposes an outline of Ephesians 1–3 in which these chapters form a chiasm, with 2:11-22 at its center.[11]

  A. Blessing of God   1:3-14
    B. Prayer for Wisdom and Power   1:15-23
      C. Gentiles and Jews (You and We) Raised to Life   2:1-10
        D. Christ is our Peace   2:11-22
      C¹· Gentiles and Jews Reconciled in Christ   3:1-13
    B¹· Prayer for Wisdom and Power Resumed   3:14-19
  A¹· Doxology   3:20-21

Since the central unit of a chiasm signals the chiasm's main concern, Yoder Neufeld provides us with a structural warrant for reading the first three chapters of Ephesians in light of 2:11-22.

There are four features of Ephesians 2:11-22 that enable us to recognize subtle cues found elsewhere in the letter. First of all, this unit employs the second person plural pronoun and verb as a way of identifying *gentiles* in contrast to Jews (Eph 2:11, 12, 13, 17, 19; see also 3:1). The first person plural in this unit refers explicitly to "us *both*" (Eph 2:14, 18)—in other words, to Jews and gentiles reconciled to God and one another in the Messiah. If the context and the use of the word "both" (*amphoteroi*) had not indicated that the first person plural referred to Jews *and* gentiles, we would have assumed—in contrast to the second person plural—that it spoke only of Jews. This point will become important when we examine Ephesians 1 and the opening verses of Ephesians 2.

Second, Ephesians 2:19-22 underlines the significance of compound nouns and verbs which include the prefix *sun-/sum-* ("with," "fellow-," "co-"). Verse 12 had spoken of the former condition of gentiles as "aliens from the commonwealth [*politeia*] of Israel." As a result of Messiah's reconciling work on the cross, these gentiles are now "citizens with [*sum-politai*] the saints"—i.e., "fellow-citizens" or "co-citizens" alongside their Jewish brothers and sisters (verse 19). Then verses 21-22 describe the new temple that is founded in Christ, "in whom the whole structure is joined together [*sun-armologoumene*] . . . and in whom you also are built together

---

10. Barth, *Ephesians 1–3*, 275; McRay, *Paul*, 338.
11. Neufeld, *Ephesians*, 21.

[*sun-oikodomeisthe*] spiritually into a dwelling-place for God." This temple includes both Jews and gentiles, whose union with the Messiah brings them also into union with one another. The *sun-/sum-* prefix will appear frequently in Ephesians 1–3, and in most if not all cases it refers to the communion of Jews and gentiles in the one Body of Christ.[12]

Third, Ephesians 2:19 also demonstrates a particular use of the word "saints" (*hagioi*) which deserves special attention. In the Pauline corpus this word normally refers to all members of the *ecclesia*. However, in this verse it identifies *Jews* in contrast to gentiles.[13] As we will see later in the present chapter, this usage of *hagioi* is not peculiar to Ephesians 2:19 but is found elsewhere in the Pauline writings.[14] This means that each appearance of the word in Ephesians should be scrutinized within its own context, with the possibility of a distinctive Jewish referent kept always in mind.

Fourth and finally, Ephesians 2:12 implies that genealogical-Israel before the birth of Christ was already joined to him in reality and in hope. This verse speaks of the desperate plight of the letter's gentile recipients in their previous pagan existence. As Catholic exegete Franz Mussner notes, the negative depiction of the gentile condition implies a corresponding positive understanding of the privileges of genealogical-Israel.

> The fundamental assertion about the Gentiles, to whom the addressees once belonged—"you were at that time without Christ"—is subsequently made explicit in detail: You were alienated from the commonwealth of Israel. You were strangers to the covenants of promise. You had no hope. You were without God (*atheoi*) in the world. If one formulates these five statements on the unsaved condition of the Gentiles in a positive way with a view to Israel, then they would sound as follows: Israel possesses the hope of the Messiah. Israel forms a "commonwealth" (*politeia*): the *qehal* YHWH. To Israel belong the covenants of the promise. Israel possesses thereby hope. Israel lives in community with God and in the knowledge of God in the world.[15]

In being separated from the "commonwealth of Israel," these gentiles were "without Christ" and "having no hope." This means that at that time the members of the "commonwealth of Israel" were already "*with* Christ" and "*having* hope" (i.e., in his coming). Mussner interprets the former privilege

---

12. On the importance in Ephesians of these compound words with the *sun-/sum-* prefix, see McRay, *Paul*, 343–44

13. Yee, *Ethnic Reconciliation*, 195–98.

14. See page 84.

15. Mussner, *Tractate*, 25.

in light of the latter, and sees Israel's prior existence "with Christ" as its "hope" or trusting anticipation of his eventual appearance. However, the phrase "with Christ" need not have only a future meaning; assuming the pre-existence of the Messiah, the author likely thinks that the Messiah dwelt with and in genealogical-Israel even before the Word became flesh in Mary's womb. Such a view is also found in 1 Corinthians 10:4, in which Paul identifies the rock which gave water to Israel in the wilderness as "the Messiah." Thus, genealogical-Israel before the incarnation enjoyed a relationship with Christ in reality and in hope.

With these four features of Ephesians 2:11–22 in mind, let us now examine Ephesians 1–3 as a whole. What do these chapters tell us about genealogical-Israel, the *ecclesia* of Jews and gentiles, and the role of the apostles?

Ephesians 1: Israel's Priestly Calling in the Messiah

After its initial salutation, Ephesians begins with a blessing (*berachah*) for divine election:

> Blessed be the God and Father of our Lord Jesus Christ, who has blessed us in Christ with every spiritual blessing in the heavenly places, just as he chose us in Christ before the foundation of the world to be holy [*hagious*] and blameless before him in love. He destined [*pro-orisas*] us for adoption as his children [*eis huiothesian*] through Jesus Christ, according to the good pleasure of his will, to the praise of his glorious grace that he freely bestowed on us in the Beloved. In him we have redemption through his blood, the forgiveness of our trespasses, according to the riches of his grace that he lavished on us. (Eph 1:3–8a)

Interpreters generally assume that the "us" in verse 3 refers to the *ecclesia* of Jews and gentiles, and that this blessing includes from the beginning the letter's gentile readers. However, in light of Ephesians 2:11–22, this assumption should be challenged. At this early point in the letter first-person plural pronouns may well refer to the uniquely privileged vocation of genealogical-Israel, in which gentiles will ultimately have a share. The "we" of these verses refers to a community of people who are the object of divine election—"he chose us" (v. 4)—and the goal of this election was that they might be "holy" (*hagioi*), i.e., "saints." This fits well with the Torah's description of Israel's election to holiness (Deut 7:6), and the priestly terminology ("to be holy and blameless before him") also fits the portrayal of genealogical-Israel in Ephesians 2:11–22 ("those who were near," 2:17).

According to Ephesians 1, Israel's priestly function derives from its filial relationship with God ("He destined us for adoption as his children [*eis huiothesian*]"). The term used in Ephesians 1:5 to refer to this filial relationship appears also in Romans 9:4, where Paul writes that his brothers and sisters according to the flesh "are Israelites, and to them belong the adoption [*huiothesia*]." Genealogical-Israel is God's eldest son (Exod 4:22), and the eldest is the family priest.[16] This is all standard Jewish thinking, as traditional as the *berachah* form in which it is couched.

However, the letter radically recontextualizes the tradition with two all-important words: "in Christ." With these words, Ephesians presents divine election as principally God's eternal delight in his eternal Son ("the Beloved"), and only subsequently as the inclusion of Israel in the Son through adoption. The eternal Son is heaven's high priest, and Israel shares by divine grace in his priestly role. Thus, from its earliest beginnings Israel is bound to its pre-incarnate Messiah, and enjoys divine favor only with, in, and through him. This fits perfectly with the description of genealogical-Israel in Ephesians 2:11–22, which always lived its life "with Christ." This also adds a new dimension to Israel-Christology: it is fitting for Jesus to sum up his people in himself, for their election "before the foundation of the world" was subsequent to and dependent upon his own.

In verse 7 the author moves forward in time to the age of the apostles, those members of the "commonwealth of Israel" who first experienced and proclaimed the redemptive work of the incarnate Messiah: "In him we have redemption through his blood, the forgiveness of our trespasses, according to the riches of his grace that he lavished on us." Ephesians 2 will likewise focus on "the blood of the Messiah" (2:13) and his cross (2:16), which grants "access" to God (2:18) for those who were already near and also for those who were remote (2:17). Thus, the first-person plural pronoun and verb of Ephesians 2:7–8a hint at the universal goal of God's work with genealogical-Israel without yet explicitly transcending the limits of that people.

The expansive scope of Israel's priestly service first becomes explicit in verses 8b–10. Through the apostles and prophets, God has revealed to Israel that the ultimate messianic goal is not merely its own redemption but the uniting of all things in the worship of God. "With all wisdom and insight he has made known to us the mystery of his will, according to his good pleasure that he set forth in [the] Christ, as a plan for the fullness of time, to gather up all things in him, things in heaven and things on earth" (Eph

---

16. According to Rashi, the "priests" referred to in Exod 19:22 are the firstborn sons of each of Israel's families. Later, the Levitical tribe will become a substitute for these firstborn sons.

1:8b–10).¹⁷ Ephesians displays here its characteristic cosmic orientation. The letter looks beyond Israel, beyond the *ecclesia*, to the furthest reaches of the created universe. Yet, it never leaves Israel or the *ecclesia* behind, for the redemption and consummation of all things occurs only through Israel and the *ecclesia*, who are the first to be united to "*the* Christ" (i.e., the Messiah of Israel). Ephesians is particularly fond of the definite article in this phrase. The word "Christ" in Ephesians serves not simply as a proper name for Jesus, but bears its full Jewish weight as a title—"*the* Messiah"—for Israel's eschatological sovereign. As the one in whom Israel originally received its vocation, he is also the one who assumes royal (and thus priestly) Jewish flesh in order to realize that vocation. As Ephesians will soon describe, he does so through death, resurrection, and ascension, by which he returns to the Father's heavenly throne, having left an indelible mark on the flesh he has born and the world in which his feet have walked.

As previewed in verse 7, the universal redemptive work of Israel's Messiah takes shape initially in the apostolic community of Jewish disciples of Jesus: "In Christ we have also obtained an inheritance, having been destined according to the purpose of him who accomplishes all things according to his counsel and will, so that we, who were the first to set our hope on [the] Christ, might live for the praise of his glory" (Eph 1:11–12). Ephesians 2:12 implicitly speaks of genealogical-Israel before the incarnation as "with Christ" and "having hope"; similarly, Ephesians 1:12 speaks of the early apostolic community as "the first to set our hope on [the] Christ." These Jewish disciples of Jesus have been "destined" (*pro-oristhentes*) to obtain an inheritance in Christ, and to "live for the praise of his glory." The use of the verb "destined" here in verse 11 parallels its use in verse 5, and confirms our thesis that the verbs and pronouns of this entire initial unit refer specifically to Jews.

Only at this point in Ephesians 1 do we encounter a second person plural pronoun. The pronominal switch is sudden and jarring, and cannot lack significance. "In him *you also* [*kai humeis*], when you had heard the word of truth, the gospel of your salvation, and had believed in him, were marked with the seal of the promised Holy Spirit; this is the pledge of our inheritance toward redemption as God's own people, to the praise of his glory" (Eph 1:13–14). In this context, "you also" means "*you gentiles*, in addition to us Jews." Through the priestly service of the Jewish apostles of Jesus in proclaiming "the word of truth," those from the gentiles have received "salvation" in Israel's Messiah, and now share in Israel's calling to live for

---

17. The NRSV often ignores the Greek definite article before "Christ." When the definite article appears in the Greek text before the word "Christ," I will insert the English definite article in brackets.

"the praise of his glory." Verses 11-14 thus present the two-fold apostolic community of Jews and gentiles as the preliminary and proleptic realization of the "plan for the fullness of the times" announced in verse 10. Just as the Holy Spirit is the "pledge" of the full inheritance that they will receive, the two-fold community itself is the "pledge" of the full inheritance that God will receive when "all things" are summed up in the Messiah.

Many commentators recognize the significance of this change in pronouns in Ephesians 1:13, and read verses 11-14 as referring to two groups within the *ecclesia*—Jews and gentiles.[18] John McRay goes further, as we have done above, and reads the entire unit of verses 3-14 in light of the Jew-gentile distinction.

> It is in the context of the role of Israel as the elect—chosen to provide the Messiah—rather than in the context of individual predestination to salvation, that Paul speaks of election. . . . Paul asserts in this chapter that the Jews, God's saints or holy ones, were "chosen" to bring the blessing of redemption to all nations in fulfillment of the promise to Abraham. It was the Jews who were foreordained unto adoption for this purpose (Eph. 1:5), chosen in the beloved (i.e., Messiah) for God's glory (i.e., to declare the sovereignty of monotheism, Eph. 1:6) before the foundation of the world to be "holy and blameless" (i.e., saints, Eph. 1:4) and to be the first to hope in the Messiah (1:12).[19]

As McRay notes, Ephesians employs the language of election and predestination in the corporate and historical mode of Jewish Scripture, rather than in the individual and timeless mode adopted by later Christian theology. Anticipating the temporal progression in the outworking of God's "plan" (*oikonomia*, 1:10) to be traced in Ephesians 2:11-22, the opening verses of the letter begin with Israel's singular privilege and culminate in a cosmic redemption that is proleptically realized in an *ecclesia* of Jews and gentiles. For Ephesians, this *ecclesia* is not an entirely new entity, separate from genealogical-Israel, but a new form of "the commonwealth of Israel," now expanded and transposed into a heightened eschatological key.

In verses 15-23 Ephesians moves from *berachah* (blessing) to *tefillah* (petitionary prayer). The focus is now on the gentile recipients of the letter, whose inclusion in the messianic redemption was signaled by the shift in pronouns in verse 13. The author prays that his gentile readers might receive

---

18. Barth, *Ephesians 1-3*, 130-35; Johnson, *Writings*, 414; Yoder Neufeld, *Ephesians*, 54. Cardinal Schönborn adopts this understanding of the pronouns of Ephesians 1:11-14 in his article, "Judaism's Way to Salvation."

19. McRay, *Paul*, 339-40.

"a spirit of wisdom and revelation" (v. 17) like that already bestowed on the apostolic community of Jews (v. 8). This "wisdom" will enable these gentiles to also partake of the "hope" (v. 18) that resided first in that apostolic community (v. 12), a hope that for them consists of sharing in "the riches of his glorious inheritance among *the saints*" (v. 18). Thus, the hope before them is a corporate reality, which individual gentiles partake of by being joined to the community of the "saints." This community is the Israel whom God chose in the Messiah before the foundation of the world to be holy and blameless before him (v. 4), as embodied now in the fellowship of the apostles.

Ephesians 2: Israel's Eschatological Expansion through the Apostolic Ministry

Ephesians 2:1-11 proceeds to speak about the impact of the resurrection and ascension of the Messiah (referred to in 1:20-23) on the daily practice of those Jews and gentiles who have become part of the apostolic *ecclesia*. If, as is likely, the shifting pronouns have the same significance as in chapter 1, the letter presents both gentiles (vv. 1-2) and Jews (v. 3) as "walking" in trespasses and sins, and suffering the judgment (i.e., death) consequent upon such a pattern of life. While both find themselves in the same predicament, the dual description maintains a distinction between them even as it emphasizes their common need.[20] Thus, these verses reflect a similar orientation as that found in Romans 1-3, where the sins of gentile and Jewish culture are characterized in starkly different ways en route to the conclusion that both are in dire need of messianic redemption.[21]

God saves both gentiles and Jews from the ultimate penalty of death by joining them to the Messiah so that they might share in his resurrection life: "But God, who is rich in mercy, out of the great love with which he loved us even when we were dead through our trespasses, made us alive together [*sun-ezoopoiesen*] with [the] Christ—by grace you have been saved—and

---

20. Yee, *Ethnic Reconciliation*, 46-58.

21. Luke Timothy Johnson perceives both the import of the shift in pronouns, and the parallel with Romans: "The argument worked out by diatribe in Romans is here presented by epitome. In 2:1-2, Paul briefly sketches the state of humanity as being subject to the power of evil (cf. Rom. 1:18—3:20). Here, the spiritual alienation is expressed in terms of subjection to spiritual forces: 'the prince of the power of the air, the spirit that is now at work among the sons of disobedience' (2:2). But Paul does not exclude from the power of sin those who possess Torah (cf. Rom. 2:17—3:20), for 'we,' the Jews, were in the same state of alienation (2:3): 'We were by nature children of wrath (cf. Rom. 1:18) like the rest of humanity'" (*Writings*, 414-15).

raised us up [*sun-egeiren*] with him and seated us [*sun-ekathisen*] with him in the heavenly places in Christ Jesus..." (Eph 2:4–6). After distinguishing in verses 1–3 between Jews and gentiles in their common plight, Ephesians now emphasizes that God delivers them *together*. Taking the *sun-/sum-* prefix employed three times in Ephesians 2:19–22 as our hermeneutical key, we should read these three compound verbs as referring not only to the fellowship of Jews and gentiles *with the Messiah* but also to their fellowship *with one another*. Yoder Neufeld catches the import of the repeated prefix and its practical implication: "To what does *together with* in verse 5 refer? In the Greek *together with* is indicated with *sun-* prefixed to this verb as well as to *raised* and *seated* in 2:6. One obvious possibility is that together refers to *you* and *we* [in verses 2:1–3].... Being made alive by God means joining a community that experiences divine life not individualistically but *together with* others."[22] The shifting pronouns of 2:1–3 and the three-fold use of the *sun-/sum-* prefix suggest that concern for Jew-gentile unity and distinction pervades the entire letter, and is not restricted to the central unit that follows.

As discussed in our hermeneutical introduction to the letter, Ephesians 2:11–22 constitutes the heart of Ephesians 1–3, and provides the essential framework necessary for understanding the letter's overall ecclesiological vision. Just as Ephesians 1–3 takes the form of a chiasm, so does its chiastic center. We thus have a chiasm within a chiasm! Verses 11–12 parallel verses 19–22 (see *politeia* in v. 12, and *sym-politai* in v. 19), verse 13 parallels verses 17–18 (see the common theme of being brought "near"), and verses 14–16 form the chiastic center. Let us examine the unit in its given order.

> So then, remember that at one time you Gentiles by birth, called "the uncircumcision" by those who are called "the circumcision"—a physical circumcision made in the flesh by human hands—remember that you were at that time without Christ, being aliens from the commonwealth [*politeia*] of Israel, and strangers to the covenants of promise, having no hope and without God in the world. (Eph 2:11–12)

We find here a devastating picture of the gentile predicament, similar to that found in Romans 1. Romans 1 implies that Jewish corporate life—though falling short of the divine purpose—was at a higher spiritual and moral level than the corporate life of the gentile-nations, since idolatrous worship and disordered sexual relations were not publicly sanctioned or visible among the Jewish people of the time. Ephesians 2:12 goes further,

---

22. Yoder Neufeld, *Ephesians*, 95. See also Barth, *Ephesians 1–3*, 220; McRay, *Paul*, 343–44; and Yee, *Ethnic Reconciliation*, 58–60, 63.

for it points beyond a superior Jewish public morality to a covenantal bond with God and the hidden but real presence of the pre-incarnate Messiah. As Franz Mussner perceived, the gentiles having been "without Christ" implies that Israel had been "with Christ"; the gentiles having been "without God" implies that Israel had been "with God"; and the gentiles having enjoyed "no hope" implies that Israel had lived "with hope" (i.e., hope in the Messiah; see 1:12). The gentiles lacked all these blessings because they had been "aliens from the commonwealth [*politeia*] of Israel and strangers to the covenants of promise" (i.e., the covenants which established Israel's *politeia* or social-and-political-order). Alienation from Israel, God's holy and priestly people, meant alienation from God and the Messiah. As argued above, this implicit picture of Israel's relationship with God before the coming of the Messiah—despite Israel's sin and the judgment consequent to it described in 2:3—justifies an Israel-centric reading of the *berachah* in Ephesians 1:3-14.

The letter follows this gloomy portrayal of gentile culture before the coming of the Messiah with the reversal that occurs as a result of his decisive intervention. "But now in Christ Jesus you who once were far off have been brought near by the blood of [the] Christ" (Eph 2:13). As is evident from verse 17 (the chiastic parallel to verse 13), the imagery of distance and proximity derives from Isaiah 57:19, which describes God's healing of Israel—subsequent to judgment—as God's gift of shalom. While the text in view is prophetic, the imagery is priestly. In the Torah, to "draw near" (*karav*) is to approach the altar or the ark (e.g., Lev 9:8; 10:5). The priests and the Levites are themselves "brought near" when they are consecrated for their service at the tabernacle (Exod 29:8; 40:12-15; Num 8:9-10). The causative (*hiphil*) form of the Hebrew verb *karav* refers to the act of offering sacrifice, and a noun drawn from the same root (*korban*) takes the meaning of "sacrificial offering." Ephesians reinforces the priestly imagery of "bringing near" with the phrase "the blood of the Messiah." Just as the consecration of the priests and Levites involved sacrificial rites, so here the "bringing near" of those from the gentile-nations occurred through the offering of a life—the life of Israel's Messiah.

But God does not draw these gentiles near apart from Israel. The shalom that the Messiah announces and effects cannot heal vertical relationships if it does not simultaneously transform horizontal relationships. This is the message at the heart of the chiasm.

> For he is our peace; he has made both [*ta amphotera*] one and has broken down the dividing wall, nullifying in his flesh the hostility between us [stimulated by] the Torah of commandments [as expressed] in [interpretive] decrees, so that he might

create in himself [from] the two one new human being, thus making peace, and might reconcile both [*tous amphoterous*] in one body to God through the cross, putting to death that hostility in him.²³ (Eph 2:14-16)

> 23. This is my own translation of Ephesians 2:14-16. The NRSV reads as follows:
>
>> For he is our peace; in his flesh he has made both groups into one and has broken down the dividing wall, that is, the hostility between us. He has abolished the law with its commandments and ordinances, so that he might create in himself one new humanity in place of the two, thus making peace, and might reconcile both groups to God in one body through the cross, thus putting to death that hostility through it.
>
> The NRSV attempts here to make sense of a Greek text that abounds in syntactic and lexical ambiguities. To highlight these ambiguities, I will translate the Greek text as a series of clauses and phrases without punctuation and with as few interpretive moves as possible:
>
>> For he is our peace,
>> he who has made both one
>> and the dividing wall has broken down
>> the hostility in his flesh
>> the law of the commandments in decrees [*en dogmasin*]
>> having nullified
>> so that he might create the two in himself as one new man
>> making peace
>> and might reconcile both in one body to God through the cross
>> putting to death the hostility through it/him
>
> The NRSV makes several critical interpretive decisions: (1) By adding "into" between "both" and "one" in verse 14, and by adding "in place of" before "the two" in verse 15, it asserts the elimination of any remaining distinction between "the two" within the "one." Thus, "the hostility" between the two groups comes to an end because they are no longer in any sense "two groups." While the Greek text permits such a reading, it is just as amenable to a reading in which "the two" become "one" without losing their distinctive properties. (2) The NRSV links the phrases "the hostility" and "in his flesh" to the preceding phrase ("the dividing wall has broken down"), and equates "the hostility" with "the dividing wall." Once again, the Greek permits such a reading, but with equal warrant one may link the two phrases to the one that follows, so that "the hostility" becomes the object of "having nullified" and "in his flesh" becomes the means of nullification. (3) Having linked "the hostility" to "the dividing wall," the NRSV interprets "the law" as the direct object of "having nullified." This is a possible reading, but it is just as probable that the phrase "the law of the commandments in decrees" is a parenthetical explanation of the root of "the hostility." (4) Following the KJV, the NRSV translates the Greek word *dogmata* with the English word "ordinances"—a term used in the NRSV translation of the Old Testament to translate a Hebrew word that refers to a category of biblical law (e.g., Exod 21:1). By doing so, it implies that "the law of the commandments *in decrees*" which is "nullified" is the biblical Torah. However, nowhere in the Greek Pentateuch is the word *dogmata* used to describe biblical commandments, and the term would more reasonably be construed to refer to the post-biblical application of biblical law. For more detailed discussion of these verses, see Barth, *Ephesians 1-3*, 283-91 and Yoder Neufeld, *Ephesians*, 111-22.

The "one new human being" that God "creates" in Christ is not a third entity equally distinct from Jews and gentiles. As the corporate expression of Israel's crucified and risen Messiah, *the "one new human being" is Israel itself*, reconfigured in a new eschatological form. In the Messiah genealogical-Israel retains its particular priestly status, and gentiles who are united to the Messiah must also be united with Israel. Yet, these gentiles do not become proselytes, but instead are incorporated *as gentiles* into an expanded and transformed commonwealth of Israel. In Christ the "two"—the Jewish people in its divinely constituted genealogical particularity, and those from the gentile-nations—are joined together, and become a new humanity, a new Adam. As indicated by the repetition of the word "both" (*amphoteroi*), the two parties remain distinct even in their unity.[24] Reconciled to God "in one body"—the crucified body of Israel's Messiah—the "two" bear witness together that God's *shalom* has the power to conquer entrenched human enmity.

The priestly language that permeates this unit of Ephesians supports the view of some commentators that the "dividing wall" in verse 14 alludes to the temple fence which barred gentiles from "drawing near" to the temple building proper.[25] The fence itself is an illustration of a legal decree (*dogma*) by Jewish communal authorities, an interpretive application of the Torah that sought to guard the holy things entrusted to Israel.[26] Such interpretive decrees drew firm lines between the holy people and the nations, and (as an unintended consequence) provoked pride, envy, and mutual animosity. While these decrees may have been necessary before the coming of Israel's Messiah, the situation has now changed. The sacrificial work of the Messiah brings Jews and gentiles near to God in fellowship with one another—and new *halakhah* must reflect the transformed conditions.

Moving out from the center of the chiasm, the next verses parallel verse 13 and elaborate on what was stated there. "So he came and proclaimed peace to you who were far off and peace to those who were near; for through him both of us [*hoi amphoteroi*] have access in one Spirit to the

---

24. Yee, *Ethnic Reconciliation*, 164–67. See also Fowl, *Ephesians*, 90, 95.

25. Johnson, *Writings*, 415.

26. Elsewhere in the New Testament the word *dogma* refers to decrees issued by the Emperor (Luke 2:1; Acts 17:7) and also to decrees issued by the apostles (Acts 17:7). In the latter case, we see a direct parallel to the type of "decrees" with which Eph 2:15 is likely concerned. The legal decrees of traditional Jewish authorities which are *rescinded* in Ephesians are those that prevented gentiles from entering into communion with Jews. Corresponding to this, the new decrees which are *issued* in the book of Acts by the apostles have the purpose of establishing such communion on a footing that is in keeping with the purpose of the Torah in the context of the new situation created by the redemptive work of Jesus.

Father" (Eph 2:17–18). Verse 13 only referred to gentiles—those who were "far off" and then "brought near." In light of the message at the heart of the chiasm (vv. 14–16), this expansion of verse 13 also refers to the people of Israel—"those who were near." Here the letter once again distinguishes sharply between the situation of Jews and gentiles before the coming of the Messiah. *Israel was already "near" to God before Jesus died on the cross.* Israel was the holy and priestly people, chosen in the Messiah before the foundation of the world. While already "near," Israel was not yet as near as God intended. Perhaps, continuing the temple imagery implicit in verses 14–16, the author is thinking of the barriers that prevented Israel from entering the holy of holies, and which in this respect resembled the fence which restricted gentile access to any of the temple structures proper. Before the coming of its Messiah Israel could draw nearer than the gentiles, but it was still barred from free and intimate access.

But now, as a result of the sacrificial offering of the Messiah, "both of us have access in one Spirit to the Father." The word "access" (*pros-agoge*) is a nominal form of the verb (*pros-ago*) that is commonly employed in the Septuagint to translate the Hebrew word *hikriv* (i.e., "to bring near") in the priestly writings of the Torah. Through the priestly work of Israel's Messiah and in a union with him mediated by the Spirit, "we both"—Jews and gentiles, the "two" of verse 15—are "brought near" to God in the heavenly holy of holies. In that lofty place (Eph 1:3, 20; 2:6) we are "both" given priestly access to the Father (3:12). For the third time in five verses we encounter that important word *amphoteroi* ("both"). Ephesians 2:18 is a classic trinitarian text, but it is also a key text for an ecclesiology that takes seriously the enduring theological significance of the Jew-gentile distinction. The two corporate entities remain identifiable, and thus distinct—it is "we both" who have access—but they are now joined together in the Messiah, and by the power of the Spirit they are able together to enter the place that had formerly been off limits to both Jews and gentiles.

The unit concludes with verses which refer back to its opening, and which contrast what is now available to gentiles with their former dismal state.

> So then you are no longer strangers and aliens, but you are citizens with [*sum-politai*] the saints and also members of the household of God, built upon the foundation of the apostles and prophets, with Christ Jesus himself as the cornerstone. In him the whole structure is joined together and grows into a holy temple in the Lord; in whom you also are built together spiritually into a dwelling-place for God. (Eph 2:19–22)

These gentiles are no longer "strangers and aliens." Strangers and aliens in relation to whom? As the chiastic connection to verses 11–12 makes evident, this refers to the "*politeia* of Israel." Through the Messiah and in the Spirit, they are now "*sum-politai* [co-members-of-the-social-and-political-realm] with the saints." The "saints" here can only be those who had been referred to earlier in verses 11–12—those who had always been members of the *politeia* of Israel, who were chosen in the Messiah before the foundation of the world to be holy and blameless before him (Eph 1:4). The priestly imagery of the unit reaches a towering crescendo as we learn that the eschatologically expanded and transformed Israel has now become "a holy temple in the Lord . . . a dwelling-place of God."

This temple rests on the foundation of "the apostles and prophets." The linking of these two terms occurs again in Ephesians 3:5 and 4:11. These latter verses suggest that the "prophets" of verse 20 are first-century Jewish disciples of Jesus rather than biblical figures such as Isaiah, Jeremiah, and Ezekiel. They are closely associated with the apostles, sharing the same definite article in both Ephesians 2:20 and 3:5. The phrase may even be a hendiadys, meaning "prophetic apostles." Regardless, emphasis in these verses falls on the apostolic office and the prophetic revelation imparted along with the apostolic commission. The apostles of Jesus receive revelation so that they can understand the way God acted in the Messiah to realize God's mysterious plan for Israel, the gentile-nations, and the entire cosmos. Having received this revelation, and having been commissioned directly by the Messiah, they become his emissaries in the establishment of the eschatological temple of God, the expanded and transformed *politeia* of Israel. What is crucial to recognize at this point is *the inextricable connection between the apostolic office and the people of Israel*. The prophetic apostles extend Israel's holy social-and-political-order (i.e., *politeia*) and bring it to eschatological fullness by mediating the Messiah to the gentile nations and by summoning Israel to acknowledge its priestly king.

Ephesians 3: The Mystery Revealed to the Apostles—Gentile Inclusion in the People of God

In chapter 3 of Ephesians we realize that the author's *tefillah* (petitionary prayer) for his gentile readers, begun in 1:15, was never concluded. The rich theological reflection found in chapter 2 was actually part of the prayer—a narration of God's mighty deeds as an act of thanksgiving and as the basis for the author's joyful intercession. It is the "reason" for his prayer.

> This is the reason that I Paul am a prisoner for [the] Christ Jesus for the sake of you gentiles—for surely you have already heard of the commission of God's grace that was given to me for you, and how the mystery was made known to me by revelation, as I wrote above in a few words, a reading of which will enable you to perceive my understanding of the mystery of [the] Christ. In former generations this mystery was not made known to humankind, as it has now been revealed to his holy apostles and prophets by the Spirit: that is, the gentiles have become fellow-heirs [*sun-kleronoma*], members of the same body [*sus-soma*], and sharers in the promise [*sum-metocha*] in Christ Jesus through the gospel. (Eph 3:1–6)

But the theological reflection and narration of God's mighty deeds are not yet complete. The end of chapter 2 spoke of the prophetic apostles as the foundation of the eschatological "holy temple in the Lord." Paul, the letter's putative author, is one of those prophetic apostles, and his "stewardship" of the good news and his suffering are for the sake of those to whom he has been sent—the gentiles. The author has already spoken of the "mystery" of God's purpose, which had been entrusted to "the saints." Ephesians 1:10 summarized the content of that mystery as God's "plan for the fullness of time, to gather up all things in him, things in heaven and things on earth." As elaborated in Ephesians 2, this cosmic unification "in the Messiah" involves at its inception and its heart the reconciliation of Jew and gentile. Now in Ephesians 3 the author speaks of this reconciliation as the essential content of the mystery itself.

Though obscured by the NRSV, Ephesians 3:6 contains the letter's most impressive string of words with a *sun-/sum-* (and here *sus-*) prefix. Since this prefix conveys the sense of "with" or "together with," we might translate it by the English prefix "co-." Adopting such a rendering, the verse could be translated in this way: "the gentiles have become *co-heirs, co-members-of-the-Body*, and *co-sharers* of the promise in Messiah Jesus through the good news." Unlike the NRSV, my translation—like the Greek text itself—raises a question: co-heirs, co-members-of-the-Body, and co-sharers of the promise *with whom*? Ephesians 2:11–22 provides the answer: with those who were already near, already in relationship to the pre-incarnate Christ, already members of the commonwealth of Israel.

To our eyes, reading almost two thousand years after this letter was originally penned, the words of 3:6 are surprising. Readers today might think that the mystery consists of Jews and gentiles becoming "Christians"— a third entity that brings them together and reconciles their differences. But this is not what the letter says. For Ephesians, the mystery consists of how

God acts to make gentiles "co-heirs" with Israel, "co-members-of-the-Body" with Jews, "co-sharers of the promise" with "the saints." Israel is already an heir, already a recipient of the promise, already "near," already "chosen in Christ before the foundation of the world." Jews and gentiles do not become a new third entity; instead, Israel's promised messianic king takes his people to the next stage of their development, and that stage involves the opening of its doors to those who were previously alienated, remote, without God, without hope, without the Messiah. The result is indeed "one new human being" (2:15), but this new Adam is but the commonwealth of Israel, in its destined eschatological fullness.

Ephesians 1–3: Apostolic Ministry and the Catholicization of Israel

The author eventually concludes his petition (3:14–19), but we need proceed no further with our exegetical comments. What we have seen in Ephesians 1–3 could be described as the "catholicization" of Israel, accomplished in principle in the death and resurrection of Israel's Messiah, and realized in history through his prophetic apostles and the work of the Holy Spirit. Catholic Israel remains "one" people, yet it now consists of a twofold reality—gentiles united to Jews, but always as "co-sharers" of the inheritance, as one of the two parties who "both" have priestly access to God through the Messiah in one Spirit. The catholic extension of Israel through the apostolic *diakonia* enlarges and deepens the realm of oneness and holiness, but in a manner that remains dependent upon Israel's core inheritance. Thus, *the one, holy, catholic, and apostolic ecclesia is the prolepsis of eschatological Israel.*

This reading of Ephesians points to a truth about the apostolic role that is rarely considered. It is common today to emphasize the Jewish identity of *the historical figure of Jesus*. It is less common to emphasize the Jewish identity of *the resurrected Jesus*, and to take account of its theological significance. It is less common still to emphasize the Jewish identity of *the apostles*. If we are reading Ephesians correctly, then the Jewish identity of the apostles is crucial. They represent the Messiah of Israel, and thus they also represent Israel itself. This connection to Israel is evident in the Gospel tradition concerning the Twelve, who are appointed and destined to rule over the twelve tribes of Israel (Matt 19:28; Luke 22:28–30). But Ephesians suggests that this connection applies equally to the entire company of apostles, including Paul. When Paul goes to the gentiles, he represents not only the Messiah but also the people who were chosen in the Messiah before the foundation of the world.

Ephesians 1–3 thus provides a biblical base for understanding the *ecclesia* in Nicene terms as one, holy, catholic, and apostolic. It does so, however, by rooting the *ecclesia* in the soil of Israel's corporate life, and by envisioning the apostles as emissaries not only of the Messiah but also of the people who were chosen in him before the foundation of the world. Ephesians is a letter about the *ecclesia*—but it is also a letter about Israel. It is both, because the *ecclesia* of Ephesians is essentially a "catholic" and "apostolic" form of the people of Israel—that genealogical community descended from the patriarchs and matriarchs which was already "one" and "holy" through its election in its Messiah before the foundation of the world. Ephesians glorifies the *ecclesia* as an eschatologically reconfigured "catholic" Israel, of which Jesus the Messiah is—and always was—the head.[27]

The Letter to the Romans: Israel's Priesthood and the Priestly Remnant

The ecclesiological vision of Ephesians suggests that the priestly role of the Jewish people takes on a new form and significance through the death, resurrection, and ascension of Jesus and the Spirit-empowered ministry of his apostles. The Jewish identity of the apostles is as essential to their ecclesiological role as the Jewish identity of Jesus is to his messianic mission. In this way Israel-Christology establishes an Israel-ecclesiology that confirms the election of genealogical-Israel and mysteriously unites the *ecclesia* and the Jewish people.

However, the apostles did not stand alone as the priestly link between genealogical-Israel and its Messiah on the one hand, and the catholic *ecclesia* on the other. The apostles were themselves participants in a wider

---

27. Stephen Fowl provides further insight into the context, intention, and implications of Ephesians: "The Church in Ephesus was overwhelmingly if not exclusively Gentile. It even appears to have had little direct contact with non-Christian Jews. Why then does Paul challenge the Ephesian Christians to remember their pagan past as a Gentile past? . . . To the extent that one can discern answers to such questions, they go to the heart of Christian identity. It appears that whether or not Christians in Ephesus or elsewhere are subject to Judaizing pressures, they must understand themselves as Christians in relation to Israel and Israel's God. They must understand their past as a Gentile past because that is God's understanding of their past. Moreover, this understanding makes sense only in the light of God's call of Israel; if there are no Jews, then there are no Gentiles. *Christian identity requires the taking or remembering of Gentile identity because Christian identity is always tied to Israel.*" Fowl, *Ephesians*, 101. Emphasis added.

community of Jewish disciples of Jesus. Some of the members of that community were direct flesh-and-blood relatives of Jesus. All of them were part of Jesus' extended family, which was the Jewish people as a whole. As we shall see from Paul's Letter to the Romans, the entire community of Jewish disciples of Jesus fulfilled a crucial priestly function in union with Israel's Messiah.

Romans 11 opens with the question, "has God rejected his people?" The apostle denies this notion, but in order to do so he must explain why the people of Israel as a whole have not embraced Messiah Jesus. He begins by presenting himself, an Israelite and an apostle of the Messiah, as a sign of God's continuing fidelity to Israel (11:1). He then points to his fellow Jewish disciples of Jesus, whom he calls "the remnant" and "the chosen," as a similar sign (11:5–7). After offering reasons why God "hardened" the rest of the Jewish people, Paul argues that this hardening is temporary and that Israel's future embrace of Jesus will usher in the eschaton (11:15). As an assurance of Israel's destined redemption, he states: "If the dough offered as first fruits is holy, so is the whole lump" (Rom 11:16).

The logic of Paul's argument in Romans 11 suggests that the term "first fruits" refers back to the Jewish disciples of Jesus of verses 5–7. In the technical language of Jewish law, the offering of first fruits does not "sanctify" the remaining dough but instead releases it for secular use. However, the offering of first fruits fits into a wider pattern within the Torah according to which a part is devoted to God as representative of the whole. The Aaronic priesthood constitutes a prime example of this pattern in which the holiness of the representative part sustains the holiness of that which it represents—the entire people of Israel. Similarly, Jewish disciples of Jesus perform a priestly service on behalf of their fellow Jews by representing them before God. As a consequence, all Israel retains its sacred status, in hope of the day of redemption when in fullness it will acknowledge its returning Messiah.

This priestly understanding conditions Paul's use of the term "remnant." A strict notion of remnant involves the substitution of a part for the whole. As a result of a judgment that destroys or disqualifies an unfaithful majority, a faithful minority—the remnant—takes their place.[28] The remnant motif fits Paul's teaching in Romans 9–11, for he stresses in these chapters the faithfulness of the Jewish disciples of Jesus in his generation, and contrasts that faithfulness with the response to Jesus offered by the rest of the Jewish community. At the same time, Paul distinguishes his use of the term from the strict notion that entails replacement. In effect, Paul adds a priestly dimension to the remnant motif. Priestly election likewise singles

---

28. See Meyer, "Remnant," 669–71.

out a minority, but it does so for the purpose of *representing* and sanctifying rather than *replacing* the whole. Paul does not portray Jewish disciples of Jesus in strict remnant terms, but instead as a *priestly remnant* that represents but does not replace the Jewish people.

A priestly reading of Romans 11:16 draws support from a curious Pauline idiom. In several texts, Paul refers to the *ecclesia* of Jerusalem as "saints" (Rom 15:25–26, 31; 1 Cor 16:1; 2 Cor 8:4; 9:1, 12).[29] This usage resembles that already seen in Ephesians, where the term "saints" sometimes refers to Israel as a whole, and sometimes to the Jewish *ecclesia*.[30] In light of Romans 11:16, we may understand this terminology as implying that the community of Jewish disciples of Jesus, especially as it was embodied in first-century Jerusalem, constituted a sanctifying first fruits not only for the Jewish people, but also for the *ecclesia* from among the nations (see Jas 1:18). They performed a priestly function on behalf of the entire people of God.

As an apostle of Jesus and a Jew, Paul himself fulfills this priestly role on behalf of the nations by bringing them the good news: "because of the grace given me by God to be a minister [*leiturgos*] of Christ Jesus to the gentiles in the priestly service of the gospel of God, so that the offering of the gentiles may be acceptable, sanctified by the Holy Spirit" (Rom 15:15–16). Here the non-Jewish followers of Jesus are the offering that Paul is presenting to God. However, in later verses dealing with the contribution he is bringing to the Jerusalem *ecclesia* on behalf of these non-Jews, Paul modifies the metaphor:

> At present, however, I am going to Jerusalem in a ministry to the saints [i.e., the Jerusalem *ecclesia*]; for Macedonia and Achaia have been pleased to share their resources [*koinonia*] with the poor among the saints at Jerusalem. They were pleased to do this, and indeed they owe it to them; for if the Gentiles have come to share [*koinoneo*] in their spiritual blessings, they ought also to be of service [*leiturgeo*] to them in material things. (Rom 15:25–27)

The Jewish Jesus-followers of Jerusalem have "shared" their spiritual treasure with those from the nations; in gratitude, those from the nations are now reciprocating by "sharing" their material treasure. As a parallel expression for this "sharing" of material resources, Paul says that those from the nations are performing "priestly service" (*leiturgeo*) by sending material gifts to the Jerusalem community.[31] The reciprocal nature of the "sharing" noted

---

29. See Tomson, *Jewish Law*, 80 (especially footnote 112).

30. See McRay, *Paul*, 346–48.

31. The English word "liturgy" derives from this Greek word which often refers to "priestly service."

by Paul implies that the "priestly service" was likewise reciprocal—since the Jerusalem Jesus-community had also performed priestly service for those from the nations by sharing with them their spiritual treasure, the good news of God. Paul's priestly apostolic service for those from the nations as a *leiturgos* (Rom 15:15–16) is related to the priestly apostolic function of the Jerusalem community, and presumably of the body of Jewish disciples of Jesus as a whole.

In Romans 15 Paul emphasizes the apostolic dimension of the priestly vocation of the first Jewish disciples of Jesus. They had received and transmitted the message of the good news. However, more is involved here. When enumerating the chief privileges of the Jewish people in Romans 9:4–5, Paul brings his list to a climax with these words: "to them belong the patriarchs, and from them, according to the flesh, comes the Messiah." The sanctified genealogical bond with both the patriarchs and the Messiah does not in itself assure the eternal destiny of individual Jews, but it does distinguish the entire people of Israel as a nation set apart for special divine service. The "flesh" has its own necessary and proper role to play—for both Jesus and his kin. We should not be surprised, therefore, to discover that those who are joined to Messiah Jesus in *both* flesh and Spirit—the chosen ones from among the chosen ones—are also summoned to a distinctive priestly vocation. According to this calling, they serve as an effective sign of the enduring *holiness* of Israel in Messiah Jesus, and of the *apostolic* foundation and *catholic* identity of the messianic *ecclesia*.

While the significance of a fleshly connection to Jesus occupies only a subordinate place in Paul's letters, it appears to have been far more prominent in the thinking of other members of the early *ecclesia*. Richard Bauckham has underlined the central role played by the relatives of Jesus in the first-century Jesus-movement, especially in its Jewish sphere.[32] James, leader of the Jerusalem community, was "the Lord's brother" (Gal 1:19). According to Hegesippus, the successor to James was Simeon, cousin of Jesus. Bauckham suggests that Simeon's election reflected "a kind of dynastic feeling, to which it seemed right that the leadership of the Church should remain in the hands of relatives of Jesus."[33] Such an emphasis on immediate kinship to Jesus among Jewish disciples of Jesus makes sense if they likewise saw significance in the less immediate kinship to Jesus shared by all Jews. If God could employ genealogical descent as a condition for priestly service in the Jerusalem Temple, and as a condition for the royal service of the

---

32. Bauckham, *Relatives of Jesus*, 86–94.
33. Ibid., 88; 125–33.

Messiah himself (Rom 1:3), might he not also set apart for special service those united to Messiah by bonds of both faith and kinship?

In addition to treating James with reverence, early tradition in the Jesus-movement stressed his priestly role. This is evident in an account from Hegesippus, preserved by Eusebius:

> He was called the "Just" by all men from the Lord's time to ours, since many are called James, but he was holy from his mother's womb. He drank no wine or strong drink, nor did he eat flesh; no razor went upon his head; he did not anoint himself with oil, and he did not go to the baths. He alone was allowed to enter into the sanctuary, for he did not wear wool but linen, and he used to enter alone into the temple and be found kneeling and praying for forgiveness for the people, so that his knees grew hard like a camel's because of his constant worship of God, kneeling and asking forgiveness for the people.[34]

Hegesippus combines Nazirite and priestly elements in his description of James. The "Lord's brother" is even presented as resembling the high priest on the Day of Atonement, who prays in the sanctuary—where he alone is permitted to enter—for the forgiveness of the nation.[35] While its historical value regarding James is doubtful, this early tradition supports our contention that James and the Jerusalem *ecclesia* were viewed widely in priestly terms.

Thus, the early Jesus movement assigned a priestly significance to the Jerusalem community, the apostles, the family of Jesus, and the entire remnant of Jewish disciples of Jesus. From one perspective, this priestly role derived from the priestly vocation of Israel as a whole. However, from another perspective it secured Israel's priestly vocation by sanctifying those who were not yet disciples of Jesus. This was necessary, since Israel's holiness ultimately derived from its Messiah, in whom it was chosen before the foundation of the world to be holy and blameless in love.

Excursus: Apostolic Succession and Jewish Peoplehood

Early in this chapter I explored the misconception of a direct analogy between Catholic priestly ministry and the Aaronic priesthood. A second misconceived analogy also arises in connection with our topic, and is worthy of a brief comment before we conclude.

---

34. Eusebius, *Ecclesiastical History* 2.23, 4–6 (171).
35. For insightful comment on this text, see Painter, *Just James*, 125–27.

PRIESTHOOD, APOSTLESHIP, AND THE PEOPLE OF ISRAEL

It is tempting to compare Catholic priestly ministry and the doctrine of apostolic succession to the office of the rabbinate and the traditional Jewish teaching concerning the transmission of oral Torah. The famous opening chapter of *Pirke Avot* presents a chain of authorized teachers, beginning with Moses and Joshua and continuing on to Hillel, Shammai, and their post-70 successors. This resembles the likewise famous comments of Irenaeus on episcopal succession in the Church (*Against Heresies* 3.3.1–4; 4.33.8). The common features can easily obscure the fact that the two offices play radically different roles within their respective "ecclesiologies." In Catholic teaching, the episcopate constitutes an essential component of the life of the Church. Without a legitimate episcopate, a Body of Christians may form an "ecclesial community," but it is not truly and fully a "Church." In Jewish teaching, however, the rabbinate does not play such a role. Though the institution is essential for the preservation and transmission of the Torah, the presence of an ordained rabbi is not a requirement for the establishment of a legitimate Jewish community.

The sacraments of holy orders and baptism function together within Catholic life as the instruments of ecclesial continuity and identity from one generation to the next. The true analogue to these sacraments among the Jewish people is neither the office of the rabbinate nor the commandment of circumcision, but *fleshly reproduction within the framework of communal Jewish life*. While the sacrament of holy orders normally involves the ordination of celibates, the sacrament of Jewish continuity involves sexual intercourse and physical birth in the context of marriage. According to Catholic teaching, the former transmits a priesthood corresponding to Jesus' resurrection by the Spirit of holiness; according to our reading of Hebrews, Ephesians, and Romans, the latter transmits a priesthood corresponding to Jesus' fleshly descent from the patriarchs and the kings of Israel.

These two priesthoods are not at odds, nor are they sequentially related (with the former replacing the latter). Rather, they are mutually interdependent, from beginning to end. Jesus' descent from David was essential to his role, but without resurrection by the Spirit his Davidic descent would have been of little value. The Spirit raised him to a new eschatological mode of life, in which "they neither marry nor are given in marriage" (Matt 22:30); but he still bears a Jewish body, and still bears the title "the son of David, the son of Abraham" (Matt 1:1) as one born of Mary (Matt 1:16). Similarly, the apostles of the Lamb will all bear transfigured physical forms when they are enthroned over the tribes of Israel in the age to come, but those forms will still show the mark of circumcision.

Conclusion

Catholic theology of the ordained priesthood claims that the sacrament of holy orders enables the priest to share in the priestly vocation of Jesus and his apostles. I have argued here that the priestly vocation of Jesus and his apostles was itself bound up with their identity as Jews, and with the priestly vocation of the Jewish people as a whole. Of course, this does not prevent gentiles who are baptized into the Messiah from sharing in his priestly service. But it does raise the question whether the absence of an explicitly Jewish episcopate governing explicitly Jewish communities of disciples of Jesus is a structural deficiency in the life of the Church.[36] It also raises the question (from a Catholic perspective) as to how to assess the ecclesial status of Messianic Jewish communities who lack an episcopate in succession to the apostles but share the Jewish flesh of the apostles.

Our discussion in this chapter of priesthood and apostleship has begun an ecclesiologically oriented examination of Catholic sacramental life and its integral connection to the Jewish people. If the thesis propounded here has merit, what might it imply about the Church's other foundational sacraments? The next chapters will offer an initial response to this question.

---

36. On this point, see the article of Fr. Jean-Miguel Garrigues in Appendix 3.

5

Israel's Eschatological Renewal in Water and Spirit

The primary thesis of this book is that the spiritual bond with the elect "stock of Abraham" which the Church discovers by "searching her own mystery" is understood best in terms of an Israel-ecclesiology rooted in Israel-Christology and entailing a special priestly role for the Jewish disciples of Jesus. In the previous chapter I offered a perspective on the sacrament of holy orders that coheres with and supports this thesis. In the current chapter I will present an interpretation of the sacrament of baptism that further confirms our fundamental contention.

At first appearance the sacrament of baptism seems to point in the opposite direction. The Catechism teaches that "Through Baptism we are . . . reborn as sons of God[,] . . . become members of Christ, [and] are incorporated into the Church" (*CCC* 1213). For most interpreters, baptismal "rebirth" suggests rupture and discontinuity with the "old" covenantal order. The field between Jews and gentiles is leveled, and both are summoned to enter on the same basis into the new community of faith—"the Church"—through becoming for the first time "members of Christ" and "sons of God." All now become "Christians," and forsake their former religious identities.

For much of Church history the sacrament of baptism has functioned in this way for Jews who received it. Upon being baptized, Jews were required to swear an oath in which they renounced all Jewish "superstitions," by which were meant basic Jewish covenantal practices such as circumcision, the dietary laws, and Sabbath observance. They were expected to exchange Jewish names for Christian ones, put off Jewish clothing and adopt

Christian garb, and forsake Jewish society to become part of a Christian social and cultural order.[1]

In this chapter I will endeavor to show that this view of the sacrament distorts its fundamental meaning. The sacrament itself and its associated concept of "rebirth" or "regeneration" actually point us back to the vocation of the Jewish people and its eschatological destiny. While baptism is for all, Jew and gentile, its significance is not identical for all who receive it. For Jews, it implies a fulfillment of their covenantal identity; for gentiles, it establishes that identity for the first time. For both, it involves a new or renewed commitment to the welfare of the Jewish people.

My study of the sacrament of baptism will begin with an examination of the baptism of Jesus by John. I will inquire as to what this event reveals about the mission of Jesus and the rite of baptism when seen against the backdrop of Israel's exilic prophecies of national restoration. I will then look at the concept of regeneration in the same prophetic context. The results of our study will confirm the ecclesiological thesis presented in the previous two chapters, and demonstrate its capacity to shed fresh light on the meaning of the sacraments.

The Baptism of Jesus

Jesus' Baptism and the Ecclesial Sacrament

One might think that the natural place to begin theological reflection about the sacrament of baptism would be Jesus' post-resurrection command to his apostles: "Go . . . and make disciples of all nations, baptizing them in the name of the Father and of the Son and of the Holy Spirit" (Matt 28:19). One could then move directly into a study of Pauline teaching about baptismal participation in Jesus' death and resurrection (Rom 6:1-11), or examine the Johannine theme of regeneration (John 3:3-5).

What seems natural to us was apparently unnatural for the church fathers of the fourth and the fifth centuries, especially in the East. For them, the starting point for all teaching about the sacrament of baptism was the baptism of Jesus in the Jordan River. Sometimes the fathers focused on how Jesus' entry into the earthly waters purified those waters so they could become the sacramental agent of his purifying power.[2] At other times they

---

1. On the history which led to such an understanding of the social, cultural, and religious implications of baptism for Jews, see Kinzer, *Postmissionary*, 181-212.

2. This theme already appears in writings of the early second century (see Ignatius of Antioch, *Ephesians* 18:2). For sources from the classical patristic period concerning

concentrated on the baptismal revelation of the Trinity, in whose name the ecclesial sacrament would be administered.[3] In most cases they showed how Jesus condescended to receive baptism at the hands of John in order to present his future disciples with the model they should follow.[4]

It was also common to stress the importance of Jesus' reception of the Spirit at the Jordan, and to see this event as the ultimate source of the impartation of the Spirit through sacramental baptism. According to Cyril of Alexandria (376-444), for example, Jesus did not need to receive the gift of the Spirit for himself any more than he needed to receive the forgiveness of sins. Jesus was conceived by the Spirit, and—as the Son of God—he lived in perpetual communion with the Father by the Spirit. When he received the Spirit at his baptism he did so on behalf of all humanity, whom he represents as the second Adam. Cyril goes so far as to state that when God gives the Spirit to Jesus at the Jordan, one can rightly assert that the Spirit has been poured out on "all flesh," as promised by the prophet Joel (2:28).[5]

Building upon this common patristic theme, Thomas Torrance has attempted to recapture the significance of Jesus' baptism for a contemporary understanding of the ecclesial sacrament: "Jesus was baptized with the baptism of repentance not for his own sake but for ours, and in him it was our humanity that was anointed by the Spirit and consecrated in sonship to the Father."[6] Torrance, like Cyril and the teachers of his era, emphasizes the representative character of Jesus' baptism, and the consequences it has for all humanity. Without denying this truth or diminishing its importance, I would propose that this universal significance is derived from a more immediate and particular meaning. The place to begin in interpreting Jesus' baptism is not with Adam-Christology, but with Israel-Christology.[7]

---

the purification of the waters, see Ferguson, *Baptism*, 503, 642-43, 710. The main point is that Jesus does not need to be cleansed by the waters of this world but they need to be cleansed by him; as a result of this cleansing, they are able to serve as the appropriate vehicle for the sacrament of baptism administered by the Church.

3. See Wilken, *Spirit*, 41.

4. Ferguson, *Baptism*, 547, 689, 710.

5. Ibid., 687-89.

6. Torrance, *Reconciliation*, 86. In underlining the signal importance of Jesus' baptism, Torrance is following his teacher, Karl Barth, who wrote that "the direct command to baptize [in Matt 28] is not a new thing, but an explication and proclamation of the institution of baptism already effected previously in the history of Jesus Christ, namely, in His baptism in the Jordan. . . . It is in this event that we are to seek the true basis for Christian baptism which is then declared and formulated as such in the saying in Mt. 28:10" (Barth, *CD IV.*4, 48).

7. Cardinal Lustiger likewise underlines the importance of John's baptism for our understanding of the ecclesial sacrament: "the baptism given by John is indeed

The Mission and Message of John the Baptist

To explore this theme, let us examine closely the narrative of Jesus' baptism as found in the Gospel of Matthew. Matthew 3 begins by describing the emergence of John the Baptist as a first-century Jewish prophet:

> In those days John the Baptist appeared in the wilderness of Judea, proclaiming, "Repent, for the kingdom of heaven has come near." This is the one of whom the prophet Isaiah spoke when he said, "The voice of one crying out in the wilderness: 'Prepare the way of the Lord, make his paths straight.'" Now John wore clothing of camel's hair with a leather belt around his waist, and his food was locusts and wild honey. Then the people of Jerusalem and all Judea were going out to him, and all the region along the Jordan, and they were immersed by him in the river Jordan, confessing their sins. (Matt 3:1–6)

John's clothing resembles that of the prophet Elijah (2 Kgs 1:8), which suggests his dual role as zealous agent of Israel's purification and as messianic precursor (Mal 4:5–6). His message of God's reign and the desert setting of his vocation evoke Isaiah's exilic prophecies of comfort and restoration (e.g., Isa 40:1–11; 52:7).

Matthew then recounts John's message of repentance:

> But when he saw many Pharisees and Sadducees coming for immersion, he said to them, "You brood of vipers! Who warned you to flee from the wrath to come? Bear fruit worthy of repentance. Do not presume to say to yourselves, 'We have Abraham as our ancestor'; for I tell you, God is able from these stones to raise up children to Abraham. Even now the ax is lying at the root of the trees; every tree therefore that does not bear good fruit is cut down and thrown into the fire. (Matt 3:7–10)

Here emphasis falls on the purification and judgment that precedes Israel's restoration. John announces a coming day of "wrath"—the fearsome "day of the Lord" anticipated by Israel's prophets (e.g., Zeph 1; Joel 1:15—2:3; Amos 5:18–20). Fiery judgment awaits not only the enemies of Israel, but also the wicked among the people of God—and especially among its leaders.

---

the origin of the baptism with which we are all baptized. It is the baptism received by Jesus and subsequently by us, too. It is the same fundamental act that inaugurates the kingdom of heaven" (*Promise*, 60). As we will see later in this chapter, the Cardinal's interpretation of the meaning of baptism in relation to Israel also resembles closely what is presented here.

ISRAEL'S ESCHATOLOGICAL RENEWAL IN WATER AND SPIRIT

John's words conclude with a contrast between his own mission and that of the one whose way he prepares. "I immerse you with water for repentance, but one who is more powerful than I is coming after me; I am not worthy to carry his sandals. He will immerse you with the Holy Spirit and fire. His winnowing fork is in his hand, and he will clear his threshing floor and will gather his wheat into the granary; but the chaff he will burn with unquenchable fire" (Matt 3:11-12).

John speaks of three baptisms: a baptism with water (which he administers), and the baptisms with the Holy Spirit and fire (to be administered by his successor). His own baptism in water fulfills a preparatory function related to repentance, ritual purification, and the forgiveness of sins (see Mark 1:4). His successor's baptism with the Holy Spirit will involve divine empowerment, sanctification, and transformation. The baptism with fire, understood in terms of the imagery of verses 10 and 12, will consist of the execution of divine judgment. Thus, John seeks to prepare Israel for the restoration and judgment, which the more powerful "Coming One" will accomplish.

What is the significance of the mission and message of John, as presented by Matthew? These verses resound with allusions to the biblical prophets, and the context and content of the prophetic sources enable us to see what might otherwise remain obscure. First, John's linkage of purifying water and empowering Spirit recalls Ezekiel 36:

> I will take you from the nations, and gather you from all the countries, and bring you into your own land. I will sprinkle clean water upon you, and you shall be clean from all your uncleannesses, and from all your idols I will cleanse you. A new heart I will give you, and a new spirit I will put within you; and I will remove from your body the heart of stone and give you a heart of flesh. I will put my Spirit within you, and make you follow my statutes and be careful to observe my ordinances. Then you shall live in the land that I gave to your ancestors; and you shall be my people, and I will be your God. (Ezek 36:24-28)

Ezekiel addresses Israel during the Babylonian exile, and proclaims what God will do for and among the people of Israel. God will bring Israel out of exile, and restore the people to its own land. This will vindicate the holiness of God's name by demonstrating God's power and covenant fidelity. But geographical restoration is insufficient, if unaccompanied by internal, relational, and behavioral transformation. Therefore, God will sprinkle water of purification over his people to purify them from the defilement deriving from the sins that drove them into exile.[8] Such ritual purification is essential, but it likewise is insufficient in itself. To complete the purification process God will place the divine Spirit within the people of Israel, which will empower them to live in covenant fidelity according to the statutes and ordinances of the Torah.[9]

As recent commentators have noted, many first-century Jews believed that the Babylonian exile had never really ended, and that the prophecies of restoration still awaited fulfillment.[10] This was true even for many Jews living in the land of Israel. According to Matthew's narrative, John holds such a view of Israel's exile and restoration, and he anticipates that the baptismal mission of his greater successor—prepared for by his own baptismal mission—will achieve the full reality about which Ezekiel prophesied.

This helps explain the baptisms of water and Spirit. But what about the baptism of fire? For this, we turn to the prophet Malachi.

> See, I am sending my messenger to prepare the way before me, and the Lord whom you seek will suddenly come to his temple. The messenger of the covenant in whom you delight—indeed, he is coming, says the Lord of hosts. But who can endure the day of his coming, and who can stand when he appears? For he is like a refiner's fire and like fullers' soap; he will sit as a refiner and purifier of silver, and he will purify the descendants of Levi and refine them like gold and silver, until they present offerings to the Lord in righteousness. Then the offering of Judah and Jerusalem will be pleasing to the Lord as in the days of old and as in former years. (Mal 3:1–4)

Elsewhere the Synoptic Gospels interpret Malachi 3:1 as referring to John the Baptist (Matt 11:10; Mark 1:2). The "messenger" prepares the way for the coming of "the Lord" to "his temple." That coming will bring a fiery purification that will refine the temple leadership and renew Israel's sacrificial

---

8. Ezekiel alludes here to the Levitical rite of purification employing the ashes of the red heifer described in Numbers 19.

9. Cardinal Lustiger sees the baptism of John in similar terms: "By confessing their sin, they [i.e., those coming for baptism by John] ask God to reestablish the Covenant, to grant the New Covenant announced by Jeremiah and Ezekiel. In this Covenant the Holy Spirit will inscribe the Law in the hearts of the people, and make it so that Israel will sin no more: Israel will be an entirely holy people, because God's own power will dwell in it in fullness, according to the prayer expressed in Deuteronomy" (Lustiger, *Promise*, 61).

10. N. T. Wright has made this theme of exile a central component of his reconstruction of first-century Judaism (e.g., *New Testament*, 268–79). While the theme may not be quite as universal for the period as Wright claims, it does appear within many streams of Jewish thought. See Evans, "Continuing Exile," 77–100.

worship. The final verses of Malachi speak again of a forerunner—this time designated "the prophet Elijah"—and of fire.

> See, the day is coming, burning like an oven, when all the arrogant and all evildoers will be stubble; the day that comes shall burn them up, says the Lord of hosts, so that it will leave them neither root nor branch.... Lo, I will send you the prophet Elijah before the great and terrible day of the Lord comes. He will turn the hearts of parents to their children and the hearts of children to their parents, so that I will not come and strike the land with a curse. (Mal 4:1, 5-6; Heb text: 3:19; 23-24)

The fire of Malachi 3:2-3 brings purification; here, the fire consumes. In both cases, the fire involves suffering and judgment. The New Testament sees Malachi's prophecy regarding Elijah, like his prophecy of the "messenger," as realized or exemplified in the mission of John (Matt 11:14; Luke 1:17).

Interpreted in the light of Malachi, the baptism of fire announced by John refers to the eschatological distress that will purify the righteous and destroy the wicked. It points not to a post-mortem judgment that all human beings must endure, but specifically to the tribulation—centered in the holy city of Jerusalem—that accompanies the "day of the Lord" and constitutes the "birth-pangs of the Messiah." Like the baptism with the Holy Spirit, this baptism of fire has as its object the restoration of Israel—understood in Malachi in terms of the restoration of Israel's worship.

Why Does Jesus Receive Baptism?

John's words make clear that he expects much from his successor, and sees his own role as insignificant in comparison. This sets the stage for the appearance of Jesus, and for a momentous dialogue between these two prophetic figures. "Then Jesus came from Galilee to John at the Jordan, to be immersed by him. John would have prevented him, saying, 'I need to be immersed by you, and do you come to me?' But Jesus answered him, 'Let it be so now; for it is proper for us in this way to fulfill all righteousness.' Then he consented" (Matt 3:13-15). John's words express more than the acknowledgement of a superior by a subordinate. John knows that he needs to be baptized by Jesus because he knows that *all Israel needs to be baptized by Jesus*—because Jesus is the "one who ... is coming," who baptizes with the Holy Spirit and with fire. He is the one who will bring Israel's purification, sanctification, and national restoration. John desires to be baptized in water by Jesus in order to inaugurate the national and cosmic renewal that Jesus' baptismal work will accomplish.

Yet, Jesus surprises John by refusing to assume the function that John assigns him. Jesus will not baptize John, but instead insists on receiving baptism at his hands. Why does he do this? Jesus responds to John without answering this question, asserting that it must be so "to fulfill all righteousness." At this point in time, God requires that Jesus receive John's baptism rather than administer his own. But why is this the case?

Another segment of the synoptic tradition may hint at the answer. Luke records the following words of Jesus regarding his mission and his inner orientation toward its fulfillment: "I came to bring fire to the earth, and how I wish it were already kindled! I have a baptism with which to be baptized, and what stress I am under until it is completed!" (Luke 12:49-50). John proclaimed that his successor would administer a baptism of fire. Jesus here asserts that he must *undergo* such a baptism! In the context of the Gospels, these words obviously refer to Jesus' suffering and death. As John anticipated, Jesus will indeed administer a baptism of Spirit and fire. But contrary to John's expectation, Jesus must first experience that baptism himself. Jesus' submission to John's baptism demonstrates from the very outset that his way of fulfilling Ezekiel 36 and Malachi 3 will defy popular assumptions of the day.

In order to grasp the full implications of this, let us continue with Matthew's narrative. "And when Jesus had been immersed, just as he came up from the water, suddenly the heavens were opened to him and he saw the Spirit of God descending like a dove and alighting on him. And a voice from heaven said, 'This is my Son, the Beloved, with whom I am well pleased'" (Matt 3:16-17). Just as Jesus must submit to a baptism of fire before administering such a baptism, so he must also receive the visible manifestation of the Spirit before immersing others in the Spirit's power. Jesus' submission to John's baptism anticipates the obedience that will lead him to the cross; the descent of the Spirit anticipates God's powerful act in raising Jesus from the dead (Rom 8:11) and enthroning him at God's right hand (Acts 2:33).

The voice from heaven addresses Jesus as the one "with whom I am well pleased." This alludes to Isaiah 42:1: "Here is my servant, whom I uphold, my chosen, in whom my soul delights; I have put my spirit upon him; he will bring forth justice to the nations." Jesus is the servant of the Lord, upon whom the Spirit rests. In Isaiah 53, this servant suffers on behalf of "many"—just as Jesus will suffer on the cross, in his own baptism of fire. But Isaiah's servant of the Lord is also presented as the people of Israel (Isa 41:8; 49:3), upon whom God will pour out the Spirit (Isa 44:1-3). Jesus is the servant whose humility and obedience please God, but in this role he represents and embodies the people of Israel as a whole. This is why he must first *be* baptized before baptizing others: if he is to identify with and represent this sinful people destined for judgment and for restoration, if he is to become the agent of their purification and renewal, he must first taste that judgment and restoration himself. The enigmas inherent in the narrative of Jesus' baptism become comprehensible when viewed in the light of Israel-Christology.[11]

Jesus' role as Israel's representative is also implicit in the opening words of the voice from heaven: "This is my Son, the Beloved." These words allude to Genesis 22—the story of the binding of Isaac: "Take your son, your only son Isaac, whom you love, and go the land of Moriah, and offer him there as a burnt offering upon one of the mountains of which I shall tell you" (Gen 22:2). Jesus is God's beloved Son, whom God will give up for the sake of Israel and the world. But he is also the descendant of Abraham whose self-offering on the cross completes Israel's sacrificial and atoning vocation implicit in the binding of Isaac and rendered explicit in Isaiah 53. He is Israel, God's Son (Exod 4:22-23). As Cardinal Lustiger writes, "The most obvious level of meaning [in the words of God to Jesus at his baptism] is that Jesus is designated as the Son *par excellence*. He is designated not as a substitute for Israel, but as the very realization of Israel's vocation. He is the one in whom the Promise destined for all of Israel is realized and by whom it can be communicated."[12] As "the Son *par excellence*," Jesus must identify fully with his people, even in its sin, and endure the judgment that Israel deserves, in order to purify and renew Israel and render its offerings acceptable—that Israel as a whole might fulfill its vocation on behalf of all the nations of the earth.

This reading of Matthew 3 is confirmed by its literary context, which constitutes the most sustained and explicit example of Israel-Christology in the New Testament. Matthew 2 presents the story of Jesus' infancy in terms of Israel's exodus from Egypt, and applies Hosea 11:1—"Out of Egypt have I called my Son"—to the return of Jesus (with Joseph and Mary) from Egypt. Similarly, Matthew 4 recounts Jesus' forty days of testing in the wilderness, in which he relives Israel's forty years of wandering before entering the land

---

11. "Baptism is not a prescription of the Law, yet Jesus views it as a divinely imposed duty (*prepon*). Why? One answer at least could run: because every strand of messianic teaching in the Old Testament depicts the Messiah as inseparable from his people. He that is 'meek and lowly in heart,' and who calls 'them that labor and are heavy burdened' to Himself, begins His ministry by identifying Himself with them in their need. He companies with sinners according to the will of God.... As Messiah, representative of people needing deliverance, Jesus demonstrates and effects his solidarity with them in their need" (Beasley-Murray, *Baptism*, 57, 60).

12. Lustiger, *Promise*, 64

of promise. The devil challenges Jesus to prove that he is "the Son of God." The biblical texts cited by Jesus in response derive from Deuteronomy, and speak of the covenantal requirements incumbent on the people of Israel. Thus, Jesus demonstrates that he is the Son of God—the true representative of Israel—not by working signs and wonders, but by obeying the Torah as Israel was called to do.[13]

The Significance of Jesus' Baptism

Thomas Torrance summarizes succinctly the main outlines of this understanding of the baptism of Jesus:

> Certainly Jesus himself linked his baptism in the Jordan with his death on the Cross, and interpreted his whole life and ministry as the baptism with which he was being baptized, identifying its completion with his passion. Hence as his death drew near, he spoke of himself as the Son of Man who had come not to be served but to serve and give his life as a ransom for many, and in the Last Supper solemnly inaugurated the New Covenant in his blood for the remission of sin. Thus his "baptism" and his "cup" both spoke of his sacrificial life and death into which he had been consecrated at the Jordan. In his crucifixion the complete solidarity of the one Righteous One with sinners, to which his baptism by John pointed, was consummated.[14]

In his baptism Jesus is indeed "consecrated" for "his sacrificial life and death" in "complete solidarity . . . with sinners." However, what Torrance—and his patristic sources—neglect to note is what is most crucial for our concerns here: those "sinners" with whom Jesus most immediately shows solidarity are *Jews*, and his purpose in doing so is to fulfill the words of the exilic prophets who promised that the nation of Israel would be restored and Zion would be glorified. As a result of Israel's eschatological renewal, all nations would come to know the Lord's saving power and worship the God of Israel in fellowship with the people of the covenant. As the church fathers and Torrance rightly perceive, the ultimate import of Jesus' baptism—and his entire mission—is universal in scope. Jesus does act on behalf of the "sinners" of the nations—but he reaches them by an indirect route that passes first through the territory of his own flesh and blood.

---

13. "It is because Jesus lives the obedience which God expects of Israel that he can thus accomplish that for which God has destined Israel" (Ibid., 67).

14. Torrance, *Reconciliation*, 85.

Jesus shows such radical solidarity with Israel because he is the Messiah whose vocation entails representing and summing up his people in his own person. Building upon the insights of the church fathers and Torrance, but interpreting them in light of Israel-Christology, we can provide our own summary of the significance of Jesus' baptism:

1. Jesus' baptism at the hands of John demonstrates his radical identification with the people of Israel, even in their sins, and expresses his calling to represent Israel in its encounter with the fire of eschatological judgment and the life-giving power of the Holy Spirit.

2. Jesus' baptism in water is a prophetic sign-act that points to the definitive baptism he will undergo in his suffering, death, and resurrection. As such, it offers insight into the meaning of those redemptive events: in them Jesus embodies and represents Israel, and he undergoes eschatological judgment and renewal on Israel's behalf.

3. The baptism which Jesus receives in his cross and resurrection—to which his baptism in water points—enables him to become the one who administers baptism with the Holy Spirit and fire. In other words, by virtue of first experiencing Israel's purifying judgment and renewal, Jesus becomes the agent through whom Israel's eschatological purification and renewal will be accomplished. He comes not to replace Israel in his person, nor to create a "new Israel" that is separate from the old, but to bring his people to its appointed destiny.

Jesus' baptism in the Jordan is oriented to his baptism on the cross, and both are further oriented to the baptism he administers in the Spirit.[15] This brings us back to the ecclesial sacrament, which is the primary concern of this chapter.

Jesus' Baptism and the Ecclesial Sacrament

What does this study of Jesus' baptism imply about the baptism that the apostles later administer? On the one hand, it supports the apostolic interpretation of baptism as an eschatological rite by which disciples of Jesus identify with and participate in the death and resurrection of the Messiah (Rom 6:3–4; Col 2:12) and are empowered by the Holy Spirit (Acts 2:38;

---

15. "Three pictures, particularly, have to be combined stereoscopically in one if *baptisma* is to be viewed in its proper dimension of depth: the baptism of Jesus in water and the Spirit at the Jordan, his baptism in blood on the Cross, and the baptism of the Church in his Spirit at Pentecost. All that stands behind the administration of baptism to us, supplies it with its ground and reality, and is effective through it" (Torrance, *Reconciliation*, 88–89).

10:47; 1 Cor 12:13; Titus 3:5). As a prophetic sign-act, Jesus' baptism in water points *forward* to his death and resurrection, and also to creation's final judgment and ultimate liberation from bondage to decay. Our baptism in water points *backward* to his death and resurrection, and binds us to those definitive acts of divine intervention while also anticipating their *future* eschatological realization.

On the other hand, this understanding of Jesus' baptism also adds a level of meaning to the baptismal rite that has remained largely hidden from the Church. When disciples of Jesus are baptized into the Messiah, they are baptized into the one who in his suffering and death represented the people of Israel, and who in his resurrection life still represents that people. As such, *baptism signifies and requires the same sort of radical identification with the Jewish people that Jesus himself displayed.* This understanding of Jesus' baptism also implies that the baptism of disciples of Jesus is itself a prophetic sign-act that points forward and not only backward: it anticipates the day when the one who received purification and renewal on Israel's behalf acts definitively as the agent of Israel's—and, through Israel, the world's—eschatological rebirth.

The New Testament and the tradition of the Church emphasize that baptism involves incorporation into the Body of Christ. As my exposition of *Lumen Gentium* in chapter 3 suggests, and the current chapter confirms, such incorporation also brings gentile disciples of Jesus into a relationship with the Jewish people. For gentiles, membership in the Body of Christ leads to participation in the commonwealth of Israel. In his commentary on the baptism of Jesus according to Matthew 3, Cardinal Lustiger draws similar conclusions:

> It is clear, in this respect, that the Spirit of Jesus can be received only on the strict condition of sharing the hope of Israel and having access to it. This is the meaning of baptism, since in baptism—according to Saint Paul's expression—we are "incorporated" into Christ. But baptism is at the same time, and inseparably—otherwise it would be meaningless—an incorporation into Israel. . . . It results that the Old Testament has not been "invalidated," according to a current expression, by the coming of the Messiah, but, on the contrary, has been made accessible and open to pagans who, without him, would not have had access to it. . . . Christian baptism is the baptism received by Jesus from John the Baptist. Through it, pagans are received into the people of Israel.[16]

---

16. Lustiger, *Promise*, 71–72, 95.

For Jews, in contrast, baptism signifies and accomplishes the realization and renewal of their already-existing identity as members of the people of God. They are to follow Jesus the Jewish Messiah, who "subjected himself to this rite so as to be obedient to God, as Israel is called to be obedient to God, and . . . [who] lives this baptism to the very end."[17] As with Jesus himself, baptism for his Jewish followers should constitute a radical act of identification with Israel, even in its sin, in prophetic anticipation of the day when the Messiah will purify and renew the people he represents and loves.

This view of the sacrament poses a profound challenge to certain ancient Catholic baptismal practices that, while falling by the wayside in the twentieth century, have never been explicitly and authoritatively rejected. For as long as anyone can remember, Christian baptism has constituted for Jews the official exit from Jewish communal life and identity. The Church insisted on it, and the Jewish community ratified the decision. Yet, our study of Jesus' baptism suggests that this was not only a tragic error, but an inversion of an important aspect of the rite's meaning. For Jewish disciples of Jesus, baptism should function not as a door *out of* Jewish life, but instead as a summons to radical identification with the people of Israel, and as a gateway through which Israel as a whole finds eschatological renewal in the Messiah.

"The Water of Rebirth"

In Catholic thought, baptism is the sacrament of regeneration. Through the waters of baptism one is "born anew." This Catholic emphasis derives from the baptismal imagery of the New Testament: "He saved us . . . through the water of rebirth [*paligenessia*] and renewal by the Holy Spirit" (Titus 3:5). According to the Gospel of John, one must be reborn in order to enter the eschatological kingdom (John 3:3, 5). In past centuries this requirement of regeneration was often assumed to nullify the religious value of Jewish identity by denying the spiritual significance of fleshly birth and genealogical descent. All must be born again through faith in Jesus and through the waters of baptism. If this view of regeneration is correct, then our conclusions regarding Jesus' baptism must be mistaken.

In fact, a closer examination of the meaning of regeneration in the New Testament actually supports the conclusions we have reached. The only other use of the word *paligenessia* in the New Testament is in Matthew 19:28: "Truly, I tell you, at the *paligenessia*, when the Son of Man is seated on his throne of glory, you who have followed me will also sit on twelve thrones, judging the twelve tribes of Israel." English translations render *paligenessia*

---

17. Ibid., 95.

in this text with such expressions as "the renewal of all things" (NRSV; NIV), "the new world" (RSV), or "the New Age" (TEV). While these translations have merit, the context more readily justifies the rendering, "when Israel is renewed/reborn." Israel's rebirth will lead to "the renewal of all things," but Matthew 19 focuses less on the universality of "all things" and more on the eschatological particularity of the people of the covenant. Jesus speaks here only of "the twelve tribes of Israel."

The other key text dealing with regeneration points in the same direction. John 3 describes the visit of Nicodemus to Jesus. Nicodemus addresses Jesus as "Rabbi," and acknowledges that he is a teacher who has come from God. Jesus responds to Nicodemus with these famous words: "Very truly, I tell you, no one can see the kingdom of God without being born from above [or, anew].... Very truly, I tell you, no one can enter the kingdom of God without being born of water and Spirit. What is born of the flesh is flesh, and what is born of the Spirit is spirit" (John 3:3, 5). This teaching of Jesus puzzles and bewilders Nicodemus. "How can this be?" (John 3:9). Yet, Jesus does not consider his words to be mysterious: "Are you a teacher of Israel, and yet you do not understand these things?" (John 3:10). Jesus will reveal heavenly mysteries, but this teaching is not among them: "If I have told you about earthly things and you do not believe, how can you believe if I tell you about heavenly things?" (John 3:12).

Why does Jesus think that Nicodemus, as a "teacher of Israel," should understand his words? What must every "teacher of Israel" know? The answer is clear: Scripture, of course! Jesus likely sees his words as a prophetic commentary on Scripture. But what text is he commenting upon? The biblical unit that fits best with this dialogue is Ezekiel 36–37. We already looked at Ezekiel 36:24–28, and proposed it as a key to understanding Jesus' baptism. These prophetic verses bring together water and Spirit, and speak of the gift of a new heart. Ezekiel 37 continues the theme of national restoration signaled by Ezekiel 36, but employs a new image: Israel in exile is like a collection of dry bones, and Israel's national restoration will be like a resurrection from the dead. The two chapters are linked by the words "I will put my Spirit within you" (Ezek 36:27; 37:14). The same Spirit who raises Israel from the dead also gives Israel a new heart, and enables the people to live in covenant fidelity. When seen together, these two chapters from Ezekiel provide all the background required for understanding Jesus' otherwise enigmatic sayings in John 3.

In light of Ezekiel 36–37, to be "born of the Spirit" is to receive the first fruits of the eschatological redemption promised to Israel in exile. It is the fulfillment of the words "I will put my Spirit within you," prophesied by Ezekiel, and as such it will lead to the realization of all that is pledged in the two prophetic chapters linked by that promise: purification from defilement, resurrection from the dead, inheritance of the land, a renewed heart, and a life of covenant fidelity—not just for individuals, but for the corporate reality of the people of Israel. Jesus calls Nicodemus, and all Jews (and, through the apostles, also gentiles), to receive the Spirit now, to experience the initial stage of Israel's national and cosmic rebirth. They do so through turning to Jesus in faith and through attachment to him in baptism.

Why does attachment to Jesus open the way to the realization of Ezekiel's prophecies? The answer is the same as that found in our study of Jesus' baptism: because Jesus is Israel's Messiah and sums up his people in his own person: "When Jesus saw Nathanael coming toward him, he said of him, 'Here is truly an Israelite in whom there is no deceit!' . . . Nathanael replied, 'Rabbi, you are the Son of God! You are the King of Israel!' Jesus answered . . . , 'Very truly, I tell you, you will see heaven opened and the angels of God ascending and descending upon the Son of Man'" (John 1:47, 49, 51). Jesus is "the King of Israel," as Nathanael confesses, and in this role he will function as the patriarch Jacob did, upon whom the heavenly ladder rested (Gen 28:11-12), and who at that time still carried all his descendants in his loins. Because he embodies the people of Israel, the death and resurrection of Jesus accomplishes in seed-form the death and resurrection of Israel, and establishes the glorified flesh of Jesus as the beginning of the eschatological transformation of all things. Those who are joined to him through the Spirit by baptism taste the first fruits of that reality.

Regeneration is rooted in Jesus' resurrection life. It is oriented to Israel's—and the world's—future rebirth (*paligenessia*). Standing between these two eschatological events, we enter even now into the world regenerated in Jesus by putting our faith in him and being baptized.

Thus, the promise of regeneration does not negate Israel's election any more that does the promise of the renewed covenant. Both promises belong to Israel according to the flesh, and point to the eschatological goal of Israel's election. For gentiles, rebirth involves a radical break with an old life and an old world, and a new connection to the covenant community of Israel, the heirs of the messianic promises. For Jews, rebirth involves a proleptic appropriation of those promises, and thus the fulfillment rather than the negation of Jewish communal identity. For gentiles, rebirth signifies rupture; for Jews, rebirth signifies eschatological self-realization.

Conclusion

This chapter reinforces a conclusion reached in chapter 3: the Jewish people are still *the* people of God (and not simply "related to" the people of God). Even more, it confirms the thesis of chapter 4: within the Body of Christ the Jewish identity of its apostolic founders and of its Jewish members retains profound theological significance. The Jewish people as a whole remain a central component of the people of God, but the life of the Jewish people is inherently ordered by God in relation to its eschatological destiny, and that destiny will be fulfilled only in and through Messiah Jesus. That is why membership in the Jewish people is eschatologically oriented to ultimate membership in the Body of Christ—and why the Body of Christ is itself the eschatological form of the commonwealth of Israel.

To understand the spiritual status of the Jewish people who are not yet fully incorporated in the body of the Messiah, we may employ an analogy from the baptismal practice of the Catholic Church. In a sense, faithful Jews who "through no fault of their own" (*LG* 16) do not yet confess Jesus as Messiah are like catechumens who are being prepared for baptism. Many may only receive their "sprinkling with clean water" (Ezek 36:25) at the ultimate end of Israel's exile, when Ezekiel 36–37 is realized fully at the resurrection of the dead. But all faithful Jews live in anticipation of the fulfillment of Ezekiel 36–37. They put their hope in the messianic redemption of Israel—and, in doing so, they put their hope in the Coming One, whom we know to be Messiah Jesus, "King of the Jews."

In light of these truths, the Church should reflect on its baptismal teaching and practice, both for gentiles and for Jews. Baptism summons gentiles to solidarity with the Jewish people, and obligates Jews to a radical commitment to Jewish life—a Jewish life renewed in Jesus. The tragic history of baptismal teaching and practice will make it difficult for the rest of the Jewish community to accept the authenticity of that commitment. But our living out of that commitment is not dependent on such acceptance. The Lamb of God, who suffered and died on the cross as Israel's representative, calls us to follow him. If we embrace the purifying baptism of fire along with him, we may become with him not only recipients but also instruments of Israel's eschatological restoration and renewal—its "baptism with the Spirit."

In conclusion, we have seen that the sacrament of baptism can readily be understood in a manner that confirms the ecclesiological claims made in our previous chapters. By focusing attention on Jesus' own baptism—both in water, and in fire and Spirit—we have developed an Israel-centered theology of the sacrament that is rooted in Israel-Christology. Furthermore, this view of baptism reinforces an Israel-ecclesiology that affirms the enduring theological significance of Jewish identity for both baptized Jews and for those not yet baptized.

Are we able to provide a similar Israel-centered interpretation for the sacrament of the Eucharist? That is the question that will occupy our attention in the next two chapters.

6

The Last Supper, The Eucharist, and the Jewish People

Our study of *Lumen Gentium* in chapter 3 underlined the document's salutary emphasis on the Church as the people of God, but questioned its implicit separation between the Israel of the "old covenant" and the Israel of the "new." Does genealogical-Israel merely foreshadow the eschatological community inaugurated by the Messiah, such that the Church more perfectly realizes certain patterns seen in Israel's life while constituting a reality independent of her predecessor? Or is the Church intended to be an eschatologically transformed consummation of Israel, with a continuity of being analogous to that found in the mortal and glorified forms of Jesus' body? In chapter 3 I proposed that the latter form of Israel-ecclesiology should be preferred over the former, and that the apparent chasm between the *ecclesia* and genealogical Israel should be bridged through Israel-Christology and a restored *ecclesia ex circumcisione*.

In chapter 4 I developed and supported this thesis by examining the Catholic sacrament of holy orders in relation to the teaching of the New Testament books of Hebrews, Ephesians, and Romans. Hebrews reinforces our emphasis on Israel-Christology by portraying Jesus' priesthood as an aspect of his messianic role—as Israel's king he embodies the eschatological realization of Israel's corporate priestly vocation. Ephesians underlines the significance of the Jewish identity of the apostles and their role in the renewal of Israel and the incorporation of gentiles in its expanded ecclesial form. Romans shows that the entire body of Jewish disciples of Jesus possesses a quasi-apostolic character, mediating Jesus' holiness to genealogical-Israel and Israel's holiness to the *ecclesia* of the nations. Apostolic priestly ministry—the substance of the Catholic sacrament of holy orders—thus links the *ecclesia* to its Jewish founders and ultimately to its Jewish Messiah, who binds his body irrevocably to his own flesh and blood, genealogical-Israel.

Chapter 5 asked if this view of ecclesiology could be squared with a Catholic theology of baptism, which appears to imply a more radical discontinuity between the "old" and the "new" people of God. Examining the baptism of Jesus and the New Testament meaning of "regeneration," I argued that this sacrament invites those who receive it to enter proleptically into the eschatological consummation of Israel and also to show radical solidarity with the Jewish people in its pre-eschatological state. This means that the sacrament of baptism has a somewhat different significance for Jews and gentiles, while summoning both to identification with and service to the community of unbaptized Jews.

In the next two chapters I will reflect on the implications of this ecclesiological perspective for our understanding of the Eucharist. My focus in the present chapter will be on the Last Supper and what it teaches us about the relationship of the Eucharist—and those who partake of it—to genealogical-Israel. In the next chapter I will consider the sacrificial dimension of the Eucharist, and its connection to the religious character of the Jewish way of life.

The Eucharist, First-Century Judaism, and the Enduring Reality of the Jewish People

For many decades Christian scholars have searched the riches of Jewish tradition in order to better understand the Last Supper and the Eucharist.[1] The most recent example of this approach is the work of Catholic biblical scholar Brant Pitre.[2] Pitre stresses the Passover setting of the Last Supper, and contends that in this meal Jesus presents himself as the new Passover Lamb who accomplishes a new exodus, establishes a new covenant, and feeds his people with new manna. Pitre likewise asserts that the Eucharist as an ecclesial rite should be seen as a "new Passover" celebration, which Jesus institutes for the community of his disciples.[3]

---

1. Classics in this modern scholarly tradition are Jeremias, *Eucharistic Words*, and Bouyer, *Eucharist*.

2. Pitre, *Jewish Roots*.

3. "[A]t the Last Supper, Jesus was not just keeping another annual memorial of the exodus from Egypt, important as that was. Instead, he was deliberately instituting a new Passover through which the new exodus would finally be set in motion" (Pitre, *Jewish Roots*, 68).

In assessing the work of Pitre or that of his predecessors, several distinctions are in order. First, sometimes these scholars propose that the ritual of the Last Supper and the Eucharist builds upon existing Jewish liturgical forms such as the Passover feast or the grace after meals. To the extent that their case is persuasive, it leads to the conclusion—which should be obvious regardless—that Jesus and his disciples lived as faithful Jews and drew upon the long-established customs of their people. While such parallels may provide new insight into the meaning of the Last Supper and the Eucharist, they do not help us grasp the significance of Jesus' life and work for the Jewish people and the Jewish way of life—which is my primary concern here.

Second, sometimes these scholars argue that in the Last Supper Jesus draws upon traditional Jewish teaching regarding the coming of the messianic age—teaching that anticipates a new redeemer patterned after the biblical figure of Moses. This new redeemer was expected to accomplish a new exodus, and to work miracles of provision like those that Israel experienced in the wilderness of Sinai. This material supplies an internal Jewish precedent for a prophetic typology of the messianic age. Thus, to view Jesus as a new Moses and his death and resurrection as a new exodus is not to depart from Judaism or to deny the enduring significance of Moses himself or the original exodus. Helpful as this is, it still does not offer any substantive guidance on precisely how Jesus and his work should be understood in relation to the Jewish people and the Jewish way of life.

Third, sometimes these scholars go beyond the specific typology of biblical figures (such as Moses) or biblical events (such as the exodus) and conclude from the general typological framework inherent in the Last Supper that Jesus sees his group of disciples as a "new Israel." The adjective "new" in this context has all the ambiguity brought to light in our discussion of *Lumen Gentium*: it could mean only that Jesus saw the community of his disciples as the nucleus of an eschatologically renewed form of the people into which he was born, in which he was raised, and among whom he spent his entire life. However, the adjective "new" could have a different and more extreme meaning: it could be an implicit assertion that the Church is a reality separate from genealogical Israel, a community and an institution foreshadowed by the Israel of the "old covenant," but essentially an *ex nihilo* creation resulting from the resurrection of Christ and the gift of the Holy Spirit. The Church would thus be fundamentally *dis*continuous with genealogical-Israel. Just as Moses was like Jesus but was also a separate individual in his own right, and just as the exodus from Egypt was like the redemption worked by Jesus on the cross and yet was a separate event in its own right, so also genealogical-Israel is "like" the Church in some ways, but, nevertheless, a separate community in its own right.

I regard this third conclusion regarding the "Jewish roots of the Eucharist" to be an assumption imposed upon the New Testament teaching rather than an inference warranted by the teaching itself. If we read the New Testament narrative of the Last Supper in light of our study of baptism, holy orders, and ecclesiology, we will discover that the Last Supper and the Eucharist shed fresh light on the intimate bond connecting the Church to the Jewish people.

Accordingly, in this chapter I will ignore most of the manifold ways that the Last Supper and the Eucharist draw upon or parallel traditional Jewish prayers, rites, or theological motifs. Instead, I will concentrate only on those features of the narrative of the Last Supper that illumine the way the redemptive work of Jesus relates to his brothers and sisters according to the flesh. I will begin by looking exegetically at the significance of the cup and the words that Jesus pronounces over it. I will then offer a brief theological reflection concerning the implications of his words over the bread. Finally, I will discuss the ecclesiological significance of the small band of disciples who surround him at this solemn meal.

The Eucharistic Cup: Israel-Ecclesiology Rooted in Israel-Christology

Tasting Judgment

According to all four canonical accounts of the Last Supper, Jesus has more to say about the cup that he blesses than about the bread that he breaks.[4] The image of the cup also arises elsewhere in the synoptic narrative with special prominence. To understand the significance of the cup at the Last Supper, we must first examine these other references in the Gospels.

The first text—Mark 10:35-45 (Matt 20:20-28)—describes the audacious request of the sons of Zebedee for privileged seats in Jesus' coming kingdom. The passage contains several features that connect it to the Last Supper—a fact recognized by Luke, who includes an abbreviated form of the story in his narrative of the Last Supper (Luke 22:24-27). Mark and Matthew, on the other hand, set this incident immediately after Jesus' third prediction of his coming suffering and death (Mark 10:32-34; Matt 20:17-19) as he marches toward Jerusalem with his disciples.

---

4. The four accounts are Mark 14:17-26; Matt 26:20-30; Luke 22:14-38; 1 Cor 11:23-25. In their description of the words of institution, Mark and Matthew manifest one stream of tradition, whereas Luke and 1 Corinthians display another.

> James and John, the sons of Zebedee, came forward to him and said to him, "Teacher, we want you to do for us whatever we ask of you." And he said to them, "What is it you want me to do for you?" And they said to him, "Grant us to sit, one at your right hand and one at your left, in your glory." But Jesus said to them, "You do not know what you are asking. Are you able to drink the cup that I drink, or be baptized with the baptism that I am baptized with?" They replied, "We are able." Then Jesus said to them, "The cup that I drink you will drink; and with the baptism with which I am baptized, you will be baptized; but to sit at my right hand or at my left is not mine to grant, but it is for those for whom it has been prepared." When the ten heard this, they began to be angry with James and John. So Jesus called them and said to them, "You know that among the gentiles those whom they recognize as their rulers lord it over them, and their great ones are tyrants over them. But it is not so among you; but whoever wishes to become great among you must be your servant, and whoever wishes to be first among you must be slave of all. For the Son of Man came not to be served but to serve, and to give his life a ransom for many." (Mark 10:35–45)

Like John the Baptist, Jesus' disciples see their master as the promised one who will restore and glorify Israel by baptizing with Spirit and fire, and they vie with one another over who will have the most authority when he establishes his rule—in their view, presumably, at the Passover that soon approaches. They thereby demonstrate that they have failed to absorb Jesus' words about his coming suffering. He now speaks again of that suffering, but for the first time he also interprets its meaning. Drawing upon the language of Isaiah, Jesus presents himself as the servant of the Lord who gives his life "for many" (Isa 53:11–12).

Jesus' question to the sons of Zebedee is crucial for understanding the eucharistic cup and its relation to his baptism: "Are you able to drink the cup that I drink, or be baptized with the baptism that I am baptized with?" As we have seen in chapter 4, the "baptism" to which he refers is his coming suffering and death. The parallelism between the images of baptism and the cup imply that the latter has the same reference. The cup he must drink is the cup of suffering and death.

This understanding of the cup is confirmed by the second text in which the image appears. Our first text was set in the period directly preceding the Last Supper. The second describes the event immediately following that meal. Jesus goes with his disciples to Gethsemane, to prepare through prayer for what is to come.

> They went to a place called Gethsemane; and he said to his disciples, "Sit here while I pray." He took with him Peter and James and John, and began to be distressed and agitated. And he said to them, "I am deeply grieved, even to death; remain here, and keep awake." And going a little farther, he threw himself on the ground and prayed that, if it were possible, the hour might pass from him. He said, "Abba, Father, for you all things are possible; remove this cup from me; yet, not what I want, but what you want." (Mark 14:32–35)

In the following verses Mark says that Jesus "went away and prayed, saying the same words" (Mark 14:39). Matthew describes this second prayer as differing slightly from the first: "Again he went away for the second time and prayed, 'My Father, if this cannot pass unless I drink it, *your will be done*'" (Matt 26:42). Once again, it is clear that the cup refers to the suffering and death that Jesus must now endure—but it also refers to the will of God, which Jesus has come to fulfill.

The image of the cup interprets the suffering Jesus must soon undergo. It does so because it served as a common biblical trope for divine judgment. We find this image, for example, in the chapter of Isaiah preceding the description of the suffering servant:

> Rouse yourself, rouse yourself! Stand up, O Jerusalem,
> you who have drunk at the hand of the Lord the cup of his wrath,
> who have drunk to the dregs the bowl of staggering. (Isa 51:17)

The judgment of exile experienced by Jerusalem is depicted here as "the cup of his [the Lord's] wrath." Thus, in the suffering and death that Jesus must endure, he will bear the divine judgment that Israel deserves, in conformity to the pattern of the Servant of the Lord in Isaiah 52–53. In this way the cup that Jesus must drink and the baptism with which he must be baptized both refer to the same events, and ascribe to those events the same meaning.

The association of the cup with Jesus' suffering and death sheds light on a peculiar feature of the Last Supper, namely, Jesus' vow to abstain from drinking wine "until the kingdom of God comes" (Luke 22:17–18; Mark 14:25; Matt 26:29). The timing of this vow in relation to the meal at hand is uncertain in Mark and Matthew, but Luke's version is unambiguous: Jesus says these words before "he took bread" (i.e., before the meal). Luke emphasizes the fact that Jesus does not eat (Luke 22:16) or drink with his disciples at the Last Supper. The words of Jesus cited by Luke suggest that it is inappropriate for him to celebrate until the joyful reality to which the meal points is established. In numerous biblical texts the image of wine carries the positive connotation of blessing and joy, even of an eschatological character.⁵ However, the association of the cup not only with celebration but also with divine judgment and with Jesus' coming suffering and death implies a second reason: the disciples can drink the cup at the Last Supper, but Jesus has only to wait a few hours before his cup of suffering—to which this meal points—would be consumed in full.⁶ The multilayered complexity of the biblical image of the cup enables it to function at the Last Supper—and in the Eucharist—as a potent symbol of both the suffering of Good Friday and the jubilation of Easter Sunday.

Before turning to the words Jesus pronounces over the cup, we must add a final observation concerning the cup of Mark 10. Jesus asks James and John if they are able to drink the cup that he will drink and be baptized with the baptism that he will undergo. They naively respond in the affirmative. Jesus then retorts, "The cup that I drink you will drink; and with the baptism with which I am baptized, you will be baptized" (v. 39). Jesus is not now speaking of their future participation in the sacraments, but of the apostolic suffering they will endure. It is their privilege to enter into communion with his own passion through suffering as his disciples.⁷ This means that while Jesus' suffering and death—and the baptism and cup that signify his bearing of divine judgment—are as unique in their redemptive power as his divine-human person, they are also inclusive. In fact, this capacity to enfold the suffering and death of others within his own highlights rather than undermines the uniqueness of his redemptive act. Moreover, other New Testament texts suggest that his suffering has an inclusive orientation backwards in time as well as forwards—he sums up and perfects all the righteous suffering of Israel's prophets and martyrs, and even those of the pre-Israelite era.⁸ As Israel's Messiah, Jesus bears the judgment that Israel deserves, but he does so in concert with others whose noble but imperfect work reaches its goal through being graciously enfolded within his own unique and definitive atoning deed.

---

5. See Gen 49:8-12; Amos 9:13-15; Zech 9:16-17.; and Hart, *Beauty*, 107-8. The association between wine and messianic joy is paramount in the story of the wedding at Cana (John 2:1-11).

6. The connection between the cup of the Last Supper and the cup which Jesus accepts at Gethsemane is underlined by the Catholic Catechism: "The cup of the New Covenant, which Jesus anticipated when he offered himself at the Last Supper, is afterwards accepted by him from his Father's hands in his agony in the garden of Gethsemane, making himself 'obedient unto death.' Jesus prays: 'My Father, if it be possible, let this cup pass from me . . .'" (CCC 612).

7. This becomes a major theme in the Pauline letters and in John's Apocalypse. See Phil 3:10; Rom 8:17; 2 Cor 1:5; 4:10-11; Col 1:24; Rev 6:9-11; 11:7-8; 12:10-11.

8. This is asserted explicitly in Hebrews 11:1—12:2, and implicitly in Jesus' parable of the vineyard (Mark 12:1-11). See also Matt 23:34-39.

The cup at the Last Supper—and thus also the cup at the ecclesial sacrament instituted at that meal—signifies Jesus' radical solidarity with his own flesh-and-blood. As such, the cup interprets his approaching death as an act in which he bears the judgment due to his people. In this light his death becomes an atoning act expressing his identity as Israel's priestly representative who bears the names of his people on his breast and carries them with him into the presence of God (Exod 28:29). The cup at the Last Supper thus calls into question any reading of this narrative that makes of it the establishment of a new and separate community lacking organic connection to the Israel of old.

Renewing the Covenant

Mark and Matthew recount that Jesus took the cup, gave thanks (*eucharisteo*) for it, passed it to his disciples, and said, "This is my blood of the covenant." Jesus thereby relates this cup—and the events of the following day to which it points—to the sacrificial blood that ratified the Sinai covenant. In that ratification ceremony Moses built an altar at the foot of Mount Sinai, and set up twelve pillars in close proximity to the altar to represent the twelve tribes of Israel (Exod 24:4). He then had animals sacrificed, and poured half of their blood on the altar (which represented God). After reading aloud the book of the covenant, he dashed the other half of the blood on the people (Exod 24:5–8). As he did this he said, "See the blood of the covenant that the Lord has made with you in accordance with all these words" (Exod 24:8). After this, Moses, Aaron, two of Aaron's sons, and seventy of Israel's elders ascend the mountain, behold the God of Israel, and eat and drink in God's presence (Exod 24:9–11).

What is the point of Jesus' allusion to the ratification of the Sinai covenant? The traditional view regards the allusion as typological in character. Just as Moses placed sacrificial blood on the people of Israel to seal the Sinai covenant, so Jesus will place his own blood on his disciples to seal the "new" covenant. This typological reading discerns a common pattern in the two actions, but also distances them from each other. It implies the existence of two separate covenants and two separate covenant peoples, with the former only foreshadowing the latter. However, the text itself does not require such an interpretation. More likely, Jesus here points to his coming death as the true sacrifice—represented proleptically by the offerings of Exodus 24—which retroactively seals and thus ultimately sustains *the Sinai covenant itself*. According to this interpretation, Jesus envisions only one covenant and only one covenant people—the people of Israel.

Joseph Cardinal Ratzinger (writing before his election to the papal office) offers a similar interpretation of the covenantal words of Jesus at the Last Supper: "With regard to the issue of the nature of the covenant, it is important to note that the Last Supper sees itself as making a covenant: *it is the prolongation of the Sinai covenant, which is not abrogated, but renewed.* Here renewal of the covenant, which from earliest times was doubtless an essential element in Israel's liturgy, attains its highest form possible."[9] Cardinal Ratzinger combines the Markan-Matthean allusion to the Sinai covenant with the Pauline-Lukan reference to the "new covenant" (1 Cor 11:25; Luke 22:20), and interprets the latter as a ritual renewal of the former that follows an existing Jewish liturgical model.

The Pauline-Lukan formulation of Jesus' words over the cup adds to the Markan-Matthean tradition an allusion to Jeremiah 31:

> The days are surely coming, says the Lord, when I will make a new covenant with the house of Israel and the house of Judah. It will not be like the covenant that I made with their ancestors when I took them by the hand to bring them out of the land of Egypt—a covenant that they broke, though I was their husband, says the Lord. But this is the covenant that I will make with the house of Israel after those days, says the Lord: I will put my law within them, and I will write it on their hearts; and I will be their God, and they shall be my people. No longer shall they teach one another, or say to each other, "Know the Lord," for they shall all know me, from the least of them to the greatest, says the Lord; for I will forgive their iniquity, and remember their sin no more. (Jer 31:31–34)

We discussed this passage in our examination of *Lumen Gentium* in chapter 3, but it merits more thorough consideration in our present context. The customary Christian understanding of Jeremiah 31 emphasizes Israel's infidelity to the Sinai covenant, which resulted in the termination of that covenant, and thus necessitated a new spiritual (rather than geographical) exodus, a new covenant, and a new people. Thus interpreted, the Jeremiah text appears to justify the merely typological connection described above between Sinai and Golgotha. However, this perspective can only be sustained by ignoring a contextual reading of Jeremiah 31, and assuming that Paul, Luke, and those who transmitted this tradition likewise used the prophetic text without reading it carefully.[10]

---

9. Benedict XVI, *Many Religions*, 62–63; emphasis added.

10. We may include Jesus in the list, leaving open the question of which formulation (the Markan-Matthean or the Pauline-Lukan) is more original. Jeremias argues for the

Three features of Jeremiah 31 are especially noteworthy for our interpretation of Jesus' words over the cup recorded by Paul and Luke. First, the only difference in Jeremiah between the Sinai covenant and the "new" covenant is a new action of God that empowers the people to faithfully observe the commandments already given. There is no indication that the requirements of the covenant have changed. The Torah is now written on the hearts of the people, but this is evidently the *same* Torah that was given at Sinai (since there is no mention here of a Torah with content differing from that of the Torah given at Sinai). Second, the intended recipients of the "new" covenant are the same as those who received the Sinai covenant—namely, the genealogical community that traced its descent from the patriarchs and matriarchs. This is not only implicit in the text, but articulated boldly and explicitly in the verses of Jeremiah 31 that follow:

> Thus says the Lord,
> who gives the sun for light by day
>   and the fixed order of the moon and the stars for light by night,
> who stirs up the sea so that its waves roar—
>   the LORD of hosts is his name:
> If this fixed order were ever to cease
>   from my presence, says the LORD,
> then also the offspring of Israel would cease
>   to be a nation before me forever.
> Thus says the LORD:
> If the heavens above can be measured,
>   and the foundations of the earth below can be explored,
> then I will reject all the offspring of Israel
>   because of all they have done, says the Lord. (Jer 31:35–37)

Third, the Babylonian exile provides the context for Jeremiah 31. The rupture in Israel's relationship with God was manifested in Israel's expulsion from the land promised to it and from the holy city where God had chosen to dwell. Correspondingly, the new covenant is part of a new exodus, which is different from the first exodus only in regards to the geographic location of the bondage from which Israel is to be redeemed. As in the first exodus, the genealogical community descended from the patriarchs and the matriarchs will be brought to the land promised to its ancestors and to the holy city associated eternally with David and his seed. This is evident throughout Jeremiah 31, both in the verses before the prophecy of the new covenant and

---

primacy of the Markan-Matthean tradition on this particular point, and his reasoning appears cogent (*Eucharistic Words*, 169–71, 189–95). However, no certainty is possible on such matters, and, as seen in our analysis above, the differences between the two traditions are in fact theologically unproblematic.

those after. These three features of Jeremiah 31 fully justify the conclusion reached by Catholic biblical scholar Norbert Lohfink: "the new covenant [of Jeremiah 31] is but the earlier one, now brilliant and radiant. . . . God pardons and institutes again and anew the old that has been lost. But it is the old. It is not another 'covenant.'"[11]

Viewed in this light, the Pauline-Lukan version of the words of institution over the cup add texture to the Markan-Matthean tradition without altering its meaning. While now residing in the land of promise, Israel's spiritual condition nevertheless resembles that of the people whom Jeremiah addressed during the Babylonian exile. They stand in need of a new exodus and a new Sinai, in which the power of God demonstrated at the beginning of Israel's national life is exerted again in order to bring to completion what those founding events were intended to accomplish. With these words over the cup Jesus implies that his coming martyrdom will be the divinely appointed means of realizing and renewing both the exodus and the Sinai covenant that was its goal.

What is there about Jesus' martyrdom that will make it effective at founding and renewing God's covenant with Israel? A clue is found in the verse of Exodus 24 immediately preceding Moses' reference to the "blood of the covenant." There the people, having heard the words from the book of the covenant, respond by saying, "All that the Lord has spoken we will do, and we will be obedient" (Exod 24:7). On the cross Jesus drinks the cup that his Father has given him (John 18:11), and in that act he demonstrates that his entire life has been an outworking of the prayer he taught his disciples, and which he himself prayed at Gethsemane: "Your will be done" (Matt 26:42). Because Jesus' life of obedient love fulfills the covenantal Torah, the climax of that obedient life will set the covenant and its Torah on an unshakeable footing.

Pope Benedict XVI understands Jesus' obedience in relation to Exodus 24 and Jeremiah 31 in just this way:

> [T]he people had responded to the reading of the book of the covenant: "All that the Lord has spoken we will do, and we will be obedient.". . . This promise of obedience, which is an indispensable element of the Covenant, was broken immediately afterward while Moses was on the mountain, through the worship of the golden calf. The entire history that follows is a tale of repeated violations of the promise of obedience. . . . The rupture seems beyond repair when God hands his people over to exile

---

11. Lohfink, *Covenant*, 48. Lohfink offers insightful exegesis of Jeremiah 31 (see 45–57).

and the Temple to destruction. At this moment, the hope of a "new covenant" arises, one that is no longer built upon the perennially fragile fidelity of the human will but that is written indestructibly on men's hearts (cf. Jer 31:33). In other words, the New Covenant must be founded on an obedience that is irrevocable and inviolable. This obedience, now located at the very root of human nature, is the obedience of the Son, who made himself a servant and took all human disobedience upon himself in his obedience even unto death, suffered it right to the end, and conquered it.[12]

The faithfulness of Israel's God calls for a corresponding faithfulness from those who are the recipients of God's gracious gift of the covenant. Israel pledges such obedience at Sinai, but—as the true representative of a wounded humanity—fails to live out that pledge in its corporate life. This sets the stage for the promise of the new covenant in Jeremiah 31, which will be founded on the "irrevocable and inviolable" obedience of Jesus—an "obedience even unto death."

Norbert Lohfink adopts a similar reading of Jeremiah 31. He notes that the mark of the renewed covenant in that chapter is the promise that the Torah will be written on Israel's heart, so that Israel can live it out faithfully and without external instruction (Jer 31:33). Has this truly happened? Do either the Jewish people or the Church manifest this reality in their corporate lives, or in the lives of their individual members? In particular, was the Torah written on the hearts of those Jews who returned from Babylonian exile and their descendants? It is clear that this was not the case. But Lohfink asks another question:

> Was the torah written . . . on the heart of one single person, in such a way that this heart was entirely one with the torah so that it had no need to be instructed anymore about it? . . . We Christians believe: there was such a heart. We refer to Jesus of Nazareth, to the "heart of Jesus." And we are convinced that all who bind themselves to this heart in faith, even when they themselves fail continually and must obtain pardon again, share in the strength of its fidelity to the torah, in its deeply rooted knowledge of God. And it is in it that we see a fulfillment of the promise of the "new covenant" which surpasses all that preceded it, *the* fulfillment of itself.[13]

---

12. Benedict XVI, *Jesus of Nazareth, Part II*, 132.
13. Lohfink, *Covenant*, 54.

Jesus himself is the recipient and embodiment of the renewed covenant with Israel, and his martyrdom seals that covenant by enacting perfectly the Torah obedience it requires and enables. He does this as Israel's Messiah, as its head and representative, so that all the covenant promises to Israel might be fulfilled. Thus, the "new covenant" brings us back once again to Israel-Christology as the basis of Israel-ecclesiology.

Atoning as Servant-Israel

Mark adds an additional phrase to the words pronounced over the cup: "This is my blood of the covenant *poured out for many*." The phrase "for many" alludes to the work of Isaiah's Suffering Servant (Isa 53:11-12). It also recalls Jesus' response to the request of James and John—"For the Son of Man came not to be served but to serve, and to give his life a ransom *for many*"—and the words of Jesus a few verses earlier concerning the cup and baptism of judgment (Mark 10:45, 38-39). Luke lacks this additional phrase, but he establishes the connection with the servant motif by inserting here—as part of his narrative of the Last Supper—an abbreviated version of the James and John incident, which concludes with the words, "But I am among you as one who serves" (Luke 22:24-27). The same motif is found in the meal of John 13, where Jesus assumes the role of a menial servant and washes the feet of his disciples (John 13:1-17). The symbolic acts of drinking (or not drinking) the cup and of washing feet, and the words which interpret those acts, together provide a way of understanding the events that will occur on the next day. They reinforce the conviction that Isaiah 53, and all the servant passages of Isaiah 40-55, are crucial for this purpose. Jesus is the righteous servant who embodies and represents servant-Israel as a whole, who in his death shoulders Israel's exilic suffering in order that his people might be glorified and the nations illumined.

What is the meaning of the phrase "poured out for many"? Who are "the many"? Pope Benedict XVI provides an enlightening comment on these words. He begins by describing an earlier scholarly consensus that the word "many" means "the totality" and "is therefore most accurately translated as 'all.'" The Pope then recounts how this position no longer holds sway.

> Meanwhile, though, this consensus among exegetes has broken down once more. The prevailing opinion today is that "many" in Isaiah 53 and similar passages does indeed indicate a totality, but it cannot simply be equated with "all." On the basis of

Qumranic usage, it is now generally held that "many" in Isaiah and on the lips of Jesus means the "totality" of Israel.[14]

This is a point of tremendous importance when viewed in light of our central thesis. According to Jesus' words at the Last Supper, his life will be poured out as a sacrifice *on behalf of his own people, the people of Israel*. Does this mean that Jesus' death has no relevance for the gentiles? The Pope draws upon the teaching of the Gospel of John to clarify Jesus' intent: "John says that Jesus will die 'for the people' (the Jews), but not only for the people: also in order to gather together into unity the scattered children of God (cf 11:50–52). Jesus died for Jews and Gentiles, for the whole of mankind."[15] Indeed, Jesus does die for "all," but the phrase "the many" conveys two crucial truths about *how* Jesus dies for all: (1) There is an ordering among those for whom he dies—he pours his life out *first* for his own people, and then also for "the scattered children of God"; (2) The way gentiles avail themselves of the atoning power of his sacrifice is by *being joined to Israel* through baptism into Israel's Messiah.

Matthew adds another additional phrase to the words pronounced over the cup: "This is my blood of the covenant, which is poured out for many *for the forgiveness of sins*" (Matt 26:28). With these words Matthew makes explicit the meaning of the Markan phrase "poured out for many." The mention of "sins" deepens the connection to Isaiah 53, and also recalls the forgiveness motif of Jeremiah 31:34.[16] The role of forgiveness in Jeremiah 31 supports the contention of N. T. Wright that "forgiveness of sins" in the Gospels refers to the restoration of individuals only in the wider context of the corporate restoration of the people of Israel.

> Centuries of Christian usage have accustomed readers of the New Testament to think of "forgiveness" as primarily a gift to the individual person, which can be made at any time. It is, in that sense, abstract and ahistorical.... What is regularly missing from analyses of forgiveness is that which, arguably, stands front and center in precisely those biblical and post-biblical Jewish texts upon which Jesus and the early Church drew most heavily. *Forgiveness of sins is another way of saying "return from exile."*... Since covenant renewal means the reversal of exile, and since exile was the punishment for sin, covenant renewal/return from exile *means* that Israel's sins have been forgiven—and vice versa. ... In the light of this, the meaning which Mark and Luke both

---

14. Benedict XVI, *Jesus of Nazareth, Part II*, 135.
15. Ibid., 137.
16. In the LXX of Isaiah 53 the word *hamartia* ("sin") appears six times.

give to John's baptism ought to be clear. It was "for the forgiveness of sins," in other words, to bring about the redemption for which Israel was longing.[17]

As Wright perceives, this meaning of "forgiveness" provides the necessary background to Matthew's version of Jesus' words over the cup: "Matthew is not suggesting that Jesus' death will accomplish an abstract atonement, but that it will be the means of rescuing YHWH's people from their exilic plight."[18] The focus is on the forgiveness of *Israel's* sins, and the renewed national life that bears witness to its efficacy. At the same time, the "many" who are forgiven will also include those from the nations who are to be joined to this expanded and eschatologically renewed people of God.

The "cup of the covenant," as both sign of judgment and of eschatological joy, is the cup that belongs to Israel. It is also the cup that belongs to Jesus as Israel's Messiah, who fulfills the covenant, bears Israel's judgment, and becomes the agent of its resurrection. Our discussion here fully bears out the words of Wolfhart Pannenberg, cited in chapter 3:

> When at the Last Supper that he held with his disciples on the night of his arrest Jesus related the promise of the new covenant to the table fellowship with his disciples that he sealed with his self-offering, he was not snapping the link of this promise to the people of Israel. Instead, he was showing that fellowship with himself is for the whole Jewish people the future of salvation that breaks in already in the fellowship of the band of disciples.[19]

The Eucharistic Bread: Israel-Christology Giving Birth to Israel-Ecclesiology

To this point I have focused on the Last Supper itself, and its implications for our understanding of the significance of the Eucharist in relation to the Jewish people. Accordingly, I have taken an exegetical approach to the material. I will resume this mode of discussion in the final section of this chapter, but in considering the eucharistic bread I will follow a different theological path.

It would distract from my purpose here to engage in a detailed exegetical exposition of Jesus' brief words over the bread, which identify it as his body. Rather than ask about the original meaning of Jesus' words, or

---

17. Wright, *Victory*, 268–69, 271.
18. Ibid., 561.
19. Pannenberg, *Systematic Theology*, 477.

the way they were understood by the New Testament authors, I will reflect upon the implications of how these words have been interpreted in Catholic tradition. I would propose that the sacramental realism of Catholic teaching points in a direction that has rarely been noted or seriously pondered.

The Catechism describes the presence of Jesus in the Eucharist as follows:

> The mode of Christ's presence under the Eucharistic species is unique.... In the most blessed sacrament of the Eucharist "the body and blood, together with the soul and divinity, of our Lord Jesus Christ and, therefore, *the whole Christ is truly, really, and substantially contained.*" "This presence is called 'real'—by which is not intended to exclude the other types of presence as if they could not be 'real' too, but because it is presence in the fullest sense: that is to say, it is a *substantial* presence by which Christ, God and man, makes himself wholly and entirely present." (CCC 1374)
>
> Christ is present whole and entire in each of the species and whole and entire in each of their parts, in such a way that the breaking of the bread does not divide Christ. (CCC 1377)

The *"whole* Christ" is present in the consecrated host, and also in the consecrated cup. This is why Catholic tradition permits communion in one kind—but, when that practice is followed, it is the host and not the cup that is taken by the faithful. In saying "this is my body," Jesus made the host an especially apt sacramental sign of his "whole" person.

Taking seriously such sacramental realism, and considering its import in light of post-Holocaust and post-Vatican II thinking about the Jewish people, Scott Bader-Saye has offered a provocative thesis concerning the Eucharist, the *ecclesia*, and the Jewish people.[20] He begins by citing and affirming the conclusion of Karl Barth regarding the incarnation and Jesus' Jewish identity. Barth writes:

> The Word did not simply become *any "flesh*," any man humbled and suffering. It became *Jewish flesh*. *The Church's whole doctrine of the incarnation and the atonement becomes abstract and valueless and meaningless to the extent that this comes to be regarded as something accidental and incidental*.... The pronouncements of New Testament Christology ... relate always to a man who is seen to be not a man in general, a neutral man, but the ... sum

---

20. Bader-Saye, "Hermeneutics," 458–74. See also Bader-Saye, *Church and Israel*, 139–40.

of the history of God with the people of Israel, the One who fulfills the covenant made by God with this people.[21]

Barth was not a sacramental realist, and so his assertion about the incarnation led him to no inference about the Eucharist. Holding a more catholic view of the sacrament, Bader-Saye takes the next logical step, and he does so by paraphrasing Barth: "If Barth is right in his claim, then we must also say that the flesh of Christ that comes to us in the sacrament is *not just any human flesh*, broken for us; it is *Jewish flesh. The Church's whole doctrine of the sacrament becomes abstract and meaningless to the extent that this comes to be regarded as something accidental and incidental.*"[22] As we noted in chapter 3, the risen Jesus remains a circumcised Jew, and this fact has explosive theological consequences that are yet to be fully appreciated in Christian theology. Bader-Saye has identified one of those consequences.

Having articulated a particular sacramental implication of Israel-Christology, Bader-Saye proceeds to show how it bears fruit in Israel-ecclesiology. He does so by drawing upon the eucharistic teaching of Aquinas and Augustine. Aquinas (citing Augustine) contrasts the physical digestive process that occurs when eating normal food with the spiritual digestive process that occurs when partaking of the Eucharist: "The difference between corporeal and spiritual food lies in this, that the former is changed into the substance of the person nourished . . . but spiritual food changes man into itself."[23] Bader-Saye presents this reverse spiritual digestive process of the sacrament as the basis for the *ecclesia*'s claim to be an eschatological extension of Israel and an heir of the covenant:

> [E]ucharistic food is not consumed by the body, but rather it consumes the body. Eucharist thereby becomes the place where God's corporeal election of Israel is extended to the Gentiles. For the Gentiles are united in the Lord's Supper to the flesh of the Jewish Jesus. By participating in Christ through Eucharist, they are made to participate in the covenant God made with Jewish flesh. The celebration of the Lord's Supper is thus made scandalous because not only are Gentiles eating with Jews, they are eating a Jew. And as his body consumes theirs, they are grafted into Israel, not just spiritually but by having their own

---

21. Barth, *CD* IV.1, 166. Bader-Saye only includes a portion of this citation in his article. Emphasis added to highlight the words which Bader-Saye will paraphrase in his assertion about the eucharistic Body of Christ.

22. Bader-Saye, "Hermeneutics." Emphasis added to highlight the wording drawn from Barth.

23. Aquinas, ST III.73.3 (*Summa*, Volume 4, 2430). See Bader-Saye, *Church and Israel*, 179, note 18, and "Hermeneutics," note 33.

bodies transformed into Jewish flesh. This practice makes visible the new life of the covenant . . . .[24]

The phrase, "having their own bodies transformed into Jewish flesh," is liable to misinterpretation, as it could imply that gentile communicants become Jews in a way that would eliminate all differentiation between them and Jewish communicants. As we saw in our study of Ephesians, differentiation between Jew and gentile endures within the eschatological commonwealth of Israel as a perpetual sign of God's reconciling power in the Messiah. However, the vivid character of the phrase has its value in underlining the enduring Jewish character of the *ecclesia* and the imperative of expressing her corporate life in concrete embodied form.

Like apostolic ministry and baptism, the Eucharist forges a link between Israel-Christology and Israel-ecclesiology. When Jesus says, "This is my body," to be honored and received by his disciples, he is establishing the ground on which Israel's renewed covenant rests, and on which those previously far away will now be drawn near.

The Twelve: The Last Supper and the Mediation of Jewish Apostles

We have already had reason to comment on the significance of the Twelve, both in relation to baptism and to the eucharistic cup. We have examined Matthew 19:28, with its promise of the *paligenessia*—the new eschatological "birth" of Israel—and the enthronement of the Twelve as rulers of the twelve tribes. According to John 3, baptism grants proleptic access to this future reality. We have also considered the audacious request of James and John (Mark 10:35-45; Matt 20:20-28). Enthronement among the Twelve was not sufficient for James and John—they wanted to have the highest of the thrones, directly beside that of the messianic king. This petition led Jesus to speak of the cup and the baptism of obedient suffering, and the apostolic vocation of sacrificial service. He makes known that he is the suffering servant who would give his life for his people, and that his disciples are called to share in his obedient suffering and his faithful servanthood.

These images and ideas coalesce at the Last Supper. All three of the Synoptic Gospels emphasize that only Jesus and the Twelve were present at this meal (Matt 26:20; Mark 14:17; Luke 22:14). This is striking in itself, as the other meals of Jesus recounted in the Gospels are wide-open affairs.

---

24. Bader-Saye, *Church and Israel*, 140.

They usually involve women, either as hosts, invited guests, or party-crashers.[25] But the Last Supper is an intimate gathering, with only Jesus and the Twelve whom he appointed to rule as servants within the people of Israel. This underlines the importance of the Twelve, and their integral connection to the symbolic act that Jesus here performs.

As explained above, Jesus' reference to the "blood of the covenant" in his words over the cup recalls the covenant ratification ceremony of Exodus 24, with its twelve pillars representing the twelve tribes of Israel. Just as the twelve pillars signified Israel's willing participation in the covenant, so the presence at this meal of the twelve chief disciples of Jesus shows that this symbolic act concerns not just them but the entire people of Israel.

Luke has shaped his narrative of the Last Supper so as to make this coalescence of images and ideas indisputable. He does this first by resituating the dispute among the Twelve over exalted positions in the messianic kingdom, setting it in the context of the Last Supper rather than the journey to Jerusalem.

> A dispute also arose among them as to which one of them was to be regarded as the greatest. But he said to them, "The kings of the gentiles lord it over them; and those in authority over them are called benefactors. But not so with you; rather the greatest among you must become like the youngest, and the leader like one who serves. For who is greater, the one who is at the table or the one who serves? Is it not the one at the table? But I am among you as one who serves." (Luke 22:24–27)

Luke's version is briefer than the narratives found in Mark and Matthew, but the parallel between the stories remains obvious. Jesus' instruction concerning servant leadership takes on heightened meaning when it follows immediately after his words over the cup and their allusion to Isaiah 53, and when it precedes Gethsemane and the narrative of the passion. Luke does not include Jesus' question to James and John: "Are you able to drink the cup that I drink, or be baptized with the baptism that I am baptized with?" Instead, the entire incident occurs directly after they *have actually drunk* from that cup (the cup that anticipates sacramentally the cup that Jesus himself will drink the following day), though they had not yet understood the meaning of what they were doing.

The Twelve are called to imitate and participate in the servanthood of their master. But they are also called to participate in his eschatological rule. To make this clear, Luke now draws upon the traditional material he

---

25. Luke is especially instructive on this point. See Luke 4:38–39; 7:36–50; 8:1–3; 10:38–42. See also Mark 7:24–30; 14:3–9.

shares with Matthew, which describes the *paligenessia*—the new eschatological "birth" of Israel: "'You are those who have stood by me in my trials; and I confer on you, just as my Father has conferred on me, a kingdom, so that you may eat and drink at my table in my kingdom, and you will sit on thrones judging the twelve tribes of Israel'" (Luke 22:28-30). Matthew inserted a similar eschatological promise in his version of the story of the rich young man (Matt 19:16-30). Luke's version lacks the term *paligenessia*, and also adds the imagery of eating at table in the messianic kingdom—imagery that fits the context of the Last Supper. Nevertheless, the promise of future enthronement and rule over the twelve tribes is identical in both texts.

The eschatological imagery of the messianic banquet is especially important in Luke. His volume contains more stories of Jesus at table and more banquet-parables than any other of the gospels. He alone begins his narrative of the Last Supper with these words of Jesus: "I have eagerly desired to eat this Passover with you before I suffer; for I tell you, I will not eat it until it is fulfilled in the kingdom of God" (Luke 22:15-16). And he alone connects the future enthronement of the Twelve with their sitting at table in the age to come, placing the saying in a context that makes the Last Supper a proleptic experience of that reality. Just as the humble service of Jesus' death and the glorious exaltation of his resurrection are mutually interpretive, so the simplicity and obscurity of the Last Supper and the splendor and cosmic scope of the messianic banquet are mutually interpretive.

The eschatological significance of the Last Supper undergirds the eschatological significance of the Eucharist. As with baptism, this is an eschatology that is Israel-centered. Just as baptism introduces those who receive it to Israel's eschatological future, so the Eucharist makes this proleptic reality an enduring—or, rather, *the* enduring—mark of ecclesial life. Jesus presents the Twelve not as the rulers of a "new Israel," but instead as those to be enthroned over the one and only Israel, the renewed people of the covenant envisioned by Jeremiah 31 and Ezekiel 36. It is thus a mistake to focus on the Twelve in themselves, as though they were the beginning of something entirely new, the "founders" of a community that was non-existent until they arose and established it. Instead, the Twelve represent the people of Israel into which they were born, whose ancestral promises they inherited, which is now entering a new stage of its existence in the Messiah, a stage that anticipates sacramentally its eschatological fullness.

Our consideration of the Eucharist thus brings us back to the topic of apostolic ministry examined in chapter 4. Both of these Catholic sacraments—which are intrinsically connected—require the perspective provided by Israel-ecclesiology and Israel-Christology in order to be understood in depth. Once again, as the Church "delves into her own mystery," she discovers her spiritual bond with "Abraham's stock."

Conclusion

This study of the Last Supper suggests that the Eucharist has more than "Jewish roots." The terminology of "roots" could imply—though admittedly it need not do so—that the sacrament has its origins in Jewish soil but ultimately transcends those origins in its universal and cosmic goal. In contrast, I contend here that the "Jewish" character of the Eucharist is essential to the enduring meaning of the sacrament and to its ultimate eschatological fulfillment. The "Jewish" character of the Eucharist has less to do with its Judaic sources and more to do with its inherent orientation to the Jewish people and to that people's divinely appointed eschatological destiny.

The Jewish people today as a religious community do not yet partake of the Eucharist—though my contention in this chapter is that the messianic future of genealogical-Israel is signified by this sacrament. However, as we will see in the next chapter, Jewish religious life in this age may have a connection to the Eucharist that neither the Church nor the Jewish people have hitherto recognized. Christians and Jews need not wait till the eschaton to share partially in central components of the eucharistic mystery—the priestly sacrificial offering of prayer for the coming of the kingdom, and the celebratory banquet which anticipates its realization.

7

Praying for Jerusalem, Feasting with the Messiah

In the last three chapters I have examined basic elements of the sacramental life of the Church in order to demonstrate their intrinsic relationship to the past, present, and future reality of the Jewish people. We cannot understand the meaning of priesthood, baptism, or the Eucharist without reflecting on the way they build upon and confirm God's covenant with genealogical-Israel while also expanding the scope of that covenant to include those from among the other nations of the world. In the terms proposed in chapter 3, I have illustrated how membership in the Body of Christ establishes for gentiles an identity as part of the people of God and renews that identity for baptized Jews.

However, chapter 3 also proposed a complementary thesis—namely, that Jewish identity even now is oriented eschatologically to membership in the Body of Christ, and that *in a certain way* the Jewish people are already participants in the life of their Messiah. If this is true, then there must exist some hidden connection between the life of the Jewish people and the sacraments of the Church. In other words, Jewish religious life must have a sacramental dimension that manifests the hidden presence of Jesus and prophetically anticipates its eschatological consummation in him. Jewish disciples of Jesus who live an observant Jewish life would in this way bear witness both to the messianic significance of the genealogical people of God and to the sacramental fullness of the radically "catholic" Body of Christ (i.e., the Body of Christ inclusive of genealogical-Israel).

In the next two chapters I will take up this second thesis. In the present chapter I will focus on the way religious Jews participate in—and, in a sense, complete—the eucharistic sacrifice of the Body of Christ. In particular, I will argue that two elements of Jewish religious life should be seen as integrally connected to the Eucharist: (1) the basic unit of Jewish prayer known as the *Amidah*; and (2) Jewish festive meals held on the Sabbath and holidays. In the chapter that follows I will widen the scope of discussion and consider the sacramental character of Jewish life as a whole.

Jewish Sacrificial Worship in the Second Temple Period

The sacrificial service of the Jerusalem Temple constituted the central act of corporate worship for the Jewish people in the time of Jesus. He witnessed and participated in that worship, as did his family and his disciples. The Temple liturgy and its accompanying rites left its mark on the post-70 worship of both the Jewish people and the Church. We must begin here if we would understand how these two traditions are sacramentally intertwined.

In essence, sacrificial worship involved the giving of a gift. According to the Torah, the Jewish people as a whole—and, in particular circumstances, individual Jews—were obligated to present gifts of domestic animals and agricultural produce to God. In this relational exchange, which could occur only in one place, the Jerusalem Temple, God was represented personally by his priests and spatially by the Temple altar. Gifts were transferred to God's distinctive domain through reception by the priests and placement (and burning) on the altar.

The purpose of these gifts was as manifold as the purpose of gift-giving in our own daily lives. We sometimes give one another gifts in order to repair a damaged relationship (e.g., a husband giving flowers to his wife after spending too much time in front of the television watching football). At other times we give gifts to express formal gratitude for a favor that has been shown to us (e.g., giving a bottle of wine to those who have invited us over for dinner), or before requesting a new favor (e.g., a child giving her parent a picture that she drew before asking if she can go to a friend's home for a sleep-over). Sometimes we give a gift to a loved one simply to say, "You are dear to me." In the same way, first-century Jews offered their gifts to God at the Temple as a way of addressing a disorder in their relationship with God, but also as a way of making a request, expressing gratitude, or demonstrating wholehearted devotion.

The transfer of the gift was the central element of sacrificial worship, but it was not the sole element. Only a minority of the sacrifices were completely consumed by fire on the altar. Most of the sacrifices also involved a banquet in which the priests—or the priests and lay-people who had donated the gift—feasted on portions of the food that had been consecrated to God but not consumed on the altar. In this way the priests and the people experienced a sacred meal that celebrated and confirmed their relationship with God. The Passover meal in first-century Jerusalem provides the most well-known example of such a sacrificial banquet, but this aspect of the Passover was typical of a wider category of sacrifices.[1]

The Torah highlights these two aspects of sacrificial worship. A third component emerges during the period of the First Temple, and develops substantially in the era of the Second Temple. This third component consists of communal prayer as an accompaniment to the sacrifice—especially in cases where the sacrifice was being offered on behalf of the entire community (as in the twice-daily offering known as the *tamid*).

All three of these elements of sacrifice in the Second Temple period—transfer of the gift, festive meal, and communal prayer—are crucial for understanding the atoning sacrifice of Jesus and the *ecclesia*'s participation in that sacrifice through the Eucharist. The second and third of these elements are also essential for understanding Jewish worship as it emerges after the destruction of the Temple in 70 CE. In the remainder of this chapter I will look first at the role of communal prayer as part of the sacrificial liturgy, and then at the role of the festive banquet. My aim is to understand how religious Jews might, along with the *ecclesia*—and, in the case of Jewish disciples of Jesus, as part of the *ecclesia*—play an important role in relation to the priestly sacrifice of Jesus and the Eucharist.

Israel's Prayer and Israel's Sacrifice

Prayer and the Jerusalem Temple

The liturgy of sacrifice at the Jerusalem Temple was a physically demanding activity, and the Hebrew term that describes this activity—*avodah* ("work," "service")—was appropriately chosen. Given the bodily exertion required, it is natural that the Bible, Second-Temple Jewish literature, and rabbinic texts have little to say about prayers recited by the priests as they performed the sacrificial ritual. The priests were occupied with much doing, but little talking. This does not mean that sacrifice was disconnected from verbal worship. While the priests were offering sacrifice, Levitical musicians sang psalms with instrumental accompaniment (1 Chr 15:16-22; 16:4-5; 2 Chr 5:11-14; 7:4-6). The priests also concluded the sacrificial ritual of the daily offering (the *tamid*) by blessing the people (Num 6:22-27; Lev 9:22-24). This act of "putting the name upon the Israelites" (Num 6:27) is the climax

---

1. For more detail on the various types of sacrifice as described in the book of Leviticus, see Levine, *Leviticus*, 4-47.

of the sacrifice, representing and completing the reality that the entire ritual was intended to accomplish.

The intimate connection between prayer and the Temple service is seen most clearly at the dedication of Solomon's Temple. The king "stood before the altar of the Lord in the presence of all the assembly of Israel, and spread out his hands to heaven" (1 Kgs 8:22). Central to the petition that follows is this request:

> Have regard to your servant's prayer and his plea, Lord my God, heeding the cry and the prayer that your servant prays to you today; that your eyes may be open night and day toward this house, the place of which you said, "My name shall be there," that you may heed the prayer that your servant prays toward this place. Hear the plea of your servant and of your people Israel when they pray toward this place; O hear in heaven your dwelling-place; heed and forgive. (1 Kgs 8:28–30)

Solomon asks that God would answer prayer directed "toward this place." This phrase refers not only to those who journey to Jerusalem and pray in the Temple courts, but also to those in distant regions who pray "toward their land, which you gave to their ancestors, the city that you have chosen, and the house that I have built for your Name" (1 Kgs 8:48). Solomon asks that this particular geographical location on earth would be so linked to God's heavenly dwelling place that prayers offered toward the earthly Temple would be received with favor in the heavenly Temple. This provides the biblical basis for Jews praying toward Jerusalem, which is attested already in the book of Daniel (6:10). It also explains why Isaiah can refer to the Temple as "my house of prayer" in the same verse in which he speaks of sacrifices being presented on the altar (Isa 56:7): the prayers of those who look to Jerusalem are mingled with the sacrifices offered by the priests, and received together by God in the heavenly sanctuary. Prayer directed to the Jerusalem Temple is counted as incense and as an evening sacrifice (Ps 141:2) because it is associated with the literal incense and sacrifice offered in that very place. Incense, sacrifice, and the Temple liturgy as a whole were not merely symbols representing an act—prayer—that was separate from them; instead, Israel's corporate offering of prayer functioned as an integral component of that complex liturgy.

While the priests were apparently silent when offering sacrifice, rabbinic literature tells us that they also offered prayer in connection with the sacrifice—and, if this tradition is historically credible, their sacrificial prayers became the basis of the post-70 Jewish liturgy. The earliest and most foundational rabbinic text, the Mishnah, records the order and details of the daily *tamid* offering presented each morning to God in fulfillment of Israel's corporate duty of worship (Exod 29:38-42; Num 28:2-8). The priests slaughtered the designated lamb, poured its blood on the sides and base of the altar, and skinned and dismembered its carcass (*m. Tamid* 4:1-2). At this point they did something surprising. Instead of completing the sacrifice by taking the pieces up to the altar to be burned, the priests instead deposited the pieces on the ramp that led up to the altar and departed from the site of sacrifice to gather in a special hall in the Temple precincts that was used by the Great Sanhedrin (*m. Tamid* 4:3). Here they conducted a short prayer service, described by the Mishnah in this way:

> The superintendent said to them, "Say one blessing."
>
> They said a blessing, pronounced the Ten Commandments, the *Shema* [Hear O Israel (Dt. 6:4-9)],[2] *And it shall come to pass if you shall hearken* (Dt. 11:13-21),[3] and *And the Lord spoke to Moses* (Num. 15:37-41).[4]
>
> They blessed the people with three blessings: *True and sure*, *Avodah*, and the blessing of the priests.
>
> And on the Sabbath they add a blessing for the outgoing priestly watch.[5] (*m. Tamid* 5:1)[6]

The priests made a blessing before reciting four paradigmatic paragraphs from the Torah that represented the Torah in its entirety. They then acknowledged the truth of what they had recited (in a declaration beginning with the words "True and sure"), and asked that God might look with favor on the *tamid* sacrifice which they were in the midst of offering (*avodah*) and grant *shalom* to the people of Israel ("the blessing of the priests"). Upon concluding this prayer service, the priests returned to the Temple courts and completed the morning sacrifice—placing the pieces of the lamb on the bronze altar, burning incense at the golden altar in the holy place, and pronouncing the Aaronic benediction.

The last two "blessings" mentioned in the Mishnah text are of special importance for our study. The first of the two—*avodah* ("Temple

---

2. As a defined unit of traditional Jewish prayer, the *Shema* consists of three paragraphs from the Pentateuch. The first paragraph is Deut 6:4-9.

3. This biblical text is the second paragraph of the *Shema*.

4. This biblical text is the third paragraph of the *Shema*.

5. The division of priests who served in the Temple in any given one-week period. There were twenty-four such divisions. See Luke 1:5, 8.

6. Neusner, *Mishnah*, 869.

Worship")—is an early version of what is now the seventeenth blessing in the daily *Amidah*.[7] In its current form it reads as follows:

> Find favor (*retzay*), Adonai our God, in your People Israel and in their prayer. And return the service-of-worship (*avodah*) to the Holy of Holies. In favor (*be-ratzon*) accept (*tekabel*) the fire-offerings (*ishay*) of Israel and their prayers in love. And may the service-of-worship (*avodah*) of Israel your People always (*tamid*) be favorable (*ratzon*). May our eyes behold your return to Zion in mercy. Blessed are You, Adonai, who restores his divine presence (*Shechinah*) to Zion.[8]

This is a prayer for the restoration of the Temple. As seen in the technical terms employed (appearing above in transliteration), the prayer is replete with priestly language related to sacrificial worship. Our current version of this prayer apparently derives from an earlier one used in the priestly prayer service (as described in the Mishnah) that consisted of a request that Israel's sacrifices be accepted. Lawrence Hoffman argues for the following reconstruction of that original prayer:

> Find favor (*retzay*), Adonai our God, in your People Israel. And the fire-offerings (*ishay*) of Israel, accept (*tekabel*) favorably (*be-ratzon*). And may you find favor (*ratzon*) in the *tamid*, the sacrificial service (*avodah*) of Israel, your People. Blessed are You, Adonai, whom we will serve (*na'avod*) with awe.[9]

The final prayer recited by the priests—referred to in the Mishnah as "the blessing of the priests"—corresponds to the final blessing in every *Amidah*. It consists of a prayer that all the good things included in the Aaronic benediction (Num 6:24–26) would be bestowed upon Israel. Thus, these two final prayers are in reality two aspects of one petition: that God would accept Israel's sacrificial worship, and manifest that acceptance by bestowing upon them the blessing of *shalom*.

In summary, the priests interrupted their sacrificial action by retreating to a private place to acknowledge the gift of the Torah and to pray for the acceptance of their sacrifice. They then returned to the Temple courts,

---

7. In the *Amidah* for Shabbat and holidays, *Avodah* is the fifth blessing. In every *Amidah* it takes the position two blessings before the final blessing (i.e., the seventeenth of nineteen blessings, or the fifth of seven blessings).

8. Hoffman, *Amidah*, 154, 157. I have changed one word from Hoffman's translation: the phrase "service-of-worship" is rendered by Hoffman as "sacrifice." The Hebrew original is "*avodah*."

9. Ibid., 162. The final line of the blessing is derived from a Genizah fragment, and was used in the old *Union Prayer Book* of the Reform movement (163).

completed the sacrifice, and blessed the people. While the priestly sacrifice and the priestly prayer maintain their distinct identities in this ritual, they are bound together so tightly as to be inextricable.

The Temple service—both of sacrifice and of prayer—was the special business of the priests and Levites. The priests and Levites were divided into twenty-four groups, each of which was called a *mishmar* (literally, a "guard" or a "watch").[10] A priestly *mishmar* would officiate in the Temple for one week at a time, and then be relieved by the next *mishmar*. Thus, in addition to their service during the festivals, they would minister in the Temple two weeks per year. While the priests and Levites bore primary responsibility for Israel's corporate worship, the Mishnah informs us that lay Israelites also played an important role (*m. Ta'anit* 4:2). Jews in the land of Israel of non-Levitical descent were divided into twenty-four groups corresponding to the priestly *mishmarot*. Together with the priests and Levites of a particular *mishmar*, these lay Israelites constituted what was called a *ma'amad* (literally a "place/group of standing")—a representative body which "stood" before God on behalf of the entire people. Some members of each lay *ma'amad* would go to Jerusalem with their corresponding *mishmar*, and attend the sacrificial service. However, most of the members would remain in their towns and villages during the week and gather daily—at the times when the sacrifices were offered in the Temple—to pray, fast, and read from the Torah. Thus, for two weeks per year ordinary Israelites had a "priestly" obligation to stand before God in prayer and study on behalf of the entire people, and to participate—onsite or at a distance—in the sacrificial service of the Temple.

The priestly prayer service in the hall of the Sanhedrin and the institution of the lay *ma'amad* together establish the groundwork for what will become the statutory pattern of Jewish prayer after the destruction of the Temple. But even before that decisive event, many Jews and God-fearing gentiles expressed their devotion to God by praying every day (and not just during their *ma'amad* weeks) at or toward the Temple, especially at the time of sacrifice. Thus, Daniel 6:10 describes the pattern of prayer of a Jewish sage in exile: "Daniel . . . continued to go to his house, which had windows in its upper room open toward Jerusalem, and to get down on his knees three times a day to pray to his God and praise him, just as he had done previously." Solomon had asked that prayers directed toward Jerusalem and the site of its Temple would be answered from on high. Acting with the

---

10. For the twenty-four courses, see 1 Chr 23:3–4.

conviction that this request of Solomon had been heard, Daniel directs his daily prayers toward the holy city.[11]

Luke-Acts provides another early witness to this Jewish practice. The first chapter of Luke tells how Zechariah, the father of John the Baptist, fulfilled the priestly function of offering the daily incense. In passing, verse 10 states, "Now at the time of the incense offering, the whole assembly of the people was praying outside." While this could simply refer to the *ma'amad*, an even more explicit text in Acts suggests that "the whole assembly" also included pious lay Israelites who voluntarily joined their prayers to the priestly service. Acts 3:1 states, "One day Peter and John were going up to the temple at the hour of prayer, at three o'clock in the afternoon." It is striking that this is called "the hour of prayer"—for it is actually the hour of sacrifice. Obviously, sacrifice and prayer were already seen as inseparable, and dedicated Jews who lived in Jerusalem made it their practice to enter the Temple precincts at the time of sacrifice in order to pray that Israel's sacrifice would be acceptable and that God would bless his people with *shalom*.

The most remarkable of the texts from Luke-Acts on this subject concerns Cornelius, the Roman centurion. This man is a gentile who is devoted to the God of Israel. He lives not in Jerusalem but in Caesarea, on the coast of the Mediterranean. Nevertheless, at three o'clock in the afternoon he pauses from work and turns to prayer (Acts 10:3, 30). He thus joins his voice to the voices of pious Jews in Jerusalem and around the world, and identifies personally with the sacrifice being offered by the priests in the Jerusalem Temple at that very hour. While the text says nothing about the direction Cornelius faces when he prays, the parallel here with Daniel 6, the universal custom of later Jewish practice, and the intrinsic meaning of his action suggests that Cornelius offered his prayer toward Jerusalem and the Temple Mount.

In response to this man's piety, an angel appears to him, saying, "Your prayers and your alms have ascended as a memorial before God" (Acts 10:4). This is the language of sacrifice: the prayer of Cornelius, empowered by charity and sincere piety, has arisen to God along with the smoke from the altar in Jerusalem, and has been accepted. Often unnoticed but just as important, four days later Peter addresses the household of Cornelius *at the same hour*—the hour of sacrifice (Acts 10:30). The gift of the Spirit to Cornelius and his household is thus like the fire from heaven that consumed the sacrifice at the consecration of the tabernacle (Lev 9:24), and like the cloud

---

11. Daniel Falk notes that "a significant amount of prayer during the Second Temple period is performed at times related to the sacrificial service in the Temple, even when one is distant from Jerusalem (*e.g.* Dn. 9:21; Ezr. 9:5; Jdt. 9:1; Acts 10:30; *cf.* Greek *Life of Adam and Eve* 7:2; 17:1)" (Falk, "Jewish Prayer," 285).

of glory that filled the Temple of Solomon at its consecration (1 Kgs 8:10).[12] The fact that this all takes place at the same hour as the sacrifice in Jerusalem underlines a basic feature of the message of Luke-Acts: the communal life of the disciples of Jesus confirms and fulfills Israel's corporate worship.

Prayer and Sacrifice in Rabbinic Tradition: The *Amidah*

After the destruction of the Temple, the Sages of the rabbinic tradition fashioned from these long-established customs a new framework of statutory prayer in which every Jewish male is obligated to fulfill the duties that had previously been undertaken primarily by the priests. This framework includes the twice-daily reading of the *Shema*, which the priests had recited in a liturgy that both interrupted and interpreted the sacrificial service of the Temple. However, an even greater connection to the Temple service exists for the second core unit of the daily liturgy, the *Amidah* (the "*Standing* Prayer"). On weekdays, this unit consists of nineteen blessings, which are eschatologically oriented petitions couched in the language of praise ("*berachah*"). As seen above, the seventeenth and the nineteenth of these blessings derive from the priestly liturgy in the Temple. When the *Amidah* is recited aloud in a congregational setting, the prayer leader chants the Aaronic benediction (Num 6:24-26) before the nineteenth blessing. Ending the *Amidah* in the same way as the sacrificial service of the Temple underlines the intimate bond that exists between the two.

This bond is emphasized in many other ways as well. First, as suggested by its name (the Hebrew verb *amad* means "to stand"), the *Amidah* is to be prayed only in a standing posture. Standing is the posture of priestly service (e.g., Ps 134:1). In contrast, the *Shema* may be recited in any posture, and the posture of sitting eventually became one of its characteristic features. Second, the *Amidah* is recited facing Jerusalem, and, if in Jerusalem, facing the Temple mount. Third, the afternoon service in which the *Amidah* is the exclusive centerpiece (since the *Shema* is read only in the morning and evening services) is called *Minchah*, a term which means "sacrificial gift" and which is associated in the Torah especially with the grain offering (Lev 2:1-16). Fourth, the hour of the recitation of the *Amidah* is ordered according to the timing of the Temple sacrifices (*b. Berachot* 26b). Just as we see Peter, John, and Cornelius praying at the hour of the afternoon sacrifice, so the *Minchah* service instituted by the sages is prayed at the hour of the afternoon sacrifice. Fifth, on special days in the calendar when an additional

---

12. This further suggests that the time of the giving of the Spirit at Pentecost (nine o'clock, the hour of the morning sacrifice) has a similar significance (Acts 2:15).

daily offering had been presented in the Temple (the *Musaf* offering), the sages established the requirement of reciting an additional *Amidah* which would include the verses in Numbers 28–29 that described the additional offering for that day. This special *Amidah* is called *Musaf*—the same name as the additional offering in the Temple.

A final sign of the bond linking the *Amidah* to Temple sacrifice will be of particular importance for our discussion of the Eucharist. As already noted, the seventeenth blessing of the daily *Amidah* originated in the pre-70 priestly liturgy as a prayer that the Temple sacrifices would be acceptable to God, and in its post-70 form consists of a prayer for the restoration of the Temple service. On Torah-mandated holidays other than the Sabbath a special petition (*ya'aleh veyavo*) is inserted within this blessing. The key word in this insertion is *zikaron* (remembrance, memorial, *anamnesis*). The prayer asks God to remember the Messiah, the patriarchs, the city of Jerusalem, and the people of Israel, and by virtue of this remembrance to have mercy and to bring redemption.[13] It is often taken to correspond to the blowing of the priestly trumpets that accompanied the special offerings presented during the holidays, and which were "to serve as a reminder (*le-zikkaron*) on your behalf before the Lord your God" (Num 10:10).[14] The opening words of the insertion (*ya'aleh veyavo*—"may it [our remembrance] *ascend* and *come* [before you]") evoke the image of smoke rising from the Temple altar. This connection between prayer, sacrifice, memorial, and ascent is identical to that seen in the angelic response to the pious life of Cornelius: "Your *prayers* and your alms have *ascended* as a *memorial* before God" (Acts 10:4).

This historical reconstruction of Second Temple Jewish prayer practices suggests that the *Amidah* should not be construed as a post-70 rabbinic substitute for the sacrificial system. Communal prayer had already developed in integral association with Temple worship before the devastation of 70 C.E. Recitation of the *Amidah* continues a traditional practice from the days of the Temple; it is not an innovation established to replace what had

---

13. The *ya'aleh veyavo* prayer is translated as follows by Jonathan Sacks: "Our God and God of our ancestors, may there rise, come, reach, appear, be favored, heard, regarded and remembered before You, our recollection and remembrance, as well as the remembrance of our ancestors, and of the Messiah son of David Your servant, and of Jerusalem Your holy city, and of all Your people the house of Israel—for deliverance and well-being, grace, loving-kindness and compassion, life and peace, on this day of [the name of the holiday is inserted here]. On it remember us, LORD our God, for good; recollect us for blessing, and deliver us for life. In accord with Your promise of salvation and compassion, spare us and be gracious to us; have compassion on us and deliver us, for our eyes are turned to You because You, God, are a gracious and compassionate King" (Sacks, *Siddur*, 126).

14. Birnbaum, *Haggadah*, 109.

been lost. In only one sense does the *Amidah* take the place of the sacrifices: in the pre-70 CE era this regimen of prayer was a voluntary practice undertaken by pious Jews, whereas in the post-70 CE era it would come to be seen as a standard practice for all Jews in fulfillment of Israel's corporate duty of daily worship. In the absence of the Temple liturgy—which had previously constituted the essential component of Israel's daily duty of worship—the prayer of the community grew in importance and became a basic requirement of fidelity to the covenant.

In the liturgy that became normative for faithful Jews, the Temple service endured as the institution that defined Israel's worship responsibilities. The Temple as a physical structure had been destroyed, yet it lived on in the Jewish imagination, and its memory continues to shape the spiritual life of the Jewish people. It does so especially through the *Amidah*, Israel's priestly prayer, in which Jews set their faces toward Jerusalem and pray for the full restoration of Israel and the coming of God's universal reign.

The Eucharist and the *Amidah*

The Jewish biblical scholar and theologian Jon Levenson has commented on the parallel roles played by the *Amidah* (in Jewish tradition) and the Eucharist (in Christian tradition):

> In the Talmud, the idea occurs that certain statutory prayers derive their authority from the laws of sacrifice in the Torah. In the case of the "prayer" par excellence, the *Shemoneh Esreh* [i.e., the *Amidah*], Rabbi Joshua ben Levi, who lived in the land of Israel in the third century C.E., said, "The prayers were instituted to correspond to the daily offerings" (*b. Ber.* 27b). The offering of two lambs every day, one in the morning and one at twilight (Exod 29:39; Num 28:4), is replaced by the recitation of the *Shemoneh Esreh* as a statutory obligation during the hours that tradition had fixed as the period for the lamb-offerings . . . in some Christian communions, most conspicuously the Roman Catholic, the eucharist is seen not only as a commemoration of the Last Supper . . . but as a ceremony of prayer and feasting that is also and most importantly *sacrifice*, an effective reenactment of Jesus' atoning death. In their different ways, both the *Shemoneh Esreh* and the mass have roots in the sacrificial ordinances of the Torah. . . . The indisputable differences between the two

great liturgical practices should not be allowed to obscure their profound commonalities.[15]

What Levenson leaves unsaid is the likelihood that key elements of the traditional eucharistic liturgy *derive from* early forms of the *Amidah*. This, at least, represents the conclusion of Louis Bouyer in his classic volume on the eucharistic prayer.[16]

Bouyer argues that the Eucharist was originally celebrated in the context of a communal meal, and that its prayers at that time were modeled on the Jewish table blessings known as the grace after meals (*Birkat HaMazon*).[17] Eventually the celebration of the Eucharist was detached from an actual meal and combined with a service of readings and prayers. Bouyer contends that at that point these early disciples of Jesus again drew upon established Jewish models of prayer and combined an adapted ancient version of the *Amidah* with its existing eucharistic liturgy. In traditional Jewish liturgy the pattern of prayer found in the *Amidah* and that seen in the grace after meals have much in common: each begins with thanksgiving for God's gracious gifts, and proceeds to petition for the realization of God's redemptive purpose for the people of the covenant and for the world. Assuming that the ancient versions of these prayers were similar in content to their extant descendants, it would have been easy to merge them into one, and to connect them both to the priestly work of Jesus in his death, resurrection, and ascension and the prayer for his return.[18]

---

15. Levenson, *Death and Resurrection*, 186. Note that Levenson describes the *Amidah* as a replacement for the daily offering only in its new status as a "statutory obligation." As a duty incumbent on all Jews, the *Amidah* replaces the communal obligation of the daily sacrifices. In itself, however, apart from its new status as a "statutory obligation," the *Amidah* continues a custom that was already common in the days of the Temple.

16. Bouyer, *Eucharist*.

17. Bouyer draws support for this assertion from the eucharistic prayers of the *Didache*, which is the earliest source outside the New Testament for the liturgy of the early *ecclesia* (ibid., 115–19). Recent scholarship on the *Didache* confirms Bouyer's hypothesis: "According to an overwhelming consensus of scholarly opinion, this prayer is a reworking of the Birkat Ha-Mazon, the prayer that concludes the Jewish ritual meal" (Van de Sandt and Flusser, *Didache*, 311–12).

18. Bouyer, *Eucharist*, 197–99. Since the publication of Bouyer's volume on the Eucharist, liturgical scholars have become far more cautious in their attempts to trace the history of the eucharistic prayer. Neil Xavier O'Donaghue argues that this caution has been excessive, and that classic treatments of this history by scholars such as Bouyer still have much to recommend them. See O'Donaghue, "Shape," 71–83. In his discussion of the Last Supper and the Eucharist, Pope Benedict cites both Bouyer (*Jesus of Nazareth: Part II*, 128) and Josef Andreas Jungmann, whose work on the history of the Eucharist was composed in the same era as that Bouyer. The Pope recalls Jungmann's

On holidays, the grace after meals and the *Amidah* share another common feature: they both include the *ya'aleh veyavo* prayer of remembrance (*zikkaron*) described above. Bouyer follows Joachim Jeremias in proposing that an early version of this prayer underlies the commandment of Jesus at the Last Supper to "do this as my memorial (*eis anamnesin*)." Jeremias states his conclusion succinctly:

> This is therefore the result of our investigation of the use of the construction *eis anamnesin* and its variants in Palestinian linguistic usage: (1) *eis anamnesin* is said *for the most part in reference to God* [i.e., that God would remember] and (2) it then designates, always and without exception, *a presentation before God intended to induce God to act*. . . . In accordance with this the command [of Jesus] for repetition may be translated: "This do, *that God may remember me*." . . . God remembers the Messiah in that he causes the kingdom to break in by the parousia.[19]

Jeremias also argues that this Jewish liturgical meaning of *anamnesis* explains Paul's teaching on the Eucharist in 1 Corinthians 11:26:

> It is in this way that Paul already understood the *anamnesis* commandment, and his words have special weight in that they represent the oldest interpretation of the commandment which we possess. After quoting the liturgical formula, 1 Cor. 11.23-25, Paul continues: "For as often as you eat this bread and drink this cup, you proclaim the Lord's death until he comes" (v. 26). . . . *The anamnesis commandment is therefore fulfilled by the proclamation of the death of Jesus at the Lord's supper*. . . . "Until he comes" apparently alludes to the *maranatha* of the liturgy with which the community prays for the eschatological coming of the Lord[;] . . . this proclamation expresses the vicarious death of Jesus as the beginning of the salvation time and prays for the coming of the consummation. *As often as the death of the Lord is proclaimed at the supper, and the maranatha rises upwards, God is reminded of the unfulfilled climax of the work of salvation* "until (the goal is reached, that) he comes."[20]

This understanding of *anamnesis*, exemplified by the *ya'aleh veyavo* insertion in the holiday *Amidah* and grace after meals, provides a sound biblical

---

statement that "The liturgy of the Mass was derived from the thanksgiving prayer after the meal on that last evening" (141).

19. Jeremias, *Eucharistic Words*, 249, 252.

20. Ibid., 252-53.

foundation for understanding the eucharistic prayer as *a liturgical prayer of petition accompanying an eschatological sacrifice.*

Just as Israel's prayer ascended as part of Israel's sacrificial offering of its gifts—and, preeminently, of itself—to God, so the prayers of the *ecclesia* ascend as part of the sacrificial offering of Jesus, who as Israel's ultimate king and priest embodies in his person Israel's corporate identity and vocation. The *Amidah* thus provided a perfect model for the eucharistic prayer. Like the *Amidah*, the eucharistic prayer was recited standing, with the one presiding facing away from the congregation and toward the altar. Like the *Amidah*, the eucharistic prayer focused on the ultimate and pen-ultimate realization of God's redemptive purposes for the world. Like the *Amidah*, the eucharistic liturgy fulfilled the *ecclesia*'s corporate responsibility of offering continual (*tamid*) worship to God.

At some point in the process of adaptation, however, two fundamental components of the traditional Jewish form of the *Amidah* disappeared. First, the content of the eucharistic prayer lost any positive reference to the Jewish people or to the land of Israel. The particular national redemption of Israel no longer paved the way for a universal redemption of the cosmos, but instead was discarded as a relic of a transcended past. Second, as a physical expression of this post-Jewish vision of ecclesial life and its eschatological goal, the congregation and the officiant no longer faced toward Jerusalem and the Temple Mount. Now they faced east (wherever in the world they were located), from which direction Jesus was expected to return. With these significant liturgical developments, the *ecclesia* of the nations ran the risk of forgetting the enduring connection between Israel's risen Messiah and his family according to the flesh, distancing herself from her own foundation in the *ecclesia ex circumcisione*, and severing the bond that joined her to the enduring reality of the Jewish people.

Matthew Levering attempts to recapture this connection by reinterpreting the meaning of the liturgical act of facing east in the recitation of the eucharistic prayer:

> It is in this way that, in solidarity with our Jewish brothers and sisters, we truly look "toward Jerusalem" in looking "toward the Lord." The Jerusalem in which Jesus went to his passion cannot be displaced by faith in the risen Lord or by a heavenly meal, let alone by an amorphous sense of sacramentality or "the sacred." Rather, Christians look "toward Jerusalem" when, with repentance, we participate sacrificially in the saving sacrifice that Jesus accomplished on earth when he turned his face toward Jerusalem (cf. Matt. 16:21), the sacrifice that both takes away sins and reveals the self-giving Love that is the Trinity.... In and

through Christ's sacrifice, we are incorporated into the communion of the new Jerusalem, the fulfillment of the cruciform desire of Israel.[21]

Given the ancient character of the Christian custom of facing eastward, perhaps such a reinterpretation is the best mode of restoring the Jerusalem- and Israel-centeredness of the eucharistic prayer. However, this approach needs to be augmented by the recognition that genealogical-Israel's recitation of the *Amidah*—with its explicit concern for the Jewish future and the land of promise, and its literal orientation toward Jerusalem and the Temple Mount—*is itself an integral component of the eucharistic sacrifice.*

I am proposing that the prayer of observant Jews is mysteriously tied to the sacrifice of Jesus and his continuing priestly work of intercession in the heavenly sanctuary. I am affirming the parallel between the *Amidah* and the Eucharist asserted by Levenson, but going far beyond his reference to their common "roots in the sacrificial ordinances of the Torah." They do have common roots, but those roots are not merely historical—they are also spiritual and heavenly. The Eucharist and the *Amidah* are inextricably bound together as enduring expressions of the sacrificial work of Jesus for and among his people. In other words, Israel-Christology leads not only to Israel-ecclesiology but also to *ecclesial-Israelology*.

The Eschatological Banquet and the Messianic Sacrifice

While communal prayer had become an essential accompaniment of the sacrificial liturgy in the period of the Second Temple, an even more basic feature of the Temple rites was the sacrificial banquet in which the people of Israel (or its priestly representatives) consumed allotted portions of the sacrifice. This dimension of sacrifice assumes great importance in the book of Deuteronomy.

> But you shall seek the place that the Lord your God will choose out of all your tribes as his habitation to put his name there. You shall go there, bringing there your burnt offerings and your sacrifices, your tithes and your donations, your votive gifts, your freewill offerings, and the firstlings of your herds and flocks. And you shall eat there in the presence of the Lord your God, you and your households together, rejoicing in all the undertakings in which the Lord your God has blessed you.... [Y]ou shall bring everything that I command you to the place that the Lord

21. Levering, *Sacrifice*, 200–1.

> your God will choose as a dwelling for his name: your burnt offerings and your sacrifices, your tithes and your donations, and all your choice votive gifts that you vow to the Lord. And you shall rejoice before the Lord your God, you together with your sons and your daughters, your male and female slaves, and the Levites who reside in your towns[;] ... these you shall eat in the presence of the Lord your God at the place that the Lord your God will choose, you together with your son and your daughter, your male and female slaves, and the Levites resident in your towns, rejoicing in the presence of the Lord your God in all your undertakings. (Deut 12:5-7, 11-12, 18)

All Israel must bring its offerings to Jerusalem—"the place that the Lord your God will choose out of all your tribes as his habitation to put his name there"—and there "rejoice before the Lord your God." This commandment to "rejoice" is equivalent to the commandment to "eat there in the presence of the Lord your God." Thus, the Torah commands that each Israelite family journey to Jerusalem at the holidays in order to share a celebrative meal with one another in the presence of God, partaking of food that had been consecrated to God at the Temple. The rites of Passover vividly exemplify the character of the sacred meal, but, as this text from Deuteronomy shows, similar sacrificial banquets took place at all the festivals.

In Second Temple Judaism the practice of the sacred meal extended beyond feasting on Temple sacrifices at the holidays. The community described in the rules of the Dead Sea Scrolls treated all their meals as holy, and many scholars believe that the Pharisees adhered to similar customs.[22] In a setting of intense apocalyptic expectation, such meals would readily become ritual anticipations of the eschatological banquet (Isa 25:6-8).[23] This provides the background to the Gospel accounts of Jesus at table, and of Jesus' parables that feature numerous banquet scenes, noted in our previous chapter. When Jesus sits with the Twelve at his final Passover, and speaks of their eating and drinking in his kingdom (Luke 22:30), he adopts the same approach as later Jewish tradition in ascribing eschatological meaning to the festival and its sacrificial meal. For readers of the Gospels, Jesus' words at the Last Supper also conjure images of the father welcoming home the prodigal son (Luke 15:22-24), of people coming from the four corners of

---

22. See Smith, "Meals," 924-26; and Dunn, "Table-Fellowship," 254-72.

23. "The motif [of the messianic banquet] seems to have been the presupposition on which the ritual meals of the Qumran community were based (see 1QS 6.4-5; 1QSa 2.17-22); those meals were understood to be anticipations of the heavenly banquet in God's kingdom" (Harrington, *Matthew*, 221).

the world to sit at table in the kingdom of God (Luke 13:28), and of the king who arranges a marriage feast for his son (Matt 22:1-14).

As noted above, Louis Bouyer asserts that the early followers of Jesus celebrated the Eucharist as part of an actual meal. Given the apostle Paul's teaching in 1 Corinthians 11, this point seems nearly certain. The apostle recounts his tradition of the institution of the Eucharist (11:23-26) in the context of instructions concerning conduct at communal banquets (11:20-22, 33-34). A meal-setting for the Eucharist likewise sheds light on Lukan references to "the breaking of bread" (Luke 24:30-31, 35; Acts 2:46; 20:7, 11); we need not choose between a eucharistic or meal interpretation of this phrase, since the former took place in the midst of the latter. As noted above, Bouyer's proposal also explains the origins of the eucharistic prayer, which he traces back to the Jewish grace after meals. The earliest followers of Jesus had already inherited a liturgy of thanksgiving and petition connected to their daily meals, and if later Jewish exemplars of that liturgy reflect the contents of their first-century antecedents, that table liturgy already contained messianic and eschatological references. The followers of Jesus only needed to make slight adaptations in that liturgy in order to render it appropriate to its new ritual purpose.

The Apostle Paul also mentions the eucharistic banquet in the chapter of 1 Corinthians immediately preceding that which recounts the eucharistic institution narrative. He does so, however, only in passing, to buttress an argument concerning a different topic—namely, the participation of disciples of Jesus in pagan sacrificial feasts. Our interest here is not in Paul's prohibition of partaking in pagan sacrifice but instead in what he assumes to be common knowledge between himself and his original audience: an understanding of the Eucharist as a sacrificial banquet.

> [F]lee from the worship of idols.... The cup of blessing that we bless, is it not a sharing in the blood of Christ? The bread that we break, is it not a sharing in the Body of Christ? Because there is one bread, we who are many are one body, for we all partake of the one bread. Consider the people of Israel [lit. Israel according to the flesh]; are not those who eat the sacrifices partners in the altar? What do I imply then? That food sacrificed to idols is anything, or that an idol is anything? No, I imply that what pagans sacrifice, they sacrifice to demons and not to God. I do not want you to be partners with demons. You cannot drink the cup of the Lord and the cup of demons. You cannot partake of the table of the Lord and the table of demons. (1 Cor 10:14-21)

Paul compares three ritual actions: (1) the Eucharist; (2) the partaking of meat sacrificed at the Temple in Jerusalem; and (3) participation in a sacrificial meal at a pagan temple. Mention of the second ritual action is necessary to establish the meaning of the first, since it is not self-evident that the Eucharist is a sacrificial meal: the Eucharist is not conducted in a temple building, no domestic animal is slain, no blood is poured out, and no body-parts are burned on an altar. Yet, for Paul, and presumably for his audience, the Eucharist is as much a sacrificial banquet as any conducted in a more obviously sacrificial context. This is crucial for the reasoning of 1 Corinthians 10, since Paul bases his argument against partaking of pagan sacrifice on the sacrificial character of the Eucharist. In summary, he cites the example of Jewish Temple sacrifice to explain the meaning of eucharistic communion, and then cites the Eucharist (understood as a sacrificial banquet) as a reason for avoiding pagan sacrificial banquets.

Notably, this argument depends for its cogency on Paul and his hearers sharing a positive view of the Jerusalem Temple and its sacrificial service. To be a "partner in the altar" is to be a partner of the God whom that altar represents. Paul speaks of this partnership in the present rather than the past tense: those who eat the sacrifices offered at the Jerusalem Temple—"Israel according to the flesh"—*are* (rather than "*were*") partners in the altar. Paul's conviction that Jews entered into communion with God when they worshipped at the Jerusalem Temple provides the foundation for his assertion that disciples of Jesus likewise enter into communion with the Messiah through the eucharistic banquet. First Corinthians 10 thus supports Paula Fredriksen's contention that "the Eucharist, for Paul, does not replace, displace or contest the sacrifices made to God by Jews in Jerusalem's temple. For Paul's gentiles-in-Christ in the Diaspora, however, the Eucharist replaces and in some sense annuls their former sacrifices to false gods."[24] If the Eucharist did not replace the sacrificial banquets associated with temple sacrifice in Jerusalem, then we have no grounds for concluding that Paul dismissed the sacred character of other Jewish table celebrations on the Sabbath or holidays, even in the Diaspora.

As the *ecclesia* grew in numbers it soon became impractical to conduct the eucharistic service in the context of an actual meal. We see from 1 Corinthians 11 that problems with such events had already arisen in Paul's time, and such difficulties would only have intensified as the decades passed. At the same time, a new need arose. The early disciples of Jesus in the Diaspora were connected to local synagogues. They would attend synagogue worship on Saturday mornings with the rest of the Jewish community, and there hear

---

24. Fredriksen, *Sin*, 39. See also Klawans, *Purity*, 219.

the reading of the Torah; later that evening they would gather on their own to celebrate the Eucharist as part of a communal meal (Acts 20:7). Once the connection to the synagogue had been damaged, it became necessary to develop a distinctive ecclesial service focused on the reading of Scripture.[25] These two pressing problems—the practical challenges of a large communal meal and the need for an ecclesial liturgy of the Word—could be resolved through a single ritual innovation: detach the rite of the bread and the cup from its original meal context and place it in a new congregational setting parallel to the Jewish morning service in the synagogue.

We can appreciate the reasons that made such a shift necessary and appropriate. At the same time, we should also recognize what was lost in this historical process of development. The reception of a consecrated host in the context of a traditional Christian worship service enables the communicant to partake of the bread of life in a sacred atmosphere of reverence and mystery. However, such a service cannot fully impart the experience of a holy communal meal which binds its participants together as an extended family and provides a vivid foretaste of the messianic banquet in the world to come. As a result, this dimension of the meals of Jesus with his disciples, and later of the disciples of Jesus in the presence of their risen Lord, has faded from the consciousness of the *ecclesia*. With it has also disappeared the pattern of domestic household worship that characterized the first disciples of Jesus (Acts 2:46) and which has remained central to Jewish religious life to the present day.

Jacob Neusner has offered a creative framework for understanding the main eras in the history of Judaism in terms of meals. He presents the first era, the period before 70 CE, as taking symbolic form in the sacrificial banquet centered on the altar of the Jerusalem Temple.[26] The second era, which encompasses all of Jewish history between 70 CE and the modern period, finds symbolic expression in the holy meals of Jewish families in their temporary places of residence throughout the world. In this second era the normal meals of ordinary Jews are sanctified by statutory ritual acts such as the priestly washing of hands and the grace after meals.

> [W]e must keep in mind that in the Judaism that took shape after the destruction of the Temple, the table at which meals were eaten was regarded as the equivalent of the sacred altar in the Temple. Before eating, each Jew had to attain the same state of

---

25. "The food of faith is the Word of God. It was therefore quite a natural process of evolution that led the Church to celebrate the eucharistic meal at the conclusion of the service of biblical readings, from the moment, or very nearly, that Christians no longer attended the synagogue" (Bouyer, *Eucharist*, 469–70).

26. See Neusner, *Short History*, 18–20.

ritual purity as the priest in the sacred act of making a sacrifice. So in the classic tradition the Grace after Meals is recited in a sacerdotal circumstance.[27]

Neusner proposes that the grace after meals effects a kind of "enchantment" in which Israel's "routine experience of hunger and satisfaction" is transformed into "a metaphor for Israel's life of anguished reality but ultimate redemption."[28] In effect, each meal—and especially those of Shabbat and holidays—assumes a sacramental character.[29]

I can attest from personal experience to the truth of Neusner's claim. I know this from my own daily meals, which are preceded by hand-washing and followed by the ritual grace, and even more from the encounter with God made possible by the holy banquets of the Sabbath, the Passover, and the other Jewish holidays. I have also witnessed Hasidic gatherings in Jerusalem where hundreds of Jewish boys and young men stand on risers and sing hymns while their beloved Rebbe and his council of elders sit at table in their midst and distribute pieces of food to be shared by all. I have likewise partaken of orthodox Jewish wedding feasts in which the eating, drinking, dancing, and praying blend together in an ecstatic mix of earthly celebration and heavenly longing. In such settings, it is easy to imagine the wedding feast at Cana, the meals of the risen Jesus with his disciples, or the joyful "breaking of bread" of the Jerusalem community after Pentecost.

I would propose that we have here more than an analogy between Jewish sacred meals in the post-70 era and the Eucharist. The risen Jesus remains in the midst of his family according to the flesh, and just as the daily recitation of the *Amidah* by observant Jews has an organic connection to the eucharistic prayer, so the holy banquets of observant Jews have an organic connection to the eucharistic feast. In these meals the Jewish people encounter Jesus in a hidden form, and gain a foretaste of the table-fellowship of the messianic kingdom. Such celebrations also provide a tangible and earthly sign of the joy of that kingdom which the Church's Eucharist on its own can no longer display in fullness. When observant Jews celebrate the sacred meals of Israel, they are *in a certain sense* participating in and fulfilling the eucharistic banquet of the Church. Once again, Israel-Christology leads not only to Israel-ecclesiology but also to *ecclesial-Israelology*.

27. Ibid., 89.

28. Ibid., 87.

29. Neusner sees the Passover Seder as the meal that represents the modern era of Jewish history. This is the one ritual occasion that continues to involve virtually all Jews who identify themselves as such, bringing them together in household units rather than in the synagogue (which only a minority of modern Jews ever attend). Ibid., 173–78.

The Church and the "Jewish Eucharist"

At the beginning of this chapter I described Israel's sacrificial system at the time of Jesus. To recall what was said there, sacrificial worship had three main components: (1) the offering and transfer of the sacrificial gift; (2) the community's prayer that God would demonstrate acceptance of the gift by the bestowal of shalom on Jerusalem, Israel, and the world; and (3) a communion feast in which Israel (or its priestly representatives) would share in the consecrated gift. The first element—the offering and transfer of the sacrificial gift—constitutes the most important of the three, but it remains incomplete apart from the other two.

According to traditional Catholic teaching, the eucharistic sacrifice contains all three of these components. In the Eucharist the heavenly high priest offers himself to the Father with, in, and through his body, the Church. On the merit of the Messiah's once-for-all sacrifice, sacramentally presented before God, the Body of Christ prays for the present manifestation and final coming of the kingdom. The Church also receives a foretaste of the messianic banquet by feasting on the sacrifice—which is Jesus himself, the bread of life. Jesus himself is the sacrifice, the priestly intercessor, and the food and drink of the banquet; but his eucharistic action is exercised in union with his people.

In this chapter I am proposing that "his people" should be understood to mean not only the Church but also the Jewish people. The *Amidah* is a eucharistic prayer that centers on aspects of Jesus' concern that have largely faded from Christian consciousness—the city of Jerusalem, the land of Israel, and the Jewish people. When observant Jews pray the *Amidah*, they do so in fellowship with the risen Messiah of Israel and as unrecognized (and unrecognizing) participants in the eucharistic liturgy. Similarly, the sacred meals of the Jewish people manifest in advance the joy of the eschatological banquet in a way that the Church's liturgy can only hint at. When observant Jews partake of these meals, they do so in fellowship with the risen Messiah of Israel, who sits among them at table, unseen yet powerfully present. Just as the Church's life is eucharistic, so the life of the Jewish people is also eucharistic.

If this is true for observant Jews in general, how much more so for Jewish disciples of Jesus who remain faithful to traditional Jewish life! When *we* pray the *Amidah*, our union with the heavenly high priest shapes and energizes our prayer and moves from the realm of hidden reality to that of acknowledged truth. When *we* sit at the Sabbath or Passover table we know and celebrate the fact that the risen Messiah sits with us as our host, much as he did with his disciples in the forty days between Easter and Pentecost

(Acts 1:4). In this way we, Jewish disciples of Jesus, consciously realize the "catholic" dimension of the eucharistic community, in which the multinational Body of Christ centers on the people of Israel; in this way we also manifest the eschatological dimension of the Jewish people, which will only come to fruition when Israel unambiguously attains its goal as part of the Body of its king.

From one perspective, the changes in the Church's eucharistic liturgy that we have considered in this chapter appear as a genuine loss. Would it not have been better if the geographical direction of the Church's prayer had maintained the Jewish focus on the earthly city of Jerusalem? Would it not have been better if the eucharistic petition for the coming of the kingdom had—like the *Amidah*—centered on the land of Israel and the restoration of the fleshly descendants of Abraham and Sarah, Isaac and Rebecca, Jacob, Rachel, and Leah? Would it not have been better if the eucharistic meal had retained all of the features of a Jewish festal banquet? From another perspective, however, these changes could have been appropriate and beneficial adaptations in the context of the Church of the nations. What rendered them problematic was the rupture between this Church and the *ecclesia ex circumcisione*, whose retention of these three Jewish aspects of the Eucharist could have complemented the liturgy of the Church and reminded gentile Christians of their dependence on the cultivated olive tree (Rom 11:17–24). The re-establishment of the *ecclesia ex circumcisione* and the renewal of communion and joint functioning of the Church's "two lungs" has the potential to transform the eucharistic consciousness of the Church of the nations without altering anything fundamental in its eucharistic practice.[30]

Even in the absence of a "messianic Jewish Eucharist," the eucharistic life of the Jewish people continues and thrives. This means that the existence and religious life of the Jewish people have an inherently sacramental character. Moreover, as reflection on the eucharistic sacrifice demonstrates, this sacramental dimension derives from and points to the ultimate sacrament—Jesus, the Incarnate Word. In the next chapter I will conclude the exegetical portion of this book by examining directly this sacramental dimension of Jewish life and the essential role it plays in the overall sacramental economy of the people of God.

---

30. On this adaptation of Pope John Paul II's image of the Church's two lungs, see Kinzer, *Postmissionary*, 310.

8

Jewish Life as Sacrament

In the previous chapter I argued that two aspects of Jewish religious life—the recitation of the *Amidah* and the celebration of holy meals—bear a eucharistic character. Initially, it might have appeared as though I were employing a Catholic concept to interpret Jewish life. As our discussion proceeded, however, I aimed to show that, while the *term* "Eucharist" is alien to Jewish religious tradition, much of the conceptual content expressed by the term is central to the meaning of Jewish religious practice.

In the present chapter I will expand my focus from two particular Jewish practices to Jewish life as a whole. Just as I am widening the scope of my study, so I will also extend the conceptual and terminological tools employed in its pursuit. If the specific ritual term "Eucharist" was appropriate to the specific practices examined in chapter 7, then the more general ritual term "sacrament" may be suitable to our expanded field of study. Like the word "Eucharist," the term "sacrament" is fundamental to Catholic thought and life, and alien to the normal discourse of religious Jews. However, as in the last chapter, I will seek to show how its conceptual content resonates with the core spiritual intuitions of Jewish religious tradition.[1]

---

1. I would like to express my gratitude to Fr. Jean-Miguel Garrigues, who early in the history of our Dialogue Group spoke to me about his belief in the sacramentality of the Jewish people and of the land of Israel. His words to me rang true at the time, and have influenced my thinking in subsequent years. I have attempted in this chapter to elaborate on his insight. Of course, Fr. Jean-Miguel is not responsible for my elaboration, which will undoubtedly go beyond what he initially intended.

Sacrament and *Kedushah*

"The sacraments are efficacious signs of grace, instituted by Christ and entrusted to the Church, by which divine life is dispensed to us" (*CCC* 1131). In these words the Catholic Catechism provides a succinct definition of the Church's sacraments. The definite article ("the") and the plural form of the noun ("sacraments" rather than "sacrament") are both important: this is a definition of *the seven sacraments* that are administered in the life of the Catholic Church. It is not a definition of the term "sacrament," which has a broader meaning. When reflecting on this broader meaning, the Catechism states that the term "emphasizes the visible sign of the hidden reality of salvation" (*CCC* 774). In this less technical—and more basic—sense, the word is appropriately applied to Jesus himself as the incarnate Logos, and to the Church as his body (*CCC* 774–75).[2]

As noted above, one rarely encounters the word "sacrament" in Jewish theological discourse.[3] When the word does arise, it is often in the context of interaction between Jews and Christians, where Jews are drawing upon Christian language to make themselves better understood. Occasionally the word is used pejoratively in internal Jewish discussion to contrast Jewish and Christian approaches to spiritual life.[4]

Despite the characteristically Christian origins and connotations of the word "sacrament," and despite polemical attempts to use the word to draw artificial lines of demarcation between Jewish and Christian religion, the reality to which the word points is an essential feature of Jewish life. It is the reality of *divine mediation*—of the infinite God's gracious self-giving within the finitude of the space-time world by means of "visible signs" (human words, human acts, and created things). In the idiom of the Torah, this reality is signified by the word *kadosh* (holy) and its cognate forms. In rabbinic literature the nominal form *kedushah* (meaning "holiness") assumes a special place as a concept central to all of Jewish religious life.[5] God is holy—utterly distinct from creation in purity and power. Yet, the Holy One also chooses certain people, places, times, and objects within the created

---

2. See footnote 9 below.

3. Martin Buber may be the most glaring exception to this generalization. See, for example, *Hasidism*, 129–44.

4. Such an approach is implicit in the following remarks by Max Kadushin, which ostensibly contrast Judaism with the mystery cults: "Communion is no more a biblical idea than it is a rabbinic idea. It is the central idea of the mystery cults, where 'the characteristic rite is sacramental—an act of communion and reunion with the daemon.' What is experienced in all the forms of Jewish worship considered here is not communion but God's nearness" (Kadushin, *Worship*, 181).

5. Ibid., 216–34.

order to belong to the Most High in a particularly intimate way and to be the locus of the special Divine Presence.[6] By virtue of this divine act of election, those people, places, times, and objects also become holy. This means that they assume the role of mediating the light and life of God within the created order.[7]

Catholic tradition recognizes well the relationship between the terms "sacrament" and "holiness." In fact, it often uses the latter term to explain the former. Thus, when Aquinas distinguishes the sacramental elements in what he calls "the old law" from the non-sacramental elements, he does so by asserting that the sacramental rites (such as the Passover meal) conferred holiness, whereas the non-sacramental rites did not confer holiness (though they might have been holy in themselves).[8] Similarly, the Catholic Catechism roots the Church's sacraments in the "holy and sanctifying [i.e., making others holy] humanity" of Jesus. The Church's sacraments are holy and sanctifying because of the relationship they have to the Incarnate Word, who is himself the true "sacrament of salvation" (CCC 774).[9]

Holiness and sacrament are likewise connected in their eschatological significance. I have argued elsewhere that the biblical category of *kedushah* is essentially eschatological.[10] The terminology of *kedushah* first appears in

---

6. Kadushin identifies divine possession as an essential component of the word's definition in Jewish thought: "what is holy is regarded as belonging to God in a special sense, as being God's own" (ibid., 224).

7. Pamela Eisenbaum captures well the connection between holiness, the divine Presence, and mediation: "biblical holiness may be defined as the space within which God can dwell. . . . Hence, when God says to Israel 'You shall be for me a priestly kingdom and a holy nation' (Exod. 19:6), holiness is the distinguishing feature that makes Israel both different from other nations and able to mediate between God and humanity" (Eisenbaum, *Paul*, 155).

8. "[T]he sacraments [of the Old Law] are, properly speaking, things applied to the worshippers of God for their consecration [i.e., holiness] so as, in some way, to depute them to the worship of God" (ST I-2, Q.102, Art. 5; Aquinas, *Summa* 2, 1068).

9. The identification of Jesus' humanity as the essential or primary sacrament, upon which all ecclesial sacraments depend, is an important insight that clarifies the meaning and significance of the term. The insight is also affirmed by Reformed theologian Thomas Torrance: "the primary *mysterium* or *sacramentum* is Jesus Christ himself, the incarnate reality of the Son of God who has incorporated himself into our humanity and assimilated the people of God into himself as his own Body, so that the sacraments have to be understood as concerned with our *koinonia* or participation in the mystery of Christ and his Church through the *koinonia* or communion of the Holy Spirit" (Torrance, *Reconciliation*, 82). Thus, sacraments involve a personal participation in the life of Jesus though the Spirit, and should not be conceived of in impersonal mechanistic terms. Viewed in this way, the sacraments (e.g., holy orders, baptism, Eucharist) become the means by which Israel-Christology issues in Israel-ecclesiology.

10. See Kinzer, *Israel's Messiah*, 91-125.

reference to the Sabbath rest of God, which is an eschatological reality. The holiness that Israel receives and bears after the exodus is a proleptic expression of the messianic age. As announced by both Israelite prophet and New Testament seer, that age will be characterized by the universal proliferation of holiness, so that all creation becomes a temple for God's glory (Zech 14:8-9, 20-21; Rev 21:9-27). Similarly, the sacraments of the *ecclesia* are eschatological in nature (*CCC* 1090, 1130). Baptism anticipates our bodily entry into resurrection glory, and the Eucharist anticipates the messianic banquet. The holiness of the world to come has invaded this world through the resurrection of Jesus and the gift of the Spirit, and the sacraments mediate this eschatological blessing.

When Aquinas explores the sacraments of "the old law," he devotes almost all of his attention to rites associated with the Temple.[11] This is common to traditional Christian treatments of "Jewish" sacraments. Such an approach accords well with an interpretation of Jewish sacramental life as obsolete, since these rites have been defunct in Jewish practice for two thousand years. In contrast to this approach, I wish to explore those sacramental elements of Jewish life whose existence and efficacy are independent of the Tabernacle and the Temple, and which have endured through the two millennia following the Temple's destruction.[12] Proposing that Catholic theology should affirm the continuing sacramental character of these elements of Jewish life, I will reflect upon their meaning and importance for Jewish disciples of Jesus and for the *ecclesia* as a whole.

Judaism's Five Fundamental Sacramental Signs

There are five expressions of holiness in this world that I will focus upon here: (1) Israel as holy people; (2) the Sabbath (and the holidays) as holy time; (3) the land of Israel and the city of Jerusalem as holy place; (4) the Torah as holy word; and (5) the *mitzvot* (i.e., commandments) as holy deeds. All five of these realities exist independently of the Jerusalem Temple, and their status in Jewish life was unchanged by the Temple's destruction.

Jews have generally approached these five realities in a manner closely resembling the way Catholics, Eastern Orthodox Christians, and

---

11. Circumcision is the main exception to this generalization.

12. As should be clear from the discussion of sacrifice in the previous chapter, in no way would I seek to minimize the significance of the Temple for our understanding of Israel, the *ecclesia*, or sacramental realities. However, I would argue that an exclusive focus on the Temple of the earthly Jerusalem—often in the context of an implicit or explicit supersessionist polemic—has tended to obscure rather than clarify other modes of divine action and self-manifestation in the midst of genealogical-Israel.

liturgically-oriented Protestants have treated Christian sacraments. By God's gracious decision and action, each of the five bears an intrinsic holiness that sets it apart from other members of its earthly class (i.e., peoples, times, places, words, deeds). The increasing influence of Jewish mystical thought and practice in the medieval period accentuated this sacramental approach. While Jews of a rationalistic bent have criticized such sacramentalism, their position represented a minority viewpoint until the modern era, and remains a minority viewpoint within the world of traditional Judaism.[13]

Holy People: Genealogical-Israel

As noted above, the terminology of *kedushah* first appears in the Torah in Genesis 2. God blesses the seventh day and "makes it holy" (*vayekadesh*). The holiness of this day represents the eschatological consummation of creation when the world will become a temple for God's glory. The world of the first six days is good, but it still awaits the holiness of the seventh day.

Holiness terminology is absent from the rest of the book of Genesis. It next appears in Exodus 3:5, as part of the narrative of Moses' encounter with God in the burning bush at Sinai: "the place on which you stand is holy ground" (*admat kodesh*). God here commissions Moses to free the people of Israel from their bondage in Egypt—but Moses is also told to bring Israel "to worship God at this mountain" (Exod 3:12). The holiness of the burning bush anticipates the holiness that awaits all Israel when it arrives at Mount Sinai.

At Sinai God reveals to Israel through Moses the purpose of their redemption: "you shall be to me a kingdom of priests and a holy nation" (*goy kadosh*). Just as every firstborn son from among the Israelites was to be "consecrated" to God (*kadesh li*, Exod 13:2), so Israel as a whole was God's firstborn son (Exod 3:22) who was consecrated by the exodus and the revelation at Sinai for the worship of their Father (Exod 3:23). As we noted in our study of priesthood in chapter 4, this corporate vocation of holiness was established before any instructions were given regarding the Tabernacle or the Aaronic priesthood. These liturgical institutions are not the condition for the realization of Israel's holiness but only the subsequent means by which it will be expressed.

13. For an enlightening discussion of this tension within Jewish thought between sacramental and non-sacramental perspectives, see Kellner, *Maimonides' Confrontation*. Kellner does not employ the language of sacrament, but instead contrasts the "ontological" or "essentialist" views of holiness expressed by the mystical tradition with the "teleological" or "normative" views advanced by Maimonides and the rationalist tradition (see 85–126).

God sanctifies the people of Israel by coming to dwell in their midst. It is the presence of God in the midst of Israel that makes it a special people (Exod 33:16). The Tabernacle embodies this reality when Israel journeys through the wilderness. Yet, as Jewish commentators often note, the purpose of the Tabernacle is that God may dwell "among *them*" (*betocham*, Exod 25:8), not that God may dwell "in *it*" (*betocho*).[14] When Israel leaves Egypt it does not merely build and carry God's sanctuary—it *becomes* that consecrated place (Ps 114:1–2). When Israel's sins cause the Divine Presence (*kavod*) to depart from the Jerusalem Temple, the Glory does not return to heaven but instead joins Israel's exiles in Mesopotamia (Ezek 10:18–22; 11:22–25; 1:1–5). God's commitment to dwell in the midst of Israel means that the Divine Presence itself must go into exile beyond the borders of the land of promise.

No Jewish thinker has perceived or articulated this truth more clearly than Michael Wyschogrod. As a theologian in constant conversation with Christian tradition, he even uses the language of sacrament to convey his insight: "If there is no need for sacrament in Judaism, it is because the people of Israel in whose flesh the presence of God makes itself felt in the world becomes the sacrament."[15] Wyschogrod goes too far in his contention that the people of Israel are the *only* Jewish sacrament. He is correct, however, in emphasizing its sacramental primacy. In the narrative of the Torah, the people of Israel becomes the first-fruits of the eschatological consummation that awaits all creation on that day when all the world will become a temple for God's glory.

While circumcision constitutes the sign of Israel's distinctive covenantal identity, it is not the means by which the individual Jew is sanctified, nor the means by which the genealogical descendants of Abraham, Isaac, and Jacob, Sarah, Rebecca, Rachel, and Leah, first join the holy people. A Jewish male possesses a sacramental character before being circumcised, and a Jewish female possesses such a character without ever being circumcised. The rite of circumcision has a sacramental dimension as one of the most important of the *mitzvot* (all of which are sacramental), but it does not stand at the same level as the five sacramental realities considered here.

Holy Time: The Sabbath

The Sabbath enjoys a privileged position in the story of holiness. As we have seen, the only usage of the terminology of holiness before the revelation

14. See, for example, *Etz Hayim*, 487.
15. Wyschogrod,, *Body of Faith*, 19–20, 25.

at Sinai is in reference to the seventh day of the creation narrative. That reference points not to a "past" event when "God rested" but instead to an eschatological reality that still awaits its fulfillment. In the meantime, God chooses Israel to be a sanctuary in the midst of the world, and commands Israel to rest on the seventh day as a sacramental sign of the holiness to come.

The holiness of the Sabbath is closely aligned with the holiness of Israel. One of the versions of the Sabbath commandment in the Torah makes this explicit: "You shall keep my sabbaths, for this is a sign between me and you throughout your generations, given in order that you may know that I, the Lord, sanctify you (*me-kadish-chem*). You shall keep the Sabbath, because it is holy for you" (Exod 31:13-14). God sets Israel apart to belong to God in a special way, and God sets the Sabbath apart to belong to God in a special way. When Israel acknowledges in practice the holiness of the Sabbath as God's special possession, it confirms its own holiness as God's special possession.

The Sabbath also corresponds to the Tabernacle. Many biblical scholars have pointed out the close connection between the creation account and the description of the construction of the Tabernacle, and the role of the Sabbath in both. Jon Levenson draws these conclusions: "The Sabbatical experience and the Temple experience are one. The first represents sanctity in time, the second, sanctity in space, and yet they are somehow the same. The Sabbath is to time and to the work of creation what the Temple is to space and to the painful history of Israel which its completion brings to an end, as God has at last given Solomon 'rest from all his enemies round about'" (1 Chr 22:9).[16]

The Sabbath commandment is reiterated twice in the midst of the chapters of Exodus devoted to the Tabernacle: once at the end of God's directions to Moses regarding the construction project (Exod 31:12-17), and once at the beginning of the unit which describes how Moses carries out those directions (Exod 35:1-3). The Sages drew a legal conclusion from this literary pattern: the types of labor required for the building of the Tabernacle are the types of labor prohibited on the Sabbath day. But if the building of the Tabernacle corresponds to the six days of the working week, so the descent of God's glory upon the completed structure corresponds to the holiness of the seventh day. As Levenson again recognizes, "Since the creation of the world and the construction of the Temple are parallel, if

---

16. Levenson, *Sinai*, 145.

not identical, then the experience of the completed universe and that of the completed sanctuary should also be parallel."[17]

But the universe is not yet complete. Israel tastes that completion on the Sabbath day, but the experience is sacramental and proleptic. The Sabbath version of the grace after meals includes the following prayer: "May the Compassionate One let us inherit the time, that will be entirely Shabbat and rest for life everlasting."[18] Faithful Jews receive a foretaste of the world to come when they observe the Sabbath, but they know that it points beyond itself—or, rather, that it grants anticipatory access to a world that remains now beyond our grasp but within the range of our hope and prayer.

Holy Place: The Land of Promise and the City of the Great King

The holiness of the people and of the Sabbath are aligned not only with one another, but also with the holiness of the promised land. Just as God gives Israel the Sabbath as an "inheritance" (*nachalah*) and as "rest" (*menuchah*), so God gives Israel the land with the same intent.[19] Both of these terms ("inheritance" and "rest") have eschatological connotations; just as the Sabbath is a sacramental foretaste of the world to come, so the land of Israel is intended to be a proleptic sign of a creation that is entirely sanctified.

Like the holiness of the people of Israel and of the Sabbath, the holiness of the land exists antecedent to and independent of the wilderness Tabernacle and the Jerusalem Temple. Its special character is evident in the call and journey of Abraham and in the lives of the patriarchs and matriarchs.[20] The special character of the city of Jerusalem is also implied by the story of Melchizedek, king and priest of "Salem" (Gen 14:18). In celebrating the exodus, the Song of the Sea refers to the goal of Israel's journey as "your holy abode (*neve kodshecha*)" (i.e., the land; Exod 15:13) and as "the mountain of your own possession . . . the sanctuary (*mikdash*), O Lord, that your hands

17. Ibid., 144.
18. Sacks, *Siddur*, 990.
19. The Bible frequently refers to the land as Israel's "inheritance" (*nachalah*; e.g., Num 26:52–56; Deut 4:21, 38); but the traditional prayer of *Kiddush*, which inaugurates the Sabbath, describes the Seventh Day in the same way ("For you chose us and sanctified us from all the peoples, and in love and favor gave us Your holy Sabbath as an *inheritance*"). The Bible also commonly associates the Sabbath with "rest" (*menuchah*; e.g., Exod 20:11; 23:12), but likewise speaks of Israel's secure possession of the land in the same manner (e.g., Deut 3:20; 12:10; 25:19).
20. Abraham takes great care that his son Isaac not leave the land (Gen 24:5–6). Jacob does depart from the land in order to flee from his brother, but he experiences extraordinary encounters with God as he leaves (Gen 28:10–17) and as he returns (Gen 32:24–32), thus underlining the significance of the place.

have established" (i.e., Jerusalem; Exod 15:17).[21] The land and its future capital were the holy destination of Israel's journey, sanctified by God before the ark of the covenant was constructed and transported to its precincts.

Leviticus 18 indicates that the land was already holy before Israel entered it under Joshua. This chapter contains the rules of sexual morality that are incumbent upon Israel as a holy people. The chapter concludes by warning Israel about the consequences of disobeying these rules:

> Do not defile yourselves in any of these ways, for by all these practices the nations I am casting out before you have defiled themselves. Thus the land became defiled; and I punished it for its iniquity, and the land vomited out its inhabitants. But you shall keep my statutes and my ordinances and commit none of these abominations, either the citizen or the alien who resides among you (for the inhabitants of the land, who were before you, committed all of these abominations, and the land became defiled); otherwise the land will vomit you out for defiling it, as it vomited out the nation that was before you. (Lev 18:24-28)

The land could only become "defiled" if it were previously holy. The land purifies itself from the defiling conduct of its inhabitants by "vomiting" them out. As Jacob Milgrom correctly infers, "by what right did YHWH have the land expel the Canaanites for polluting the land (18:24-30)—unless the land was already his!"[22]

The holiness of the land—like the holiness of the Sabbath—is antecedent to the holiness of the Tabernacle. However, again like the Sabbath, the land and its holy city correspond to the Tabernacle and are the fitting site for its residence. The labor that goes into the construction of the wilderness Tabernacle and the Jerusalem Temple displays the human participation required in the transformation of the created order into a sanctuary for the glory of God, and the end-product provides hints of what that transformed world will be like. The holy land and the holy city are the initial workplace for this sanctifying eschatological activity. When the holy people live in the holy land and the holy city, their aim should be to make their entire communal existence a temple in the midst of the world. That temple is itself but the proleptic sign of what God desires for the entire creation.[23]

---

21. Jacob Milgrom draws the appropriate conclusion from Exodus 15: "the epic (JE) Song of the Sea expressly states that 'you brought them and planted them in the mountain of *your* inheritance' (Exod 15:17a; cf. Ps 78:54). Again, the land must have been YHWH's even before Israel's arrival" (Milgrom, *Leviticus 17-22*, 1404).

22. Ibid., 1404.

23. Pope John Paul II appreciated the enduring sacramental vocation of the land of Israel and the city of Jerusalem: "What a blessing it would be if this Holy Land, where

Holy Word: The Torah

By divine election Israel, the Sabbath, and the land are holy. In themselves they are but another people, another day, another place; but God has graciously designated them as his own and chosen them to mediate his illuminating presence. Is there anything that is of this world and yet so intrinsically holy that we cannot conceive of it apart from its relationship to the one who calls it his own? The answer to this question leads us to the most important of all the holy realities of this world: the name of God.

The holiness of God's name is a basic assumption of Scripture.[24] The revelation of the divine name to Moses at the burning bush coincides with the first appearance of the Hebrew root *k-d-sh* after the creation narrative.[25] From this point on the divine name is linked with the people of Israel. God establishes an eternal connection between the divine name and the people who have received the covenant, so that Israel's disobedience and humiliation profane the name that dwells among them.[26]

In Jewish tradition this name is so holy that it can only be spoken by the high priest (the holiest Israelite) in the Jerusalem Temple (the holiest place) on the Day of Atonement (one of the holiest days). While in all other circumstances it is unspeakable, it can be written down, and the transcription of God's name within the Torah and the other Jewish scriptures—in the language in which it was originally spoken to Moses—is the fundamental event that renders those texts holy.[27] In fact, after the destruction of the

---

God spoke and Jesus walked, could become a special place of encounter and prayer for peoples, if the Holy City of Jerusalem could be *a sign and instrument* of peace and reconciliation" (*Spiritual Pilgrimage*, xxxiv. Emphasis added). According to Gregory Vall, the Pope here likely alludes to the opening paragraph of *Lumen Gentium*: "the Church is in Christ like a sacrament or as *a sign and instrument* both of a very closely knit union with God and of the unity of the whole human race." Vall suggests that "It may be, then, that John Paul's choice of words is aimed at directing our attention to one facet of the relationship between Israel and the Church." Just as the Church is a sign and instrument of vertical and horizontal reconciliation, so the holy land—which Voll sees as a "'sacrament' of God's covenant with Israel" and of "Israel's unique vocation to mediate knowledge of the true God to the gentiles"—is meant to be a summons to "peace and reconciliation" for all nations. Sadly, the land and the city have enjoyed and conveyed too little of the sacramental blessing of peace which they signify. See Vall, "'Man Is the Land,'" 131, 133, 144.

24. See Lev 20:3; 22:2; 22:32; Ezek 36:20–23; 39:7; 39:25; 43:7–8; Isa 29:23; Amos 2:7; 1 Chr 16:10, 35; 29:16; Pss 33:21; 103:1; 105:3; 106:47; 145:21.

25. Exod 3:5, 13–15.

26. Lev 20:3; 22:2; 22:32; Ezek 36:20–23; 43:7–9.

27. According to the Jewish mystical tradition, the Torah as a whole manifests or is equivalent to the divine name. See Scholem, *Kabbalah and Its Symbolism*, 32–86. Still, as Scholem demonstrates, a distinction remains in the mystical tradition between the

Jerusalem Temple the only objects that are truly holy are those that include writing sanctified by the divine name, transcribed by an appropriate person in an appropriate manner. Max Kadushin provides a clear summary of the traditional halakhah regarding these holy objects:

> Certain things—a *sefer-Torah*, *tefillin*, *mezuzot*, and *sefarim* (scrolls of the Prophets or *Ketubim*)—are classified by the Halakhah as *Kedushah*. Even objects directly used in connection with these holy things, objects which are characterized as *tashmishe Kedushah* [i.e., holy utensils], such as the receptacles or cases for the holy things, are to be stored away when no longer used, and not just thrown aside carelessly. (This applies all the more, of course, to the holy things themselves.) On the other hand, a second group of objects ... [which are employed in rites governed by the Halakhah]—*sukkah*, *lulab*, *tzitzit*, and *shofar*—may be thrown away when they can no longer be used, and this applies not only to them but also to "others like them." Classified by the Halakhah as *tashmishe Mitzvah* [i.e., utensils for the fulfillment of a mitzvah] the objects in this second group are thus regarded as merely being essential to a particular rite and nothing more. They are not holy in themselves. If, in contrast to *tashmishe Kedushah*, they may be finally thrown away, it is because they are basically of an ordinary character.[28]

Elsewhere Kadushin describes the hierarchy that exists among these holy objects, and the transcriptive acts that render them holy:

> In descending order, that hierarchy [of holy objects] consists of a *Sefer Torah* (a scroll of the Pentateuch), *tefillin* (four specified passages from the Pentateuch), *mezuzot* (two specified passages from the Pentateuch on parchment), *sefarim* (scrolls of Prophets and *Ketubim* [from Psalms to Chronicles]), a synagogue [i.e., a place where sacred texts are kept and publicly read]. Failure to conform with but a single one of the many rules for the writing of a *Sefer Torah* and for the preparation of its parchment is enough to disqualify it, and similar rules apply to the making of *tefillin* and *muzuzot*. A number of those rules have to do with the *kavanah*, intention, and one rule in particular reminds us of *kavanah* in the case of sacrifices and of tithes: names of God in a *Sefer Torah*, *tefillin*, and *mezuzot* must be written with

---

heavenly Torah (which is fully equivalent to the eternal uncreated name of God) and the earthly Torah (which expresses that eternal name in the created order of time and space).

28. Kadushin, *Rabbinic Mind*, 171–72.

> *kavanah*, that is, each name must be written with the idea in mind that it refers to God.[29]

The scribe (*sofer*) is thus like a priest, who takes that which is ordinary and renders it holy by bringing it into contact with the Holy One, in one case through the mediation of the transcribed name of God, in the other through the mediation of the Temple altar.

For anyone familiar with Catholic piety and practice, Kadushin's discussion of holy objects calls to mind the eucharistic elements. There is, in fact, an analogy between the sanctifying activity of the scribe (the *sofer*) and that of the Catholic priest, and of the reverence shown to the *Sefer Torah* and to the eucharistic elements. The analogy breaks down when reckoning with the difference between reverence and adoration—but the similarity is nonetheless striking. There is also an analogy between the role played by the Torah service in the synagogue liturgy, and that played by the eucharistic service in the Catholic liturgy. The analogy can also be extended to the qualifications for contact with the *Sefer Torah* (i.e., one must be a Jew) and those for eucharistic communion (i.e., one must be a Catholic).

We should also note the significance here of the Hebrew language. The sacred writings only maintain the summit of holiness in their original form. Translations are esteemed and employed, but they are not holy in the same way as the Hebrew text. This means that the holy text is bound closely to the holy people, who guard and transmit the language through which the Holy One is revealed and in which the holy name is inscribed.

Holy Deeds: The Mitzvot

For Jewish tradition, the *mitzvot* (commandments) constitute the heart of the Torah. They provide the framework for Israel's holy life in fulfillment of its priestly vocation. The connection between the *mitzvot* and holiness appears in Numbers 15:38–41, which is recited twice daily as the third paragraph of the *Shema*. These verses speak of the fringes which Israelites are to affix to the four corners of their garments, and which represent "all the commandments (*mitzvot*) of the Lord" (v. 39). When Israelites look upon the fringes, they are to remember to "do all my commandments" (v. 40). The latter verse ends with these words: "and you shall be holy to your God."

These words at the conclusion of verse 40 could be taken as a relational reason for keeping the *mitzvot*. In this reading, the keeping of the *mitzvot* is the behavioral imperative implicit in a holy status: if one is holy

---

29. Kadushin, *Worship*, 221.

(i.e., belongs to God), then one observes the commandments of God. In contrast, Jewish tradition has generally understood the latter as a promise contingent upon fulfillment of the former: "if you observe my *mitzvot*, then you shall be holy." In this view, observance of the *mitzvot* becomes a means of sanctification rather than its result. This is the interpretation reflected in the blessing recited before performing any ritual commandment: "Blessed are you, Lord our God, King of the universe, who has sanctified us by your *mitzvot*, and commanded us to . . . ." As the Sages state, "With every new *mitzvah* which God issues to Israel he adds holiness to them."[30] As Abraham Joshua Heschel realizes, this means that the *mitzvot* are sacramental. "The *mitzvot* are the Jewish sacraments, sacraments that may be performed in common deeds of kindness."[31]

In the eyes of Jewish tradition, why do the *mitzvot* have sanctifying power? One explanation comes from a midrashic interpretation of the phrase "my *mitzvot*" (Lev 26:3), which takes it to mean "the *mitzvot* which God observes."[32] Thus, the *mitzvot* represent the characteristic behavior of God, and to keep them is to imitate God. The Sages depict God as one who visits the sick, feeds the hungry, and comforts mourners; when Israel observes the *mitzvot* that command such behavior, they are entering into God's own way of life. Heschel takes this interpretation one step further:

> A mitzvah is an act which God and man *have in common*. We say: "Blessed art Thou, Lord our God, King of the universe, who has sanctified us with *His* mitzvot." They oblige Him as well as us. Their fulfillment is not valued as an act performed in spite of "the evil drive," but as an act of *communion* with Him. The spirit of mitzvah is *togetherness*. We know, He is a partner to our act.[33]

According to Heschel, the *mitzvah* does not merely bring us into God's characteristic way of acting; it also implies a promise that God will *join with us* in our actions when we make the *mitzvot* our characteristic way of life. By emphasizing the co-operative nature of the *mitzvot*—God acting in and with our acting—Heschel heightens the sacramental dimension of the *mitzvot* that is already central to the tradition.

As a member of one of the great families of the Hasidic world, Heschel's spiritual orientation reflects the mystical approach to the *mitzvot* that

---

30. *Mekhilta de-Rabbi Ishmael* on Exod 22:30.

31. Heschel, *Moral Grandeur*, 278. Paul Mendes-Flohr likewise uses the language of sacrament to characterize Franz Rosenzweig's understanding of the *mitzvot* and Jewish ritual observance ("Law and Sacrament," 326–32).

32. *Leviticus Rabbah* 35:3.

33. Heschel, *God in Search of Man*, 287.

crystallized in the teaching of Isaac Luria (sixteenth century). According to Luria, the *mitzvot* are God's instruments for effecting a *tikkun* (repair) of the broken cosmos. When Jews observe the *mitzvot*, they participate in the process whereby the world is redeemed. For Luria, this is not an empirically observable humanitarian venture by which we improve the world through our own efforts, but instead a hidden divine process in which God brings cosmic effects in response to the fulfillment of *mitzvot*. In this view, the *mitzvot* become the instruments by which Jews sanctify the world, and not merely themselves.[34]

Just as the *Sefer Torah* of Jewish tradition resembles the eucharistic elements of Catholic tradition, and the Torah service in Jewish liturgy resembles the partaking of those elements in communion, so the *mitzvot* in Jewish practice—at least among those, like Heschel, influenced by the mystical tradition—resemble the sacrificial dimension of the Eucharist discussed in our previous chapter. Catholics understand the eucharistic sacrifice as an offering that affects the world, and not just themselves. It has eschatological and sanctifying power. From a Catholic perspective, the Eucharist is the ultimate act of *tikkun olam*, in which the atoning self-offering of the Messiah is presented before God as the Messiah's own prayer for the redemption of the world.

Jesus, Jewish Sacramental Signs, and the *Ecclesia*

The sacramental character of these five realities as bearers of *kedushah* should be evident from the biblical text and from Jewish tradition. But what is their relation to the person and work of Jesus, and to the sacramental order of the *ecclesia*? In response to this question, I propose three basic theses for consideration: (1) Jewish sacramental signs find their messianic realization in and through Jesus; (2) Jewish sacramental signs have enduring significance and efficacy in and through Jesus; and (3) Jewish sacramental signs are integral to the life and identity of the *ecclesia*.

Realization in and through Jesus

Writing as a Catholic theologian on the topic of the "sacramentality of the Land of Israel," Gregory Vall asserts the following: "Ultimately, to call something a 'sacrament' is to specify its relation to Christ, the Incarnate Logos,

---

34. See Dan, *Jewish Mysticism*, 107–13. Dan proposes that "The concept of the *tikkun* is the most powerful idea ever presented in Jewish thought" (107).

who is the definitive sacrament of God's presence to the world."[35] As one who shares Vall's faith in Jesus as "the Incarnate Logos," I concur with his understanding of the term "sacrament." What precisely, then, is the relation between these five Jewish sacramental realities and Jesus?

As the Word made flesh and the bearer of the divine name, Jesus is the incarnate expression of the heavenly *holy Torah*, the one to whom the earthly scroll bears witness.[36] As the messianic king who represents and embodies his people in himself, and carries them into the next stage of their eschatological destiny by means of resurrection from the dead, Jesus is *holy Israel*.[37] As the one whose perfect obedience to the commandments of the Torah culminates in his atoning martyrdom on the cross, and whose gift of the Spirit enables his disciples to follow the same path, Jesus brings the messianic realization of the *holy mitzvot*.[38] As the one whose Spirit is the pledge, seal, and first-fruits of the world to come, and who will in the fullness of time return to reign over a transformed creation, Jesus is the Lord of the *holy Sabbath*, the new Joshua who brings Israel into the promised *holy land*, and the new David who establishes the *holy city*.

Jesus' role as the incarnation of the heavenly Torah underlines his divinity, whereas his role as the individual embodiment of Israel highlights the particularity of his humanity. His realization of the *mitzvot* reflects his redemptive life and death, and also the way of discipleship that participates in his work of *tikkun olam*. The proleptic holiness of Shabbat and the land point to his resurrection life given by the Spirit, and to the inheritance of a renewed cosmos of which his resurrection is a first-fruit and the Spirit a deposit. These five Jewish sacramental realities thus inscribe prophetically—and in the form of a mystery—the substance of the creed in the daily life of the Jewish people.

Christian theology has traditionally treated these five Jewish expressions of holiness under the heading of typology. Theologians have agreed that they point forward to the coming of Jesus and the new era he would inaugurate. They have disagreed over whether such types were truly sacramental in character, enabling those living before the incarnation to participate proleptically in the messianic realities they prefigured.[39] While admitting a

---

35. Vall, "Man is the Land," 136.

36. This is the Torah-Christology taught by Pope Benedict XVI.

37. This is the Israel-Christology taught by Cardinal Lustiger.

38. "What then is the Christian vocation? . . . It is to observe the totality of the commandments. Jesus is the one who fulfills these commandments to perfection and gives strength to those who follow him so that they, too, can fulfill them perfectly" (Lustiger, *Promise*, 10).

39. For a discussion of this disagreement and an argument in favor of seeing types

distinction in the degree of participation in the Messiah available through the sacraments which anticipated his coming and those which he himself instituted, I am proposing here that the people and land of Israel, the Sabbath, the Torah, and the *mitzvot* are truly sacramental and truly grant such participation.[40] As the pre-incarnate Messiah was the "spiritual rock" that quenched Israel's thirst in the wilderness with "spiritual drink" (1 Cor 10:4), so the same pre-incarnate Messiah was active in and through all the "types" of the Torah, and most especially those five realities discussed above.

Typology, so conceived, provides a useful but still limited perspective on these five expressions of *kedushah*. The limitation arises because typology normally concerns two distinct realities—type and anti-type—whose relationship is unidirectional rather than reciprocal. Displaying a pattern that derives from its anti-type, the type draws its essential import and power from that which it anticipates or embodies; in contrast, the anti-type has its import and power independent of the type. Thus, Joshua as the one who leads Israel into the land is a type of Jesus who leads his people to its messianic inheritance. Joshua is like Jesus, and one might even say that the pre-incarnate Messiah was himself active in and through Joshua, but we would not say that Joshua was active in and through Jesus. The relationship between them is unidirectional. However, the situation is otherwise with our five primary expressions of Jewish *kedushah*. Israel and Jesus are not two distinct realities; Jesus is an Israelite, and as the Messiah he embodies the entire people in himself. He was present and active in Israel's life before the incarnation, but, as Cardinal Lustiger has argued forcefully, genealogical-Israel is also present in the life of Jesus the incarnate Son.[41] In other words, Israel-Christology has deeper meaning and more radical theological implications than Israel-typology.

Similarly, the Torah does not merely prefigure Jesus or grant proleptic access to his pre-incarnate presence. Jesus studied the Torah, taught the Torah, loved the Torah, and embodied the Torah. The Torah lived in him, just as Israel lived in him. Jesus and the Torah are not two separate realities, one of which points to the other. They are so bound together that wherever Jesus is, there is also the Torah. Israel and the Torah are ordered in relation to

---

as sacramental, see Leithart, "Old Covenant," 174–90.

40. It is worth noting that, according to Catholic teaching, partaking of the sacraments of the Church does not ensure the eternal beatitude of those who so partake. The effectiveness of the "grace" conveyed by the sacrament may be thwarted by the evil disposition of the one who receives it. This would likewise hold for the sacramental realities of Israel which I am considering here.

41. See pages 13–16.

Jesus—he is the master of Torah and the King of Israel, just as he is the Lord of the Sabbath. But he is never apart from Torah, Israel, and the Sabbath.

Enduring Efficacy in and through Jesus

The five sacramental signs described above have remained the pillars of Jewish life and thought through the last two millennia, undiminished by the destruction of the Temple in 70 CE. I have proposed that they were efficacious signs of the Messiah and of the messianic age before the incarnation. What about after the incarnation?

In this second thesis I am proposing that these five realities retain their sacramental status in the new order established through the death and resurrection of Jesus. In fact, I would even suggest that the initial realization in Jesus of their messianic significance *intensifies* their sacramental character. The Messiah has been raised from the dead, the Holy Spirit has been given, and the next stage of Israel's eschatological journey has begun—though this world has not yet been transformed into the world to come. In light of these events, there is no obvious reason why these five primary expressions of *kedushah* would be nullified rather than intensified.

Philip Cunningham and Dieder Pollefyt propose the same thesis in regards to the overall framework of "Jewish covenantal life," a term which encompasses the five sacramental realities that have been our focus here.

> [T]he Catholic Church now teaches that Jewish covenantal life was "never revoked by God." From a Christian viewpoint this must mean that even after the time of Christ, the people of Israel have been interacting covenantally with the Triune One[;] . . . it might even be said that God's covenantal sharing-in-life, dwelling within the flesh of the people of Israel, became even more focused, more intimate with the incarnation of the Logos in Jesus, the "authentic son of Israel."[42]

As noted in our opening chapter, Hans Hermann Henrix argues that the Torah-Christology of Pope Benedict XVI, understood in the context of the teaching of Pope John Paul II, implies that faithful Jews who observe the *mitzvot* and honor the Torah enter thereby into communion with Christ:

> If Christians trust in God's blessing upon Jewish walking in accord with Israel's Torah and if this halakhic "walking" can be considered salvific only when related to the fundamental Christian belief that every salvation is the salvation of Jesus Christ,

---

42. Cunningham and Pollefyt, "Triune One," 197-98.

> then saying that Jesus Christ is the living Torah can be understood as denoting such mediation. Then that which for Jews is salvific—life according to the Torah, trust in God's Word, faith in God's promise—would be in contact with Jesus Christ and would be taken up in him in a way that confirms, reaffirms, or reinforces, since Jesus Christ is obedient to the Torah and fulfills it. . . . Whoever obeys the Torah as a Jew and strives toward the goal "to be an incarnation of the Torah," walks on his or her way in a manner that, because of Jesus Christ's link with the Torah, Christians believe to be salvific communion with Christ as the Torah incarnate.[43]

Henrix's focus upon "salvific communion" should be understood in the broad Catholic sense of God's healing and transformative power at work in the renewal of human life, rather than in a narrow sense restricted to the question of inheriting the world to come. What he asserts about *mitzvot* and the Torah, and what Cunningham and Pollefyt assert about "Jewish covenantal life," would apply likewise to the Sabbath and the land of Israel which take their meaning from their role as covenantal signs and gifts.

In support of this thesis is the fact that the *ecclesia ex circumcisione* of the first century continued to honor these five traditional expressions of *kedushah*. They circumcised their sons, indicating their continued identification with genealogical-Israel (Acts 21:20–24; 1 Cor 7:18). They observed the Sabbath (Luke 23:56; Matt 24:20) and revered the city of Jerusalem (Matt 4:5; 5:35; Acts 24:11). They studied the Torah and kept the *mitzvot* (Matt 5:17–19; 23:23; Acts 21:20).

Why did they act in this way? I have argued in *Postmissionary Messianic Judaism* that they did so out of obedience to the commandments of God, which had not been cancelled.[44] While gentile disciples of Jesus were exempt from the distinctive obligations incumbent only upon genealogical-Israel, Jewish disciples of Jesus continued to treat "Jewish covenantal life" as a sacred responsibility. Cardinal Lustiger suggests the same, and emphasizes the point through repetition.

> In this early Church, the status of the Pagan-Christian assemblies begins to be established. They are not dispensed from observing the Law. . . . But the gift of the Holy Spirit, a grace of the Messiah, enables pagans to observe the Law differently from Israel, *which remains charged with this "delightful" burden of observance.*[45]

43. Henrix, "The Son of God," 137–38.
44. Kinzer, *Postmissionary*, 48–96.
45. Lustiger, *Promise*, 6–7. Emphasis added.

> Undoubtedly, there are several ways of observing certain precepts and practices in religious life: that of the Church of Jerusalem, as described in the Acts of the Apostles in the first days of Christianity, a community composed of observant Jews[,] ... whereas the Pagan-Christian communities do not have the same *obligations*.[46]

> Pagans also have a right to the Law, as a holy law inscribed in their hearts. ... The discipline of the Church dispenses them from Israel's observances, a burden too heavy for them, and *which remains Israel's privilege*.[47]

For Cardinal Lustiger, the redemptive work of the Messiah did not grant these Jewish disciples of the Messiah "freedom" from the *mitzvot* any more than it emptied the Sabbath or the land of their holiness. Genealogical-Israel was still "charged with this 'delightful' burden of observance," which "remains Israel's privilege." The Cardinal sees the decision of the Jerusalem Council of Acts 15 not as a nullification of the differences between Jews and gentiles but as a ruling in which "the first apostles had generously allowed the pagans to keep a distinct status ... alongside the Jews."[48]

But what was the purpose of those commandments incumbent only on Jews? If the Messiah had come to fulfill the commandments and promises—to "fill them up" to their fullness—and if those commandments and promises had previously anticipated the Messiah's work and granted proleptic access to it, would the Jewish followers of Jesus not look for an even richer encounter with him through their engagement with Shabbat, the land and the city, the Torah, the mitzvot, and the corporate life of the people of Israel?

This thesis receives further support from the Apostle Paul's vision of the eschatological significance of the Jewish people. The apostle to the gentiles asserts that genealogical-Israel will welcome Jesus as part of the final act in the drama, which culminates in the Messiah's return (Rom 11:25–27). He also expresses his conviction that Jews who have not yet embraced Jesus remain "holy" (Rom 11:16) because of their connection to the patriarchs and matriarchs (Rom 11:16b, 28–29) and to the priestly remnant (Rom 11:16a). The enduring holiness of genealogical-Israel explains their role in the eschatological drama: the people who are set apart for the Messiah, who lived their life in his presence even before his coming (Eph 2:12), must welcome back their king with open arms and hearts if he is to return to reign

---

46. Ibid., 15. Emphasis added.
47. Ibid., 105. Emphasis added.
48. Lustiger, *On Christians and Jews*, 131.

over them (Matt 23:39). If genealogical-Israel retains its sacramental status to the end, despite its ignorance of the risen Messiah, why should we expect the abolition of any of the other four Jewish sacramental realities that are oriented to this most basic one?

The faithful engagement with these five sacramental realities by the early Jewish disciples of Jesus and the enduring holiness of genealogical-Israel suggest that these expressions of *kedushah* have a sacramental role in God's dealings with all Jews, baptized or not. Jesus lives on in the midst of genealogical-Israel, and he does so—at least in part—through these five sacramental realities. Just as the sacraments of the *ecclesia* translate Israel-Christology into Israel-ecclesiology, so the sacramental life of the Jewish people translates Israel-Christology into ecclesial-Israelology.

Integral to the Church's Identity

My final thesis is the most radical of the three: I propose that these five Jewish sacramental realities are not only of enduring validity, but are integral to the identity of the *ecclesia* as the mystical Body of Christ.

In the previous two theses I have presented a view of the sacramental character of Jewish life that is thoroughly messianic in orientation: all five embodiments of holiness find their perfect realization in Jesus the Messiah, and all five continue after his incarnation, death, and resurrection to mediate his presence and power among the people to whom he is eternally bound. In this way they are analogous to—and oriented toward—the sacraments that he explicitly institutes in the *ecclesia*. For example, as I argued in chapter 5, the sacrament of baptism is intended as initiation into the next stage of Israel's eschatological vocation. As such, for Jews it functions as a re-affirmation of their status as members of the people of Israel and as a re-commitment to its eschatological mission and destiny. Thus, the sacrament of Jewish identity—an identity that is already messianic in character—is to be realized in, but not replaced by, the sacrament of baptism into the Body of Israel's risen Messiah.

If there are no Jews within the Body of Christ whose baptism functions as a realization rather than nullification of their Jewish identity, an identity that was already inherently sacramental and messianic, then the *ecclesia* loses something of fundamental importance. We can see this most clearly in the case of the baptism of gentiles. The sacrament of baptism is intended to initiate them into an expanded eschatological Israel, which retains its intimate relationship to genealogical-Israel. If the social, cultural, and religious connection to genealogical-Israel for Jews is severed by their baptism rather

JEWISH LIFE AS SACRAMENT

than affirmed and renewed, then gentile members of the *ecclesia* are left stranded, cut off from the extended community to which their baptism was supposed to join them. In this way ecclesial denial of Jewish sacramental life results in damage to an ecclesial sacrament instituted by Jesus.

As another example, let us look at the Eucharist. In its character as a sacrifice the Eucharist involves remembrance before God of the atoning death of Jesus as part of a prayer for the final coming of the messianic kingdom. Jesus' act of martyrdom—in Hebrew, *kiddush Hashem* ("sanctification of the name")—was the culmination of a life lived in accordance with the *mtizvot*, an act that represented the fullness of that life. As we saw in chapters 6 and 7, the Eucharist is based on Jesus' realization of the *mitzvot* and has in view the eschatological renewal of Israel. In this light, Jewish practice of the *mitzvot* within the *ecclesia* would function naturally as an extension of the Eucharist; in their observance Jewish disciples of Jesus would remember and share in Jesus' petition to the Father for the redemption of Israel and the repair of the entire world (i.e., *tikkun olam*). The Eucharist would not render the *mitzvot* irrelevant any more than baptism would render Jewish identity irrelevant. However, if the *ecclesia* fails to offer the Eucharist with genealogical-Israel in view, and if Jews within the *ecclesia* fail to observe the *mitzvot*, something of fundamental importance disappears from the community that calls Jesus Lord.

If these five Jewish sacramental signs are integral to the identity of the *ecclesia* as the mystical Body of Christ, then what should we conclude about the state of the *ecclesia* since its early centuries, when it unambiguously rejected their validity? We may conclude, as I did in *Postmissionary Messianic Judaism*, that the *ecclesia* has been as wounded by its attitude to Jews and Judaism as the Jewish people has been wounded by its attitude to Jesus. As Cardinal Lustiger has stated, "The blinding pains of history have obscured the vision of both Christians and Jews, so that we fail to recognize Israel in its Messiah or the Messiah hidden in Israel."[49] But we may also conclude something more positive in nature: if the *ecclesia* remains the Body of Christ, despite her failure to acknowledge the sacramental character of Jewish life; and if the Jewish people remain the people of God, despite their failure to acknowledge their Messiah; then we must conclude that God views these two bodies as one complex reality, locked together against their will for a joint future that neither can evade.

The sacramental realities of Jewish life within the *ecclesia ex circumcisione* of the New Testament era embodied the spiritual link binding genealogical-Israel to its appointed Messiah while simultaneously joining the

---

49. Lustiger, *On Christians and Jews*, 135.

Body of Christ to genealogical-Israel. This is why these Jewish sacramental realities are integral to the identity of the *ecclesia*: it is because *the relationship with genealogical-Israel is integral to the identity of the ecclesia*. In the anomalous situation created by the disappearance of a recognized *ecclesia ex circumcisione*, we must believe that God accounts the practice of this life by the Jewish people—even without the sacramental mediation of the priestly remnant of Jewish disciples of Jesus—as though it were realized directly by the *ecclesia*. The risen Messiah is integral to the identity of the Jewish people; however, in the anomalous situation created by the disappearance of a recognized Jesus-believing community within the Jewish people, God accounts the honoring of Jesus by the *ecclesia*—again, even without the sacramental mediation of the priestly remnant—as though it were done by genealogical-Israel.[50] Each needs the other, and each has the other, if only by God's merciful methods of accounting—merciful, but not entirely a matter of legal fiction, since the two divided partners are joined ontologically in a unity that lies at the heart of the mysterious identity of each. The *ecclesia* rightly discovers the "stock of Abraham" when she delves into the mystery of her being, but genealogical-Israel also discovers its Messiah and his *ecclesia* when it searches its own hidden depths.

Nevertheless, God's gracious accounting does not render superfluous the *ecclesia ex circumcisione*. The loss of a visible community of Jewish disciples of Jesus has wounded both the *ecclesia* and genealogical-Israel. Its restoration would facilitate their healing, and open a new chapter in the relationship between the Church and the Jewish people.

Conclusion

Jewish thought would benefit greatly from reflection on the Catholic understanding of sacrament, and from its employment as a conceptual tool in the analysis of Jewish life. The category is especially helpful for Jewish disciples of Jesus, as it offers a way of thinking about Jewish realities that unites those realities indissolubly to the person and work of Jesus without diminishing their intrinsic significance. In fact, such a sacramental perspective actually deepens the meaning ascribed to various aspects of Jewish life, and increases motivation for faithful adherence to them.

Of course, appropriation of a Catholic understanding of sacrament also poses a serious challenge for participants in the Messianic Jewish

---

50. As should be evident, I am speaking here of the sacramental status of the Jewish people and of the *ecclesia* as communal entities, and not of the spiritual condition of the individuals within them.

JEWISH LIFE AS SACRAMENT

movement. Take, for example, the sacrament of the Eucharist: as Messianic Jews grow in appreciation for a Catholic understanding of the Eucharist, we will need to assess our own practice of this rite, and ask if it is worthy of the holiness of the sacrament. Most of us, I think, will find that the answer is "no." If the approach presented above is accepted, this has implications for the integrity of our *Jewish lives*—since Jewish life now is inseparable from Jesus. I have proposed that Messianic Jewish observance of the *mitzvot* be viewed and lived as an extension of the Eucharist. If we are not celebrating the Eucharist appropriately, then our observance of the *mitzvot* will also be affected.

At the same time, a sacramental understanding of Judaism likewise poses a serious challenge to Catholic self-understanding. The absence of Jewish sacramental life within the Catholic Church—and, historically, its active suppression—becomes a problem of tremendous urgency and importance, which has implications for the integrity of her own ecclesial sacraments. Thus, for both Messianic Jews and for Catholics the collapse of sacramental compartmentalization offers rewards and risks, hopeful prospects and fearful tests.

In the early chapters of this book we presented a form of Israel-Christology that undergirds Israel-ecclesiology while at the same time upholding the irrevocable election of genealogical-Israel. The adoption of such an Israel-Christology would better enable the *ecclesia* to discover her spiritual bond with the Jewish people by probing the depths of her own mystery. In these last two chapters we have considered how that Israel-Christology can also undergird an ecclesial-Israelology. This view of genealogical-Israel upholds the enduring theological significance of Jewish religious life and lays a spiritual foundation for the Jewish people to discover its bond to the *ecclesia* through the resurrected Jew, Jesus the Messiah, who dwells unrecognized in its midst. All that remains for us now is to gaze at the path ahead as we seek to transform these theological propositions into concrete visible realities.

9

The Task of Mutual-Indwelling

Ontological Mystery and Sacred Task

I have attempted in this book to offer a particular way of construing the theological implications of Vatican II's teaching regarding the relationship between the Church and the Jewish people and between the Church's faith and the Jewish way of life. *Lumen Gentium* raised the necessary questions by presenting an Israel-ecclesiology that depicts the Church as the people of God, a "new Israel." At the same time the document also affirmed the irrevocable election of genealogical-Israel. *Lumen Gentium* set these two affirmations side-by-side, but shed little light on how one was related to the other.

Nostra Aetate restated the Church's belief in the enduring election of the Jewish people in an even more unambiguous fashion. Moreover, in its introductory remarks on the topic (as authoritatively interpreted by Pope John Paul II) it also opened the way for reflection on the relationship between this belief and the Israel-ecclesiology of *Lumen Gentium*. Those remarks spoke of a "spiritual bond" that connected the Church to the "stock of Abraham." Furthermore, they asserted that the Church discovered this "spiritual bond" by plumbing the depths of her own mystery. The document thus refused to view the Church and the Jewish people as two externally related religious communities and traditions, pursuing their historical journeys on parallel but separate tracks.

Nostra Aetate speaks of the bond linking two peoples—the "people of the New Covenant" and the "stock of Abraham." It says nothing explicit about the relationship between the Church's faith and the concrete reality of Jewish religious life. Some Catholic thinkers, both before Vatican II and since, have affirmed the election of the Jewish people and at the same time

THE TASK OF MUTUAL-INDWELLING

denied the enduring covenantal significance of Jewish religious practice.[1] It is therefore striking that Pope John Paul II paraphrases the introduction to *Nostra Aetate* 4 in words that speak of the Jewish *religion* and not only the Jewish *people*. "The *Jewish religion* [as well as the Jewish people] is not 'extrinsic' to us, but in a certain way is 'intrinsic' to our own religion. With *Judaism* [and not just the Jewish people], therefore, we have a relationship which we do not have with any other *religion*."[2] Pope John Paul II refuses to drive a wedge between the Jewish people and the Jewish religion, honoring one while devaluing the other. Bruce Marshall draws a stark contrast between the Pope's views and those of Catholic thinkers less appreciative of Jewish religious life:

> [T]hese thinkers affirm the Church's ongoing and uniquely intimate relationship with the Jewish people, and indeed God's electing love for the Jews, in spite of their religion—their Judaism—not because of it. For Pope John Paul II, by contrast, the Church professes a unique intimacy with the Jewish people in good part precisely because of their religion. And this means, it would seem, that Christians need to see Jewish faith, the practice of the Jewish religion after Christ, not as a humanly imposed obstacle to God's electing love, but as in some deep way the very fruit of that love.[3]

This teaching of Pope John Paul II complicates further the questions raised by *Lumen Gentium* and *Nostra Aetate*. Both the Jewish people and the Jewish religion have covenantal significance and an intrinsic connection to the life of the Church. How can this be, when the Jewish people corporately rejects the claims of Jesus and has cultivated a religious life in which his name is unmentioned and sometimes unmentionable?

Neither the documents of Vatican II nor the writings of Pope John Paul II answer this question directly. However, the answer we have offered in this volume takes its starting point from the words of the latter.

> According to the teaching of the Second Vatican Council, she [the Church] could better understand her bond with you [the Jewish people], certainly thanks to fraternal dialogue, but also by meditating upon her own mystery (*Nostra Aetate*, 4). Now

---

1. Bruce Marshall singles out Jacques Maritain and Charles Journet as two prominent examples of such a view before Vatican II (Marshall, "Elder Brothers," 118–19). Since Vatican II a similar position has been advocated by many Hebrew Catholics. See Friedman, *Jewish Identity* and Schoeman, *Salvation*.

2. John Paul II, *Spiritual Pilgrimage*, 63. Emphasis added.

3. Marshall, "Elder Brothers," 119.

that mystery is rooted in the mystery of the person of Jesus Christ, a Jew, crucified and glorified.[4]

The Pope here asserts that the one who ostensibly marks the point of division between the two communities and religious traditions is in reality the "spiritual bond" that joins them together, albeit at an ontological level discerned only through profound self-searching. He can fulfill this role because he is the "Christ" (i.e., the Messiah of Israel), "a Jew, crucified and glorified." He was crucified not only as "a" Jew, but, in accordance with the words of the *titulus* inscribed over his head, as "*the King* of the Jews." Moreover, his Jewish and royal identity did not end with the cross. In his resurrected, "glorified" form, he remains a Jew and the King of the Jews. In a mere seven words—"Jesus Christ, a Jew, crucified and glorified"—the Pope has provided us with a compact formula pointing toward the type of Israel-Christology articulated concisely by Cardinal Lustiger and elaborated in the preceding chapters.

This Israel-Christology entails a relationship of mutual-indwelling. Just as Jesus dwells among his disciples and they also dwell in him (John 14:20; 15:4–5), so Jesus dwells among the Jewish people and also carries them in himself. Jesus guides and cares for his family as a mediator of divine blessing whose identity remains hidden from them, like that of Joseph providing for his brothers. Embodying genealogical-Israel in his own person, Jesus represents his kin before God and before his gentile disciples.

This is why Jesus serves as the "spiritual bond" between the "people of the New Covenant" and "the stock of Abraham." When the Church fails to grasp the significance of the Jewishness of the crucified and glorified Messiah, she likewise fails to understand or honor her relationship with the Jewish people and its covenantal way of life (i.e., Judaism). Once the Church begins to sense the import of his Jewish identity, she realizes that she cannot embrace him without also embracing his flesh-and-blood family whom he represents; she cannot appreciate the richness of his teaching without seeing the way he has continued to shape the corporate life of those who are often reluctant to speak his name.

In other words, *Jesus is as much the mystery hidden in the depths of the Jewish people and the Jewish way of life as he is the mystery of the ecclesia.* The relationship of mutual-indwelling that Jesus has with both communities creates the "spiritual bond" that joins each to the other. Because he dwells in them both, they also dwell in one another. Through the unbreakable relationship that Jesus forges with his own flesh-and-blood, genealogical-Israel abides in the heart of the *ecclesia*. Through her baptismal union with Jesus,

---

4. John Paul II, *Spiritual Pilgrimage*, 126–27. Emphasis added.

the *ecclesia* likewise abides in the heart of the Jewish people. Only through humble and persistent self-searching can either discern this mutual-indwelling, but once it is perceived, new vistas open to the eyes of faith.

At first appearance, such a claim could easily be taken as a condescending expression of Christian triumphalism. "You Jews have value because *our Jesus* gives it to you. We understand you and your significance far better than you understand yourself!" However, Christians who truly discern the spiritual bond joining them to the Jewish people will respond with mortification rather than self-congratulation, for they will recognize the judgment this renders on the Christian past. As Cardinal Lustiger explained with unequivocal and prophetic clarity, Christians of former generations who mistreated Jews and mocked Judaism were showing contempt for the Messiah whom they claimed to know and follow. Christians today who honor the Jewish people as "the elder brother" and acknowledge the work of Jesus in the unfolding of Jewish religious tradition must therefore adopt the attitude of penitent disciples who seek a better understanding of their master. They cannot call the one they now discover dwelling among his own flesh-and-blood family members "*our* Jesus," for *this* Jesus was formerly a stranger to them. In a sense, they are meeting him for the first time.

In such an ecclesiology of mutual-indwelling, Jewish disciples of Jesus play a unique role. If we embrace our Jewishness as a spiritual vocation, identify with the Jewish people as well as the *ecclesia*, and seek to live a distinctively Jewish mode of discipleship informed by Jewish religious tradition, then we become a sacramental sign of the spiritual bond joining the *ecclesia* to genealogical-Israel. We become, like the holders of the episcopal office in Catholic teaching, contemporary representatives and embodiments of the Jewish apostles and the apostolic *ecclesia*, just as those apostles and their fellow Jewish disciples of Jesus were themselves representatives and embodiments of the Jewish Messiah who commissioned them. Through our lives we manifest the reality that genealogical-Israel abides in the midst of the *ecclesia*, and that Jesus abides in the midst of the Jewish people and the Jewish tradition.

The mutual-indwelling of Jesus and the *ecclesia* entails a relationship of love and communion, and this is also the divine purpose for the relationship between the *ecclesia* and the Jewish people. In historical terms, the latter relationship has fallen far short of its goal. However, the same can be said for the unity of the *ecclesia* itself, whose explicit vocation entails the communal manifestation of the unity of the Father and the Son (John 17:20–21). The unity of the *ecclesia* depends upon an established ontological foundation— "There *is* one body and one Spirit . . . one Lord, one faith, one baptism, one God and Father of all, who is above all, and through all and in all" (Eph

4:4–6). At the same time, this unity remains a task to be accomplished—"until all of us come to the unity of the faith and of the knowledge of the Son of God" (Eph 4:13)—a task in which the *ecclesia* has often fallen short. Similarly, the mutual-indwelling of the *ecclesia* and genealogical-Israel is founded on an ontological truth—namely, the person of "Jesus Christ, a Jew, crucified and glorified." Sadly, this underlying spiritual reality has usually taken the historical form of intense struggle, so that what should have been an embrace of love became instead the inextricable entwinement of two wrestlers, each seeking to subdue the other. The task remains of transforming the struggle for dominance into a covenant of peace. Vatican II constituted a decisive turning-point in the recognition of this task, but its historical realization still lies on the road before us.

Sacramental Sign or Syncretistic Sect?

As an essential part of the fulfillment of that task, I have proposed that Jewish disciples of Jesus who identify as Jews and who express that identity in their way of life serve as a sacramental sign of the mutual-indwelling of the *ecclesia* and the Jewish people. I have also argued that this fits well with the teaching of Pope John Paul II on the nature of the "spiritual bond" that joins the *ecclesia* and genealogical-Israel. However, the Pope also issued a warning that might seem to suggest otherwise. When addressing the Jewish community of Rome in his landmark visit to its synagogue in 1986, he stated that each of these two related religious traditions "wishes to be recognized and respected in its own identity, beyond any syncretism and any ambiguous appropriation."[5] Would the Pope have considered Jewish Catholicism or Messianic Judaism to be guilty of such illegitimate syncretism?

I am confident that Pope John Paul II did not have Jewish Catholics or Messianic Jews in mind when he uttered those words. If this had been his intent, he would never have spoken of Edith Stein as he did at her beatification.

> For Edith Stein, baptism as a Christian was by no means a break with her Jewish heritage. Quite on the contrary she said, "I had given up my practice of the Jewish religion as a girl of fourteen. My return to God made me feel Jewish again." She was always mindful of the fact that she was related to Christ "not only in a spiritual sense, but also in blood terms." She suffered profoundly from the pain she caused her mother through her conversion to

---

5. Ibid., 64.

THE TASK OF MUTUAL-INDWELLING

Catholicism. She continued to accompany her to services in the synagogue and to pray the psalms with her.[6]

> Her own life and the cross she had to bear were intimately connected with the destiny of the Jewish people. In a prayer she confessed to the Savior that she knew that it was his cross that was now being laid on the Jewish people and that those who realized this would have to accept it willingly on behalf of all the others.[7]

Was Edith Stein guilty of syncretism when she identified as a Jew, attended synagogue with her mother, and interpreted the suffering of the Jewish people as a sign of their enduring connection to their Messiah? The Pope evidently did not think so.

My confidence on this point also derives from the fact that it was Pope John Paul II's own theologian, Georges Cardinal Cottier, who initiated the Roman Catholic–Messianic Jewish Dialogue Group. Cardinal Cottier reported on his activities to the Pope, who evidently gave them his blessing. If Pope John Paul II had viewed the Messianic Jewish movement as a syncretistic sect, he would never have permitted his personal theologian to launch such a project.

Jewish disciples of Jesus are not practitioners of syncretism, but instead legitimate heirs of two intimately related religious traditions and legitimate members of two intimately connected communities. As I have argued here, this is possible because the "people of the new covenant" are but an eschatological expansion and realization of the "stock of Abraham." The wider Jewish community does not yet accept this claim, but the thesis is fully in keeping with the teaching of the late Pope.

What, then, does the Pope mean when he warns of the danger of "syncretism"?[8] I would suggest that we can make most sense of his concern by recalling the ruling of the Jerusalem Council in Acts 15. The apostles and elders determined that only Jewish disciples of Jesus were obligated to observe all the particulars of God's covenant with genealogical-Israel. Gentile disciples of Jesus were subject merely to those prescriptions that Leviticus 17–18 applied to non-Jews who dwelt "in the midst of Israel." They were

---

6. Ibid., 95.

7. Ibid., 94.

8. In speaking of Judaism and Christianity as distinct religions, and in referring to inappropriate mixtures of the two as "syncretism," Pope John Paul II communicates effectively by employing terminology that is familiar to both a Jewish and Christian audience. At the same time, his own subtle treatment of the relationship between the two traditions challenges the notion that they are totally separate religions, or can be properly understood independently of one another.

otherwise free—and called—to embody the life of Israel's Messiah in ways that would draw upon the divinely-bestowed cultural riches of the nations. This ruling cleared the way for a bilateral ecclesiology in which the *ecclesia* of the circumcision and the *ecclesia* of the uncircumcision could develop distinct corporate patterns of life and yet maintain full communion.

Members of the *ecclesia* of the nations participate in an expanded commonwealth of Israel, but they are not Jews. It would therefore be inappropriate for them to adopt practices that were distinctive marks of membership in the Jewish people. When gentile Christians circumcise their sons on the eighth day as a sign of the covenant, wear the ritual fringes of the *talit* (the Jewish prayer shawl), employ a handwritten Torah scroll in their worship, and sound the *shofar* (rams horn) as part of their prayer, they are transgressing a boundary that they should be honoring.[9] When Jewish disciples of Jesus do these same things, they are upholding that boundary and assuming their appointed role as a sacramental sign of the ecclesiology of mutual-indwelling.[10]

Steps Forward

What are the next steps forward on the road of this ecclesiology of mutual-indwelling? They will vary depending on our specific communal context and commitments. I will address here the steps ahead for the Catholic Church in general, for Catholic Jews in particular, for Messianic Jews, and for the wider Jewish world.

The Catholic Church

The Catholic Church has been a pioneer on this road. Vatican II changed the game for all players, and the Jewish and Christian worlds have not been

---

9. These are all what Jewish tradition refers to as "positive commandments," i.e., prescribed practices that require a particular action. Gentile Christians may learn from such practices, but any elements they adapt for their own use should be clearly distinguished from the distinctive Jewish covenantal signs. In the case of "negative commandments" (i.e., prohibited behavior) of a ritual character, the situation is more flexible. Thus, if gentile Christians decide to refrain from work on the Seventh Day, or to eliminate pork or shell-fish from their diet, they are free to do so, as long as they acknowledge that these abstentions are voluntary rather than compulsory.

10. In this paragraph I am not addressing the situation of gentiles who participate in Messianic Jewish or Jewish Catholic environments. The determination of what is appropriate for gentiles in such settings is a complicated matter which goes beyond the aims of this chapter or this volume.

the same since. Catholic leaders have also been pioneers in theological and personal engagement with the Messianic Jewish movement, as I described in chapter 2. Catholics feel most strongly the weight of the Christian past in its legacy of contempt for Jews and Judaism, and they have accordingly taken their place at the forefront of efforts to repair the damage and to clear a new path for the future.

At Vatican II the Church affirmed the irrevocable election of the Jewish people, and in the teaching of Pope John Paul II she acknowledged the spiritual riches of Jewish religious life. Through the reiterated statements of that Pope—and, most strikingly, through his visit to the holy land in the year 2000—the Catholic Church also acknowledged the past sins of her sons and daughters in their dealings with the Jewish people. However, one significant element of that past has remained unaddressed. I speak here of a pattern of behavior deeply rooted in the Church's canonical and theological history, which has been noted more than once in the preceding pages—namely, the suppression of distinctive Jewish practice among baptized Jews.

Of course, Jews who seek baptism in the Catholic Church are no longer required to renounce all "Jewish superstitions" (i.e., basic Jewish covenantal practices such as the dietary laws). If a Jewish Catholic wants to observe basic Jewish covenantal practices, he or she is unlikely to receive a reprimand from a parish priest for having committed a mortal sin, as would have once been the case.[11] Torah-observant Jewish Catholics no longer fear the inquisition or the threat of capital punishment—as was the fate of baptized Jews in the Iberian peninsula who secretly practiced Jewish rites during the age of Torquemada. They will be tolerated by local Catholic authorities and parishioners, though probably seen as eccentric and as victims of inadequate catechesis.

If, however, my thesis in this volume carries any weight, such a response is only a modest improvement over the earlier Catholic position. While it may be unrealistic to ask the Catholic Church to *require* baptized Jews to live a distinctively Jewish life, one could readily imagine a future in which Jewish Catholics were taught the value of such a life and *encouraged* or even *urged* to consider it for themselves. One could also imagine the Church establishing explicitly Jewish ecclesial environments that fostered Jewish forms of Catholic life and preserved Jewish identity for Jewish Catholic children and grandchildren.[12]

---

11. See Aquinas, ST I–II Q103 Article 4.

12. One model for such an environment would be the establishment of a Jewish Catholic rite. This was the aim of Fr. Elias Friedman, a Jewish Carmelite priest who founded the Association of Hebrew Catholics. "The Jewish convert should be encouraged to correct the deficiencies of his situation by common action with other converts.

In 2008 Christoph Cardinal Schönborn wrote a short article on the Christian responsibility to bear witness to Jesus among the Jewish people. He argued that such a responsibility exists, but that Christians must realize that Jews do not receive salvation in Christ in the same way as gentiles. As those already in covenant with God, Christ comes to them as the realization of their own existing identity. The same is not true for gentiles. This has implications for the way the message of salvation is proclaimed and for the way those who receive it are instructed.[13]

> God's choice of the Jews in his plan for the world—"the gifts and the calling of God are irrevocable" (Romans 11:29)—calls for particular attention on the part of the Church regarding the way in which the Gospel message is proclaimed to the Jews by her children. . . . [T]his twofold way of receiving salvation calls for a twofold way of bearing witness to the Gospel message for Christians *and a twofold catechumenal way to prepare for the same baptism in the one Jesus.*[14]

What might this Jewish catechumenate look like? Fr. Elias Friedman offers his own proposal:

> Every Jewish convert needs to be registered as an Israelite at the moment of baptism and his descendants likewise. During his catechism he should be taught the doctrine of the Church concerning the identity of the Jewish people. After all, the existence of the "election factor" places an obligation on the Church to act in consequence by encouraging converts to associate in order to build their new identity in continuity with their past.[15]

These words of Fr. Friedman were published in 1987. No substantial progress toward their actualization occurred between that date and the publication

---

Together, they would endeavor to establish a policy for their own collective future and another for relations with Jewry. The ultimate object of their associating would be to petition the official Church to set up a Hebrew community, juridically approved by the Holy See" (Friedman, *Jewish Identity*, 171).

13. Walter Cardinal Kasper agrees with this view: the "command for mission is as valid for Jews as for pagans, but it must be put into effect differently among Jews and pagans" ("Foreword," xvi). In the same volume Christian Rutishauser offers this comment on the New Testament's approach to this question: "The claim of Jesus Christ, as preached by the first believers in him after his resurrection, was truly a claim for Jews and also for other people, but in the differentiated way already seen in the Gospel of Matthew with its two different mission texts" (Rutishauser, "Old Unrevoked Covenant," 242).

14. Schönborn, "Judaism's Way to Salvation," emphasis added.

15. Friedman, *Jewish Identity*, 172.

of Cardinal Schönborn's short article in 2008. Perhaps the time has now come for the Catholic Church to officially recognize the difference between the baptism of a Jew and the baptism of a gentile, and to provide instruction and ecclesial environments suited to these differentiated identities in Christ.

The appropriateness of such a positive pastoral approach to Jewish Catholics sets in stark relief the ancient practice of suppressing Jewish identity within the Church. With a new awareness of the way this practice ran counter to the gospel itself, the Church should publicly and officially take responsibility for her past canonical order which penalized those who were seeking to fulfill their divine vocation as Jewish disciples of the Jewish Messiah. The leaders of the Catholic Church have shown a penitent spirit in their acknowledgement of past sins toward the Jewish people and the Jewish religion *outside* the Church's own boundaries. It is now time to show the same spirit in acknowledging past sins toward Jews and Judaism *within* those boundaries. Such action would make it far easier for the Church to discern the mystery of Israel through searching the depths of her own mystery.

A new public posture toward the covenantal responsibilities of Jewish Catholics would be well complemented by a formal and institution-wide engagement with the Messianic Jewish movement—or at least with those segments of the movement which are ready for such engagement. To this point very few Catholics know anything about this movement, and most of those who do treat it as merely another marginal evangelical sect. The personal, spiritual, and theological encounter which began in the autumn of 2000 with a handful of Catholics and Messianic Jews needs to expand to encompass a wide representation from both sides.[16]

In particular, Jewish Catholics could learn much from Messianic Jews about integrating Jewish life with faith in Jesus. Messianic Jews, in turn, would benefit greatly from the ecclesial consciousness of their Catholic brothers and sisters. This leads to our next set of recommendations for the coming journey.

---

16. While I write this book especially for Catholics and for Messianic Jews (whose concerns and perspectives I seek to represent), I also hope that Christians from other ecclesial settings will consider this work relevant and applicable to their varied contexts. All Christians can learn from the ecclesiology and Israelology of *Lumen Gentium*, *Nostra Aetate*, the Catholic Catechism, Pope John Paul II, Pope Benedict XVI, and Cardinal Lustiger. All Christian traditions need to come to terms with the sacraments/ordinances of baptism and the Lord's Supper and their relationship to the Jewish people. All Christian communions have Jews in their midst, and must decide whether these Jews retain a distinctive theological significance as members of genealogical-Israel.

Jewish Catholics

In the summer of 2008 I gave a lecture in Jerusalem concerning my book, *Postmissionary Messianic Judaism*. Attending that lecture was a Jewish disciple of Jesus from France, who also happened to be a Catholic priest and theologian of the Dominican Order. Fr. Antoine Levy introduced himself to me that evening, and so began a friendship and collaboration that has shown me how much Messianic Jews and Jewish Catholics can enrich one another's lives.

Such was, in fact, Fr. Antoine's intention from the beginning. He had met with Messianic Jews and Jewish Catholics in Israel, and was convinced that we needed one another. Fr. Antoine believed passionately in the enduring theological significance of Jewish identity within the Body of Christ, but he also knew from personal experience how difficult it was for Jewish Catholics to express that identity in concrete ways. On this matter, Fr. Antoine thought Jewish Catholics could learn from their Messianic Jewish brothers and sisters. On many other matters, he thought that Messianic Jews could learn from Jewish Catholics. Furthermore, if the two groups could forge an alliance around a set of common convictions, he believed that our united voice would be amplified and our message would receive a more serious hearing from both the Christian and the Jewish worlds.

Fr. Antoine enlisted the support of Fr. David Neuhaus, a Jewish Jesuit, an Israeli citizen, and the Vicar of the Latin Patriarch for Hebrew speaking Catholics in the land of Israel. Fr. David viewed Jewish identity from a different angle than Fr. Antoine, but he was no less committed to the principle that baptized Jews have a distinctive and important role to play within the Body of Christ. I, in turn, enlisted the help of some ecumenically-minded and theologically astute Messianic Jews. Together, we established the Helsinki Consultation for Jewish Continuity in the Body of Christ.[17] The Consultation also includes Jews from other Church traditions, but it originates as a joint initiative of a Jewish Catholic and a Messianic Jew.[18] I do not believe that it could have begun in any other way.

Many Jewish Catholics lack consciousness of the theological significance of their Jewish identity, and have never given a moment's thought to the question of whether or how to to live a distinctively Jewish Catholic life. One of the goals of the Helsinki Consultation—and of this book—is to make the question of Jewish identity a challenge faced by all Jewish disciples

---

17. For a set of statements produced by the Helsinki Consultation, see Appendix 2.

18. The Helsinki Consultation is also a joint initiative of the two institutions with which Fr. Antoine and I are affiliated, namely, The Studium Catolicum of Helsinki and Messianic Jewish Theological Institute.

of Jesus. Some Jewish Catholics are aware that their Jewish identity is important, but their particular understanding of Catholicism leaves no room for learning from a movement arising beyond the borders of the Catholic world. One of the goals of the Helsinki Consultation—and of this book—is to demonstrate the fact that all Jewish disciples of Jesus, regardless of their particular ecclesial commitments, need one another. As men and women united by both our faith in Jesus and our membership in his flesh-and-blood family, we have the potential to practice and model an ecumenism unlike any other.

Messianic Jews

Messianic Jews cannot avoid Catholicism with the ease that Catholics show in avoiding Messianic Judaism. We are all vividly aware of the presence of the Catholic Church and her unique role in the world. Yet, most Messianic Jews see this imposing institution as having little relevance for their own lives or for the mission of the movement to which they belong.

When encountering dedicated Roman Catholics, some Messianic Jews respond with mistrust. "These Catholics want to convert us and absorb us." (Of course, many Catholics feel the same way about Messianic Jews—but we all overlook the fears that afflict people of whom we are afraid.) Messianic Jews also often react with confusion and bewilderment at the elaborately developed terminology of Catholic religious culture. They do not understand or speak "Catholic." The Sacred Heart? The Blessed Sacrament? Days of holy obligation? The Immaculate Conception? The Assumption? Messianic Jews have learned to understand and speak "evangelical," but this new language baffles them. It seems to be a different religion altogether.

In my experience, the attitude of Messianic Jews changes drastically once they have learned of the Roman Catholic–Messianic Jewish Dialogue Group, and of the openness toward Messianic Judaism demonstrated by leading Catholic authorities. These prominent Catholics do not view Messianic Judaism as a Protestant sect, but see it instead as a divine initiative that poses a prophetic challenge to the entire Church. Accustomed to institutional marginality, Messianic Jews marvel at such a humble and spiritually receptive orientation, and wonder if perhaps their previous assumptions about Catholicism need to be re-examined.

I can only imagine what the response would be among Messianic Jews if the Roman Catholic Church publicly and officially acknowledged the grave error of suppressing Jewish practice among baptized Jews, and then encouraged all baptized Jews to find suitable ways to express their commitment to the Jewish people and their respect for the Jewish religious tradition. If the Catholic Church went further and proceeded to initiate a formal process of engagement with the Messianic Jewish movement in which the Church recognized the existence of this movement as a work of the Holy Spirit, the impact among Messianic Jews would be profound. Many would feel compelled for the first time to acknowledge the powerful work of the Holy Spirit in and through the Catholic Church, and would realize their need to add another religious language to their repertoire.

The benefits for Messianic Jews would be enormous. They would learn to see the evangelical Protestant language they inherited from their mentors as only one possible framework for interpreting and expressing the teaching and work of Jesus—in other words, as a particular tradition with strengths and weaknesses. They would prove through experience that the Christian tradition is wider than evangelicalism, and offers a rich variety of ways of articulating and living the good news. This insight into the value of the *Christian* tradition as a whole could also shed light on the significance of *Jewish* tradition, and help Messianic Jews to avoid a naïve biblicism that denigrates all practices and perspectives which lack explicit scriptural sanction. Moreover, engagement with Roman Catholicism could help Messianic Jews realize that genuine spirituality is aided rather than hindered by rigorous intellectual inquiry.

In this volume I have argued that Roman Catholicism has much to learn from Messianic Judaism. However, this volume likewise points to specific areas where Messianic Jews may learn from Roman Catholics. In particular, Messianic Jews should take note of the sacramental sensibility of the Catholic Church. Our movement has given little thought to the significance of baptism, the Eucharist, and the historical continuity of apostolic ministry. Similarly, we have given little thought to how the concept of sacrament might illumine our practice of Judaism. Our life as Messianic Jews would be deepened and enriched by the acquisition of a sacramental sensibility resembling that displayed by our Catholic brothers and sisters.

Messianic Jews should not fear that engagement with Catholicism will lead to our being subsumed under the Roman Catholic Church. Our fundamental message of bilateral ecclesiology calls for the restoration of the *ecclesia ex circumcisione* as a partner to the *ecclesia* of the nations, and we will stay faithful to that message. Furthermore, our Catholic friends-in-dialogue want us to stay faithful to that message. They realize that our prophetic vocation and our distinctive contribution would be nullified if we simply all "became Catholics." We must live a corporate Jewish life as disciples of Jesus if we are to be a blessing not only to the Church but also to the Jewish people as a whole.

The Wider Jewish World

My primary audience in this volume consists of Catholics and Messianic Jews. However, I hope that some mainstream Jews who are committed to improving Jewish–Christian relations, and to theological reflection for that purpose, will also give ear to what has been said. It would be unreasonable to expect assent from such readers for what is proposed in the preceding chapters. Jews who consider Jesus to be a non-Messiah, a failed Messiah, or a false Messiah cannot find in him the divinely-revealed meaning of Jewish existence.[19] On the other hand, it is conceivable that mainstream Jews might judge my theological proposal to be a constructive step forward in Jewish–Christian relations *for Catholics*. If my Jewish brothers and sisters can be so persuaded, I will be content.

Why should mainstream Jews respond in a positive manner to my proposal? To begin with, it offers a way for Catholics to be faithful to their Jesus-centered religious life and to affirm the election of genealogical-Israel and the essential value of Jewish practice *because of that Jesus-centered life, rather than despite it*. Jews want Christians to adopt such a theological position vis-à-vis the Jewish people and Judaism, but they should not be pleased when Christians offer it at the expense of violating the core convictions of their own tradition. Belief in the universal salvific mediation of Jesus is as central to the Catholic tradition as any other article of faith.[20] What I have proposed here is as far as orthodox Catholics could go in their affirmation of Judaism without betraying the cardinal tenets of their own Catholicism.

Second, my proposal enables Catholics to see Jesus in the midst of the Jewish people and Jewish religious life without falling prey to condescension and triumphalism. As stated above, this encounter with Jesus leads to penitence and humility, for it reveals the gaps in the tradition of the Church of the nations which need to be filled by Jewish tradition.

Third, I concur with the Jewish theologian Michael Wyschogrod in contending that a theologically consistent Christian renunciation of supersessionism demands that Christians take Jewish identity seriously both beyond *and within* the boundaries of the *ecclesia*.

---

19. On Jesus as a "failed Messiah" rather than a "false Messiah," see Greenberg, *Heaven and Earth*, 176–80.

20. This is the main point of the declaration, *Dominis Iesus: On the Unicity and Salvific Universality of Jesus Christ and the Church*. An attempt to reconcile this conviction with *Nostra Aetate*'s affirmation of the covenantal status of Judaism and the Jewish people stands at the center of the Vatican initiated project that resulted in the volume *Christ Jesus and the Jewish People Today*.

> [T]he Church claims to be the new people of God, Abraham's sons according to faith.... From the point of view of the Church, it appears, the election of Israel is thus superseded in God's plan by a new election. Does this mean that the old Israel, the sons of Abraham according to the flesh, ought to disappear from the stage of history? This is not clear. It would seem that the answer is "Yes" because the Church, with the exception perhaps of the very first decades, did not insist that Jews who embraced Christianity retain their identity as Abraham's offspring. Instead, Jews who entered the Church intermarried and their descendants quickly lost knowledge of their origins.
>
> Had the Church believed that it was God's will that the seed of Abraham not disappear from the world, she would have insisted on Jews retaining their separateness, even in the Church. ... Since the Church did not assign to the Jew who became a Christian such special status, it can be inferred that ... the Church seriously holds that its election superseded that of the old Israel.[21]

Admittedly, Wyschogrod's argument makes many Jews (and Christians) uncomfortable, since it challenges the artificial construct that defines Jewish and Christian identity as mutually exclusive alternatives.[22] Nevertheless, its logic is compelling. If Christians consider Jewish identity as theologically significant outside the *ecclesia*, then they should also consider it significant inside. The proposal set forth in this volume lays a theological foundation for this conclusion. If Wyschogrod is taken as seriously as he deserves, my proposal should be good news rather than bad news to Jewish ears.

Fourth, assuming that my mainstream Jewish audience holds a reasonable suspicion of my intentions, I must state not only what my proposal *is* but also what it is *not*: the preservation of Jewish identity within the *ecclesia* advocated here is not motivated by a Christian missionary agenda. My fundamental concern here is ecclesiological, not missiological. As in a previous book, I have argued here that Jesus is *already* at the heart of the Jewish people and the Jewish religious tradition.[23] Of course, this view implies the conviction that the Jewish people would benefit from acknowledging this hidden messianic reality, a reality that not only reveals the mystery of Jewish identity today but also provides the key to the eschatological realization of the divine promises to genealogical-Israel. However, I have no expectation

---

21. Wyschogrod, *Abraham's Promise*, 183–84. See also 202–10.

22. For extended discussion of Wyschogrod's argument, see *Modern Theology* 11.2 (1992) 163–241.

23. I refer here to my 2005 volume, *Postmissionary Messianic Judaism*.

that the restoration of such Jewish ecclesial environments will result in a massive influx of new Jewish disciples of Jesus. The Catholic Church should take this step because it expresses appropriately her own identity and because it repairs a past wrong. While the *ecclesia* as a whole must ever bear witness to Jesus as the Messiah of Israel and the Savior of the world, she would fail to grasp the profound truth of her own identity if she established Jewish ecclesial environments with the primary intent of gaining new Jewish adherents.[24]

Fifth and finally, acceptance of my proposal among Catholics would encourage their support for causes that are dear to the Jewish community—and especially to those segments of the community that remain rooted in the Jewish religious tradition. Catholics would be disposed to see the continuity of Jewish communal life as a priority deriving not only from charity to an external ally but also from loyalty to the faith that animates the Church's inner being. Catholics would look for ways to foster and strengthen Jewish religious life and would be reluctant to take initiatives that would undermine its integrity. Catholics would be more attuned to the love Jews hold for the land of Israel, and would grasp more readily the theological significance of a Jewish country in that sacred place. Catholics would be even more zealous to purge from their midst anti-Jewish prejudice and interpretations of Scripture that denigrate the Jewish religious tradition.

My theological proposal in the previous chapters has much in common with the contributions of Catholic scholars presented in *Christ Jesus and the Jewish People Today*, the recent volume resulting from a set of meetings initiated by a suggestion from the Vatican Commission for Religious Relations with the Jews. Therefore, I consider the response of one of the volume's Jewish observers to be relevant in considering how mainstream Jews should respond to my work:

> To a Jew, it is at once scandalous and also—I recognize—unavoidable for Catholic authors such as Cunningham and Pollefyt to say that "rabbinic Judaism and Jewish religious life up to today must therefore be seen as expressions of the divine Logos and Spirit" even if "Christ incarnates the divine Logos." . . . [T]he authors . . . naturally perceive religious reality in *their* "own terms." But those terms are not the terms that Jews use, though it should be observed that Jews also inevitably must seek to understand Christians through Jewish categories. . . . Still, from my perspective, this is a signal improvement. . . . The belief that Jewish covenantal life is in "unity with the glorified

---

24. It should also be obvious that I, as a Messianic Jew and a non-Catholic, have no interest in persuading Jews to become Catholics.

humanity of the Jew Jesus" . . . , while undoubtedly not at all the way that Jews understand their covenant, is much less problematic than denying validity to Jewish covenantal life at all.[25]

In responding to the theological papers of his Catholic colleagues, Adam Gregerman writes with candor, sobriety, and hopeful realism. Just as he sees these Catholic views of Judaism to be "a signal improvement" from the supersessionism of the past, so mainstream Jewish readers of my volume have good reason to view its contents as an advance rather than a retreat.

I submit that my theological proposal should be welcomed by members of the wider Jewish community as a constructive step forward in Catholic–Jewish relations, even though they cannot themselves embrace its core affirmations.

A Notre Dame Inscription

In 2011, basking in the early-summer beauty of Paris, I walked the streets of the French capital with a distinguished Jewish Catholic philosopher from Hungary. A holocaust survivor who lost both parents during the Second World War, Miklos Vetö embraced the Catholic faith as a teenager. He participated in the Hungarian revolt against the Russians in 1956, and evaded arrest by escaping to France. At the Sorbonne he met a Catholic chaplain whose background resembled his own. That new friend went on to become the Archbishop of Paris.

Miklos guided me through the streets and alleys of a Jewish neighborhood near the center of the city. While we walked, he told me the story of his life, and expressed intense admiration and affection for Cardinal Lustiger. Finally, he led me to Notre Dame de Paris, the Cathedral of the Archbishop of Paris. I followed him to the front of the sanctuary, where he stopped in front of a pillar. Inscribed on the pillar, in French, was the following epitaph.

> I was born Jewish.
> I received the name
> Of my paternal grandfather, Aaron
> Having become Christian
> By faith and by Baptism,
> I have remained Jewish
> As did the Apostles.
> I have as my patron saints
> Aaron the High Priest,

---

25. Gregerman, "A Jewish Response," 224–25.

THE TASK OF MUTUAL-INDWELLING

> Saint John the Apostle,
> Holy Mary full of grace.[26]
> Named 139th archbishop of Paris
> by His Holiness Pope John Paul II,
> I was enthroned in this Cathedral
> on 27 February 1981,
> And here I exercised my entire ministry.
> Passers-by, pray for me.
> † Aaron Jean-Marie Cardinal Lustiger
> Archbishop of Paris

The Cardinal had composed these words in 2004, three years before he passed to the next life. At his funeral his cousin recited the mourner's *Kaddish* at the portal of the Cathedral, just as the Cardinal had recited that same prayer in synagogue for his own mother.

As a young Jew who had come to believe in Jesus, I never expected that the course of my life would bring me into close contact with Cardinals of the Catholic Church. As described in chapter 2, what I never expected has in fact come to pass. However, the Cardinal who intrigues me most is this French Jew whom I never had the privilege of meeting during his lifetime. On that summer evening in Paris, his beloved city, walking and talking with Miklos Vetö, his friend, and reading the words he had written as his epitaph, I felt as though we had finally been introduced.

By faith and baptism, this man had become a disciple of Jesus. He was born a Jew and he died a Jew, as did the apostles before him. In his bold and unwavering confession of this uncomfortable truth, Cardinal Lustiger bore witness to the spiritual bond that links the "people of the new covenant" to the "stock of Abraham." May his memory be for a blessing, and may the truth to which he bore witness also be remembered, that the two communities he loved might dwell in one another in the eternal shalom of Israel's Messiah.

---

26. "When I chose my Christian names, I chose three Jewish names: Aron-Jean-Marie. It's obvious if you look at the Hebrew forms. I kept the name I had received at birth" (Lustiger, *On Christians and Jews*, 10–11).

APPENDIX 1

Nostra Aetate 4[1]

As the sacred synod searches into the mystery of the Church, it remembers the bond that spiritually ties the people of the New Covenant to Abraham's stock.

Thus the Church of Christ acknowledges that, according to God's saving design, the beginnings of her faith and her election are found already among the Patriarchs, Moses and the prophets. She professes that all who believe in Christ—Abraham's sons according to faith[2]—are included in the same Patriarch's call, and likewise that the salvation of the Church is mysteriously foreshadowed by the chosen people's exodus from the land of bondage. The Church, therefore, cannot forget that she received the revelation of the Old Testament through the people with whom God in His inexpressible mercy concluded the Ancient Covenant. Nor can she forget that she draws sustenance from the root of that well-cultivated olive tree onto which have been grafted the wild shoots, the gentiles.[3] Indeed, the Church believes that by His cross Christ, Our Peace, reconciled Jews and gentiles, making both one in Himself.[4]

The Church keeps ever in mind the words of the Apostle about his kinsmen: "theirs is the sonship and the glory and the covenants and the law and the worship and the promises; theirs are the fathers and from them is the Christ according to the flesh" (Rom 9:4–5), the Son of the Virgin Mary. She also recalls that the Apostles, the Church's main-stay and pillars, as well

---

1. Declaration on the Relation of the Church to Non-Christian Religions (*Nostra Aetate*), proclaimed by his Holiness, Pope Paul VI, on October 28, 1965. For the complete text of the document, see http://www.vatican.va/archive/hist_councils/ii_vatican_council/documents/vat-ii_decl_19651028_nostra-aetate_en.html

2. See Gal 3:7.
3. See Rom 11:17–24.
4. See Eph 2:14–16.

as most of the early disciples who proclaimed Christ's Gospel to the world, sprang from the Jewish people.

As Holy Scripture testifies, Jerusalem did not recognize the time of her visitation,[5] nor did the Jews in large number accept the Gospel; indeed not a few opposed its spreading.[6] Nevertheless, God holds the Jews most dear for the sake of their Fathers; He does not repent of the gifts He makes or of the calls He issues—such is the witness of the Apostle.[7] In company with the Prophets and the same Apostle, the Church awaits that day, known to God alone, on which all peoples will address the Lord in a single voice and "serve him shoulder to shoulder" (Zeph 3:9).[8]

Since the spiritual patrimony common to Christians and Jews is thus so great, this sacred synod wants to foster and recommend that mutual understanding and respect which is the fruit, above all, of biblical and theological studies as well as of fraternal dialogues.

True, the Jewish authorities and those who followed their lead pressed for the death of Christ;[9] still, what happened in His passion cannot be charged against all the Jews, without distinction, then alive, nor against the Jews of today. Although the Church is the new people of God, the Jews should not be presented as rejected or accursed by God, as if this followed from the Holy Scriptures. All should see to it, then, that in catechetical work or in the preaching of the word of God they do not teach anything that does not conform to the truth of the Gospel and the spirit of Christ.

Furthermore, in her rejection of every persecution against any man, the Church, mindful of the patrimony she shares with the Jews and moved not by political reasons but by the Gospel's spiritual love, decries hatred, persecutions, displays of anti-Semitism, directed against Jews at any time and by anyone.

Besides, as the Church has always held and holds now, Christ underwent His passion and death freely, because of the sins of men and out of infinite love, in order that all may reach salvation. It is, therefore, the burden of the Church's preaching to proclaim the cross of Christ as the sign of God's all-embracing love and as the fountain from which every grace flows.

---

5. See Luke 19:44.
6. See Rom 11:28.
7. See Rom 11:28–29.
8. See Isa 66:23; Ps 65:4; Rom 11:11–32.
9. See John 19:6.

APPENDIX 2

Documents of the Helsinki Consultation on Jewish Continuity in the Body of Christ[1]

2010 Helsinki Statement on the Purpose of the Consultation

We thank God for bringing us as Jews to the knowledge of Jesus the Messiah, and we express a debt of gratitude to those from the Nations who have transmitted the knowledge of Christ from generation to generation. While we seek to speak on behalf of those who share our Jewish identity and faith in Christ, we have no official mandate from our respective communities. In what follows we are expressing our own deeply held convictions.

At this unprecedented event, we have experienced the depth of our bond, and at the same time we have wrestled with the diversity of our ingrained theological and cultural constructs. In spite of Church divisions, we have come together as Jews who believe in Jesus. We hope that sharing the fruit of our common efforts will benefit our brothers and sisters in Christ. We do not aim to issue a definitive declaration, but to initiate an ongoing process of discussion.

There are many Jewish people in the Body of Christ. We believe that this reality reflects God's intention that Israel and the Nations live as mutual blessings to one another. In fact, the Church in its essence is the communion of Jews and those from the Nations called to faith in Christ.

In light of this truth, we think that the life of Jews in the Body of Christ has theological significance for that body as a whole. Their presence serves as a constant reminder to the body that its existence is rooted in the ongoing story of the people of Israel. This story resounds throughout the celebration of the liturgical life of the community. We believe that this story finds its

---

1. For these documents and additional information on the Helsinki Consultation, see http://helsinkiconsultation.squarespace.com/.

center in Israel's Messiah. We believe that Jews within the body are a living bond between the Church and the people of Israel. Accordingly, we would like to explore concrete ways in which Jewish people may live out their distinctive calling in the Body of Christ.

Finally, we wish to express to our Jewish brothers and sisters who do not share our faith in Jesus the Messiah that we consider ourselves to be part of the Jewish people and are committed to its welfare.

2011 Paris Statement on "Am Israel—Our People"

The theme of this year's consultation was *"Am Israel*—our People." As the many papers demonstrated, the identity of the Jewish People is complex, consisting of historical, familial, ethnic, cultural, and spiritual components that are all essential and inseparable. The paradoxical nature of Jewish identity challenges us to avoid reductionist interpretation and to explore further the mystery of our people.

As Jewish believers in Jesus, we affirm our identity as part of both the people of Israel and of the Body of Christ. We recognize the pain this affirmation may cause to some of those of our people who do not believe in Yeshua. We are also aware of the misunderstanding that can occur in the Church when we state that we continue to be part of the Jewish people.

Nevertheless, we believe that we are a living witness to the mysterious and invisible bond which persists between the Church and Israel. Our dual membership brings us into a unique relationship with one another, and also entails weighty responsibilities and formidable challenges. Our two communities have been separated, but belong together. We bear witness to the tragedy of their division and herald the hope of their future reconciliation.

We are exploring how this unique relationship to one another as Jewish believers in Jesus might take visible form as a wider fellowship dedicated to the service of the Jewish people and the body of Messiah.

2012 Berlin Statement on Torah

We, the members of the Helsinki Consultation, bear living witness to the recent emergence of Jewish believers in Yeshua (Jesus) who affirm their Jewish identity and acknowledge its theological significance. We are increasingly recognizing the intrinsic connection between this identity and Torah, the dynamic reality that has shaped the life of the Jewish people throughout its historical journey. We are also increasingly challenged to understand the continuing significance of the Torah encountered in the light of the gospel within the life of the Body of the Messiah.

The complex nature of Jewish existence reflects the multifaceted and paradoxical character of the Torah. Torah is both the historical revelation of God to Israel, and Israel's window to the eternity of God; once-for-all transmitted truth, and ever new process of discovery; the fashioner of human institutions, and the secret of the cosmic order; the absoluteness of the Divine Word, and the relativity of its human interpretation; the vulnerable letter of the written text, and its invulnerable spirit; defining mark of Israel's singular path and destiny, and wisdom for all nations of the earth.

From an early period, many Christians have not fully grasped the Torah's paradoxical unity. They have limited its relevance to what they deemed "moral precepts" whilst rejecting the so-called "civil" and "ceremonial" practices that are foundational to Jewish life. They have frequently viewed Torah through the dualistic lens of grace and law, contrasting faith and works, and thus overlooking the Torah's enduring value.

Recent scholarship has shed new light on the Jewish context of Yeshua and the early Yeshua-movement which challenges traditional Christian understanding of the Torah and brings renewed appreciation for its positive significance. Many now recognize that Yeshua, Sha'ul (Paul), and the other early Jewish followers of Yeshua were Torah-observant. This historical reality carries significant theological implications.

We as Jewish believers in Yeshua acknowledge the special bond that unites us with Israel's Torah. This bond with Israel's Torah witnesses in the Church to the irrevocability of God's gifts and call to Israel (Rom 11:29). For Yeshua said, "Think not that I have come to destroy the Torah, or the prophets: I have not come to destroy, but to fulfill" (Matt 5:17). We believe in the continuing validity of the Torah even as it is fulfilled in Christ. Moreover, we see Christ as the incarnate Torah, the eternal Wisdom of the Father in human flesh. He alone lived out the Torah in perfect form, and he calls his disciples to walk in his ways.

As Jewish believers in Yeshua we are in the process of working out the meaning and concrete implications of this bond that we collectively experience. We find ourselves in a variety of different ecclesial and Jewish communal contexts, and we hold different understandings and definitions of Torah observance. Some of us consider the observance of mitzvot such as Shabbat, Jewish holidays, and the dietary laws as an essential component of fidelity to Torah. Yet we all understand that our attempt to live in radical discipleship to Yeshua (in conformity to teaching such as that found in the Sermon on the Mount) is the foundational principle of Torah observance.

Furthermore, we all understand our faithfulness to Israel's Torah as a commitment to promote an awareness of the Jewish roots of the Church.

In the midst of our different approaches we have experienced through our deliberations and fellowship the dynamic and unifying power of Christ as Torah. Continuing to reflect on the Torah's role in our lives, we desire to grow together as Jews and as disciples of Yeshua. We hope these insights will resonate with other Jewish believers in Yeshua, and we invite them to join us on our journey.

2014 Ede Statement on Jewish and Christian Tradition

As Jewish disciples of Yeshua we inherit and respect both Jewish and Christian traditions. Jewish tradition, rooted in the Torah and developed through the centuries, guides the life of our people Israel and remains a vital source of our identity. Christian tradition, rooted in Christ and unfolding over time, shapes the life of the Body of Christ and is therefore an indispensable source for our shared faith and life in Messiah.

Tragically, Jewish denial of the legitimacy of Jewish belief in Yeshua as Messiah and Christian denial of the reality of his ongoing relationship with the Jewish people have been central in the development of these two traditions. We recognize the need to challenge these core denials.

Although the Messiahship of Yeshua is not recognized in Rabbinic tradition, we believe that the Spirit of Yeshua is at work within it. Conversely, Christian tradition, founded on Yeshua's teaching and redemptive work, has often propagated a distorted understanding of Christ by failing to acknowledge his Jewish identity and his ongoing relationship with the Jewish people and their tradition. As heirs of both traditions, our faith in Yeshua and our commitment to our people summon us to receive each tradition with filial deference and with the critical freedom of mature sons and daughters.

As Jews who believe in Yeshua, we represent a spectrum in our concrete expression of the Jewish and Christian traditions we have inherited. Each of us embodies in some way fidelity to the core practices of these traditions, such as Shabbat and the Lord's Supper. We experience an increasingly harmonious and natural integration of these two traditions as we search for an authentic way of being Jewish disciples of Yeshua. At the same time, the tensions that exist between Jewish and Christian traditions pulsate within us. As diverse as our practices might be (and diversity is a mark of both traditions), these practices express our shared commitment to honor the Lord Yeshua and identify as members of the Jewish people.

Therefore, we undertake to bear witness to and transmit a life of faithfulness to Torah and Messiah in which Jewish and Christian tradition are not opposed but rather mutually enriching. We believe this witness has significance for the entire people of God, both Israel and the Church. We aim to foster and embody a living community in which, even as both traditions are respected and upheld, the historical division between them is challenged and transcended.

APPENDIX 3

The Jewishness of the Apostles and Its Implications for the Apostolic Church[1]

Jean-Miguel Garrigues, O.P.

Jewish Mediation as Structural Dimension of the Church

In recent decades Catholic thought has become increasingly aware of the implications of the Jewishness of Jesus for the Christian faith. Though less attention has been given to the Jewish character of the apostolic Church and its significance, much in the New Testament suggests that the Jewish connection is as important to ecclesiology as it is to Christology. The olive tree mentioned by Paul in Romans (11:17–24) is likely the people of Israel as it is united to the Messiah in the new covenant. It is a nation whose "roots are holy" (11:16), from the patriarchs to Jesus; its "first fruits" are also holy (11:16) in the person of the "saints of Jerusalem" (Acts 9:13; Rom 15:26), that is, the Jewish believers in Jesus. Since both the roots and the first fruits are Jewish, Paul implies that the mediation of the Jews on behalf of the gentiles is structurally connected to the mediation of Jesus. According to Paul, if a gentile is incorporated by baptism as a member of Christ, he is at the same time grafted onto the cultivated olive tree "among its natural branches, so that he can benefit, together with these, from the root and the sap of the olive tree" (Rom 11:17), that is, from the fulfillment in Jesus of the promise

---

1. Reprinted from *Nova et Vetera*, English Edition, Vol. 12.1 (2013) 105–21. The reflections I propose in this paper have emerged in the course of my participation in a Catholic–Messianic Jewish dialogue group that has met annually since 2000, rotating between Jerusalem and Rome. My friendship and theological exchange with the Messianic Jewish theologian Mark Kinzer has played an important role in the development of these insights.

that Israel possesses. And so we must ask: is this mediation of the Jews who believe in Christ an enduring structural dimension of the Church, or is it simply an historical circumstance related to the origins of the Christian Church?

The first community of the Church was made up of Jews, and the gentiles who converted were associated with them. This was true both in the land of Israel and in the Diaspora, where, according to Acts, Paul always visited the synagogues first and addressed himself to his fellow Jews, some of whom were persuaded (see Rom 11:14). If those Jews had failed to believe in Jesus, there would have been no Church at all; this is a point on which all Christians agree. But was this founding role a mere chance occurrence of history, or is it really an enduring structural component in Christ's mediation with regard to his entire body? It seems difficult to construe the emphatic words of Paul concerning Jews and gentiles in the Church as a mere metaphor, intended only to describe the concrete historical situation at the beginning of the apostolic mission. We need to reread Paul's words in connection with the question we have raised.

Paul bases himself on what Christ said to him on the road to Damascus, when Paul first received his mission as an apostle: "so that the nations to whom I am sending you . . . may obtain, by faith in me (Jesus), the forgiveness of their sins, and a portion in the inheritance of those who have been sanctified" (Acts 26:17–18). Paul continually repeats the same idea in his own words: "The gentiles are admitted to the same inheritance [the one intended for the Jewish people and which Jews who believe in Christ have actually received], they [the gentiles] are members of the same body" (Eph 3:6). The gentiles—who formerly were only "strangers and sojourners" (Eph 2:19), separated from Christ (without a Messiah), excluded from the commonwealth of Israel, strangers to the covenants of the promise" (Eph 2:12)—have now become in Christ "fellow citizens with the saints, members of the household of God" (Eph 2:19). Indeed, "the Father has qualified [them] to share in the inheritance of the saints" (Col 1:12). For the Body of Christ that is the Church, the Jewish believers in Christ are the heirs of the promises made by God to Israel. And thus, by the fact of their election they have a role in communicating God's blessing in Christ to the gentiles who convert. In the Church, they constitute a living witness to the way in which "Christ became a minister to the circumcised, in order to show God's truthfulness" (Rom 15:8); thanks to this faithfulness of the Lord towards them (the people of Israel), "the nations glorify God for his mercy" (Rom 15:9). And thus, in Paul's view the double vocation of Jews and gentiles remains at the very center of the unique Body of Christ. The duality between Jews and gentiles is not erased in the unity of the Church: Christ wants to "create

APPENDIX 3

both of them in himself as one New Man" (Eph 2:15) and to "reconcile *both* of them in one body" (Eph 2:16); and, above all, "through him we *both* have access in one Spirit to the Father" (Eph 2:18).

It appears that Paul considers this association of Jewish believers in Christ with Christ's mediation to be a structuring dimension of the Church. Indeed, he does say that in virtue of baptism "*you are all* sons of God through faith in Christ Jesus; for as many of you as were baptized into Christ have put on Christ. There is neither Jew nor Greek, . . . neither male nor female . . . for you are all one in Christ Jesus" (Gal 3:26-28). However, this holds true only with regard to the baptismal gift of grace by faith, which brings salvation: "for there is no distinction between Jew and Greek: all have the same Lord, who bestows the riches (of his grace) upon all who call upon him" (Rom 10:12; see Rom 3:22-24). By the same token, there is no longer "either male or female" with regard to the baptismal priesthood. However, there still remains a distinction between the vocations, missions, and ministries of men and women, a distinction that the Catholic Church steadfastly guards. Similarly, the distinction between the vocations and missions of Jew and gentile continues to exist in the Church.

To repeat, for Paul this distinction of ecclesial vocations and missions appears to play a structural role. Paul employs an inclusive "we" when referring to salvation, which is common to Jewish and gentile believers. Thus, when evoking baptismal typology in his letter to the Corinthian Church, which consisted mainly of gentiles, Paul indicates that they too have been included in Israel by Christ: "*Our* fathers were all under the cloud; and all passed through the sea" (1 Cor 10:1). On the other hand, when he explains the forms of mediation involved in the realization of God's plan of salvation, he distinguishes between "we [the Jews]" and "the rest of you [the gentiles]" (Eph 1:11-13). Later in this same epistle, he says to the converted gentiles, "Remember that at one time, you, the gentiles . . ." (Eph 2:11). And this distinction holds true not only for the past, the era preceding their entry into the Church. It continues to exist in the present life of the Christian community: "Now I am speaking to you gentiles" (Rom 11:13).

Today the Catholic Church encounters a new (yet old) development: Messianic Jews who share with us the New Testament faith in Jesus as the accomplishment of God's promises. These contemporary Jewish believers in Jesus are confronting the Church of Christ with the following decisive question: is the mediation exercised by the Jews at the birth of the Church a mere historical accident, or does it have a deeper significance? Does it represent an enduring structural element for the Church? At first glance, this mediating function would seem to have disappeared with the apostolic or sub-apostolic generation, when the Judeo-Christian community of Jerusalem held the role of the Mother Church.

Modern historical studies provide a resource for responding to this important question.[2] They have shown the great extent to which the sacramental and liturgical rites and the priestly institutions of the sub-apostolic Church—the very "frühkatholischen" elements that would mark her from the second century onwards as the "Catholic Church"—received the structural imprint of Judeo-Christian models which can come only from the original apostolic community. Unfortunately, with the influx of gentiles into the Church, the Judeo-Christians became marginalized and gradually disappeared. In light of the emergence of the Messianic Jewish movement in the twentieth century, we should ask ourselves whether this treasure of Christian community and spiritual life which goes back to the apostles, and which the Catholic Church guards as the apple of her eye, can really yield its full meaning and fruit for the benefit of all Christians without being assumed by the Jews who believe in Jesus as the accomplishment of the messianic promises carried by the people of Israel.

On an even deeper level, we need to ask ourselves whether the multitude of believers coming from the nations can fully express its own baptismal incorporation into the Messiah of Israel, without taking root, through Christ-believing Jews, in the people of Israel, which God preserves as the trustee of the promise for its final fulfillment in view of the glorious coming of the Messiah (Rom 11:15). "If you want to boast, remember that it is not you that support the root, but the root that supports you" (Rom 11:18). The Catholic Church can only respond to these questions with the assistance of the Holy Spirit, whose mission is to "introduce [the Church] into the entire truth" (John 16:13), and to glorify Christ in her, through fellowship among a diversity of members.[3]

---

2. For example, Jean Daniélou, *The Theology of Jewish Christianity*, trans. John A. Baker (London: Darton, Longman & Todd, 1964); Louis Bouyer, *Eucharist*, trans. Charles Underhill Quinn (South Bend, IN: University of Notre Dame Press, 1968); Carmine Di Sante, *Jewish Prayer: The Origins of the Christian Liturgy* (New York: Paulist, 1991).

3. Up to this point the text has mainly been taken and translated from my book *Le Saint-Esprit sceau de la Trinité: le Filioque et l'originalité trinitaire de l'Esprit dans sa personne et dans sa mission*, coll. «Cogitatio fidei» n°276, (Paris: Cerf, 2011), 125–28 and 142–45.

APPENDIX 3

The Jewishness of the Apostles

As noted above, the Catholic Church has made a considerable effort in recent decades to account for the Jewishness of Jesus in its Christological teaching. Nothing comparable has yet been undertaken to integrate the Jewishness of the apostles of Christ, and of the Mother Church of Jerusalem, into Catholic ecclesiology. Greater attention to these factors might well have major consequences for both the theory and the practice of the apostolic ministry in the Church.

All the apostles were Jews. This holds true in the first place for the "twelve apostles" (Matt 10:2). These are most often designated as the collective body of "the Twelve" (Mark 3:14)—an expression employed even for the period when the group included only eleven members (1 Cor 15:5). They are also sometimes called simply "*the* apostles" (Luke 6:13) par excellence. But in addition, there is the larger group of "*all* the apostles," as St. Paul calls them (1 Cor 15:17), and of which he himself is the "last" (1 Cor 15:7). This group too is entirely made up of Jews. It is composed of those to whom the risen Christ appeared and whom he himself sent to be his witnesses (see 1 Cor 9:1; Rom 1:1, 5; Gal 1:16). James, "the Lord's brother" (Gal 1:19), must be counted among these, because Christ appeared to him personally (1 Cor 15:7). In this larger group of apostles we also find Barnabas (see Acts 14:14) who is "a Levite from Cyprus" (Acts 4:36) and Andronicus and Junias, kinsmen of Paul (Rom 16:7). These "apostles," like the Twelve, received their mission directly from Christ, without having to submit to any ordination "through man" (see Gal 1:1), as will later be the case, for example, with Timothy (see 1 Tim 4:14; 2 Tim 1:6). This larger group of apostles was undoubtedly quite sizable, since Paul speaks of an appearance of the risen Christ to "five hundred brethren at once" (1 Cor 15:6).

Christ calls the apostles to be witnesses of his resurrection according to the order that he himself established before his death. The most primitive *kerygma* includes Peter and the Twelve as foundational to the testimony concerning the resurrection (see 1 Cor 15: 5). Only those who were called to associate with Jesus from the beginning of his ministry until his death can validly testify that it is the same Jesus who is now risen from the dead (see John 15:27). This is why the ministry of "all the apostles" is based on the testimony of the Twelve (see Acts 13:31), who are the "foundations" (Rev 21:1). Paul himself receives from them the *kerygma* (see 1 Cor 15:3) as well as Baptism and the Eucharist; before embarking upon his apostolic mission, he goes up to Jerusalem "to see Peter, spending fifteen days with him" (Gal 1:18).

THE JEWISHNESS OF THE APOSTLES

Christ instituted the college of the twelve apostles in order to correspond to the twelve tribes of Israel. They are the leaders of the people of Israel in its new messianic and eschatological era. In Matthew, the formula "The names of the Twelve are..." (Matt 10:2) is reminiscent of the language employed by the books of Kings in describing the twelve prefects appointed by Solomon at the head of all the people (see 1 Kgs 4:7–8). This status of the Twelve is inseparably historical and eschatological, extending over the entire time span of the new covenant inaugurated by the resurrection of Christ and including the last judgment, which will establish the kingdom of future glory: "In the new world (παλιγγενεσίᾳ), when the Son of Man will sit on his glorious throne, you also shall sit you on twelve thrones, judging the twelve tribes of Israel" (Matt 19:28). In Hebrew the verb "to judge" (*shafat*) means both to rule and to exercise judgment. The Greek equivalent (*krino*) is employed here in Matthew to refer both to the time of history during which the Eucharist is celebrated (i.e., "until he comes" [1 Cor 11:26]), and to the eschaton when God will be "all in all" (1 Cor 15:28). When he instituted the Eucharist, Jesus said to the Twelve: "It is you who have been continually with me in my trials; and I assign to you the kingdom as my Father has assigned it to me, that you may eat and drink at my table in my kingdom, and sit on thrones judging the twelve tribes of Israel" (Luke 22:28–29).

The book of Daniel prophesied that in the messianic age "the saints would possess the kingdom" (Dan 7:22) and "thrones would be placed" (Dan 7:9) so that the saints could exercise judgment with the Son of Man. We see this fulfilled in the Apocalypse: "I saw thrones and seated upon them were those to whom judgment was entrusted" (Rev 20:4). In the eschatological Jerusalem the Twelve exercise judgment because the city has "twelve foundations, and on them are the names of the twelve apostles of the Lamb" (Rev 21:14). The wall of Jerusalem, of which the Twelve are the foundations, is endowed "with twelve gates, and at the gates twelve angels, and on the gates the names of the twelve tribes of the children of Israel" (Rev 21:12). The twelve ensure the messianic structure of the people of Israel up to and into the age to come. This people is visibly represented in the Apocalypse by those who are chosen from "all the tribes of the sons of Israel" (Rev 7:4). The expression is too precise to apply to a "spiritual Israel." It obliges us to see, in the immediately subsequent vision of a "great multitude that no one could count, from every nation, tribe, people, and language" (Rev 7:9), the multitude of the gentiles, who are considered as distinct, even in the age to come, from the twelve tribes of the eschatological Israel.

The Twelve are destined by Christ to judge the twelve tribes of Israel in the world to come. In the meantime, they already have a permanent mission to govern the people of Israel as embodied in its messianic *kahal* (assembly or Church). The faithful from the gentiles are joined to this *kahal*, with its Jewish roots in the mother community of Jerusalem. On the Apostolic Sees, from which the Twelve judge the twelve tribes of the messianic Israel, bishops (most often gentiles) have succeeded one another throughout the history of the Church. But these bishops represent the twelve apostles in their ministry, because it is always through them that Christ "keeps [his flock] under his constant protection through the apostles, guiding it still through these same pastors who continue his work today."[4] The apostolic ministry of the Church is indeed Jewish in its historical origin, and this is not a purely contingent fact of history, but instead a stable disposition established by divine providence and by the will of Christ in an eschatological perspective.

What may seem at first sight paradoxical is that these Jewish apostles, whose ministry is based on the twelve tribes of Israel, are all sent by Christ to the gentiles: "All power is given unto me in heaven and on earth. Go therefore and make disciples from all nations, baptizing them in the name of the Father, Son, and Holy Spirit. And behold, I am with you until the end of the world" (Matt 28:18–20). We find the same universal mission in the final chapter of the Gospel of Mark: "Go into all the world and preach the gospel to the whole creation" (Mark 16:15). Only Luke notes that the preaching of the gospel to all nations requires a "beginning at Jerusalem" (Luke 24:47). This serves as a reminder to the gentiles that they must not cut themselves off from the Mother Church, the Church of the eyewitnesses of Jesus and of Pentecost, which is attached directly to the Jewish people. The opening up of the messianic Jewish *kahal* to the gentiles is clearly revealed through the interdependence of the three key apostolic figures of the early Church: Peter (inseparable from John and from the college of the Twelve), Paul, and James.

Peter and Paul as Jewish Apostles

Peter, the rock upon which Christ founded the Church (Matt 16:18) and the one who loved the Lord Jesus "more than the others" (John 21:15), is the pastor of the entire flock (see John 21:15–17). It is he who is responsible for "strengthening his brethren" (Luke 22:32). Even before the coming of the Holy Spirit, Peter took the initiative to complete the college of the Twelve

---

4. *Catechism of the Catholic Church*, no. 1575 quoting the Preface of the Apostles of the Roman liturgy. The *Catechism* further states: "The college of bishops . . . makes the college of the Twelve an ever-present and ever-active reality until Christ's return" (no. 1577).

by presiding over the election of Matthias (Acts 1:15). Peter is the one who speaks to the people of Israel on behalf of the Twelve. He does this alone at Pentecost (Acts 2:14), and acts together with John during the first miraculous healing (Acts 3:11–12). He is the one who, with John (Acts 4:7–13) and the apostles (Acts 5:27–32), speaks twice on behalf of the apostolic Church before the Sanhedrin. His universal ministry is also evident in the initiative he takes at the home of Cornelius, where, in obedience to the Holy Spirit, he "ordered that [the gentile believers]" be baptized (Acts 10:48). Later he departs from Jerusalem, leaving James to preside over the Church of this city (see Acts 12:17). He goes first to Antioch (see Gal 2:11), then to Rome (see 1 Pet 5:13).

The geographical itinerary of Peter's apostolic mission between Jerusalem and Rome expresses the eschatological extension of the nation that was desired by the risen Christ. However, this universal ministry, which is ultimately established in Rome, the first world metropolis, is exercised by Peter as "the apostle to the circumcised" (Gal 2:8). His point of departure and of reference is the singularity of the divine election of the Jewish people. His first epistle is addressed "to the foreigners [or exiles] in the Diaspora: Pontus, Galatia, Cappadocia, Asia, and Bithynia" (1 Pet 1:1). From Rome, Peter is writing either to the Jewish believers of the Diaspora who reside in these nations, or more probably to all "Christians" (1 Pet 4:16) who in this world are "strangers and sojourners" (1 Pet 2:11 citing Gen 23:4 and Ps 39:13). In any event, it is clear that he is addressing his recipients as a Diaspora of the people of Israel, thus implicitly referring them to Jerusalem. Passing from Jerusalem to Rome, Peter does not enact a simple geographic transfer of the Church, in the way that historians would later speak of a *translatio imperii* by Charlemagne. Peter accomplishes his apostolic mission received from Christ, a mission that goes from Jerusalem to the nations, not in order to start a "gentile Church," replacing the people of Israel presumed to have been rejected by God, but instead to gather the nations together and, at the right time, to integrate them into Israel.

Paul, who is the "last" to whom the risen Christ appeared (1 Cor 15:8), describes himself as "the least of the apostles" (1 Cor 15:9). He is not a member of the college of the Twelve, in which Peter has John as his usual companion, both before and after Pentecost. Nevertheless, Paul has received from Christ a mission to the gentiles, parallel to the mission Peter has received to the Jews, and this puts them is a symmetrical position (Gal 2:7–9). This explains why tradition has come to honor them together as the two "princes of the apostles." When Paul describes his mission in the Letter to the Galatians, he employs the same terms found in St. Mathew's episode of Peter's confession at Caesarea: "When [God] was pleased to *reveal* his *Son* in me" (Gal 1:15-16) is parallel to the Gospel's "You are the Christ, the *Son of the living God*. . . . This has been *revealed* to you by my Father who is in heaven" (Matt 16:17). It is even more striking to note the parallel between St. Paul's expression, "without consulting flesh and blood" (Gal 1:16), and Jesus' words in the Gospel, "this revelation came to you not from flesh and blood" (Matt 16:17).

Even though for Paul the Twelve were "apostles before me" (Gal 1:17), he does not go to Jerusalem to meet them immediately after his encounter with the risen Christ. However, before embarking on his apostolic mission to the gentiles (Gal 1:18-21), he does go up to Jerusalem "to visit Cephas and stay with him fifteen days" (Gal 1:18). Paul's recognition of the apostolic authority of Peter and, at the same time, his awareness of the symmetry of their missions stand out simultaneously in the confrontation that later occurs between the two apostles at Antioch. Paul "opposed [Peter] to his face" because, the latter "stood self-condemned" (Gal 2:11), having concealed the fact that up until then he had been in the habit of "eating with the gentiles" (Gal 2:12). Paul openly opposes him in this, because Peter's authority is such that "other Jews [i.e., Jewish believers in Christ] followed him and began likewise to dissimulate, to the point that even Barnabas was carried away by their dissimulation" (Gal 2:13). In Paul's eyes, Peter "stood self-condemned" in hiding "for fear of those from the Circumcision" (Gal 2:12) the true conviction of his faith, which he had expressed openly up until then by "living like a gentile and not like a Jew (ἐθνικῶς καὶ οὐχὶ Ἰουδαϊκῶς)" (Gal 2:14) and by eating together with the gentile believers.[5] This dissimulation led his fellow Christ-believing Jews astray, and seemed to "compel the gentile converts to adopt Jewish practices," contrary to the decisions of the apostolic assembly of Jerusalem (see Acts 15:28-29) and to Peter's own speech on that occasion (see Acts 15:7-11).

Paul further pursues the parallel between himself and the "apostle to the circumcised" (Gal 2:8) by seeking to go to Rome, where Peter had probably already established himself along with his two longtime disciples Silvanus and Mark (1 Pet 5:12-13). Paul does this despite the fact the he usually "makes it his ambition to limit [his] apostolate to the regions where the name of Christ has not been invoked, in order not to build on the foundations laid by others" (Rom 15:20, see 2 Cor 10:15-16). At first glance it might appear that Paul considers this visit to Rome as a mere stopover on a mission to Spain (see Rom 15:24, 28; Acts 19:21). But the manner in which Christ reveals to Paul the meaning of his upcoming journey to Rome (Acts

---

5. Contrast this with Peter's exclamation when God asks him to share the table of the gentile Cornelius: "Oh no, Lord! Because I have never eaten anything profane or unclean" (Acts 10:14).

23) helps us understand the reason why both of these apostles must come to the capital of the Roman Empire. In the course of a dream that Paul has while a prisoner in Jerusalem, Jesus says to him: "Courage! Just as you have testified about me in Jerusalem, so must you testify in Rome" (Acts 23:11). There is a striking correlation here ("just as . . . so") between Rome and Jerusalem, as well as between the mission that Christ assigns to Paul "in Rome as in Jerusalem"—a mission requiring that Paul "testify about him." In this context, the expression seems to imply that there will be persecution. This is why the book of Acts, which begins in Jerusalem, ends with the arrival of Paul in Rome.

It is therefore no accident that Peter and Paul, the "princes of the apostles," bore witness to Christ together through the martyrdom they endured under Nero.[6] In the second century, Irenaeus of Lyons refers to "the very great, very ancient and universally known Church, which the two most glorious apostles, Peter and Paul, founded in Rome."[7] The Church of Rome, as the Church marked forever in blood by the *charisma* of Peter and Paul, is *the* Apostolic See not merely because it is the Church of the capital of the Roman Empire. It has this status because this same empire, as it already manifests itself under Caligula and Nero, is the first draft of a false pagan universality or an antichristic Babylon, which represents its historical and eschatological struggle among the nations, as Peter in his first epistle (5:13) and the Apocalypse (chapters 17 and 18) indicate. This Church, through the gospel preaching and the martyrdom of Peter and Paul, received the gift of being not only the Church whose bishop exercises the ministry of Peter, the universal pastor,[8] but also the Church of Peter and Paul, linking together the two modalities of their respective apostolic missions—the mission to the Jews, who represent the "first fruits" (Rom 11:16) of the Church rooted in Israel, and the mission to the multitude of nations, to whom Christ sent the apostles in order to evangelize them.

---

6. Before the end of first century, Clement of Rome already attests to this fact in his *Letter to the Corinthians* (5:3–5).

7. Irenaeus, *Adversus haereses*, III,3,2.

8. "For with this Church, by reason of her pre-eminence, the universal Church, that is, the faithful everywhere, must necessarily be in accord, since she is that Church in which, for the benefit of people everywhere, the Tradition which comes from the Apostles has always been preserved" (ibid.).

APPENDIX 3

James as Jewish Apostle

This presentation of the interaction between the two main apostles would be incomplete without reference to a third apostle, James, "the brother of the Lord" (Gal 1:19; see Mark 6:3). Whereas in the first eleven chapters of the Acts of the Apostles the Twelve are omnipresent and Peter takes all pastoral initiatives, in chapter 12 a shift occurs in the narrative. When Peter returns after being miraculously delivered from his third arrest, he asks that "James and the brethren" be informed of what has occurred (Acts 12:17). The same verse concludes enigmatically: "Then he departed and went to another place." Although Peter had previously been the book's main protagonist, he now fades into the background, leaving James as the head of the Church of Jerusalem. Paul mentions that on the first trip he made to Jerusalem as a believer in Christ he had already seen James, but insists that he had come "to visit Peter and remain with him fifteen days" (Gal 1:18–19). Relating his second visit to Jerusalem, fourteen years later, Paul says that James extended to him his hand as a sign of communion. This time James is mentioned alongside Peter and John, as an "acknowledged pillar of the Church" (Gal 2:9).

The full importance of James appears at the Council of Jerusalem (see Acts 15:7–29). Peter speaks first to recall his initiative, in obedience to the Holy Spirit, of receiving the gentiles into the Church: "In the early days, God chose me from among you, so that I should be the one through whom the gentiles would hear the message of the good news and become believers" (Acts 15:7). The silence that follows signifies the adherence of the entire assembly, something that the Occidental text of Acts recounts in this way: "As the elders gave their assent to what Peter had said, the whole assembly fell silent" (Acts 15:12, Syriac). Paul then proceeds to describe, together with Barnabas, their common mission to the gentiles. James is the last to speak, and his words put an end to the debate: "I myself judge . . ." (Acts 15:19).

If the words of James at this council were so decisive, it may be due in part to the fact that the original challenge which gave rise to the meeting had came from "some people in the entourage of James" (Gal 2:12). In the book of Acts these are referred to as "some people from the party of the Pharisees" (Acts 15:5). More importantly, James appears here as the one who ensures that the opening to the gentiles is not acquired at the price of making the Church cease to belong to the people of Israel. James presents the entry of the gentiles into the apostolic Church as their integration into the people of Israel, raised up once again by the Messiah according to the prophetic promise:

> Simon [Peter] has described how, early on, God has taken care to draw from the gentiles a people dedicated to his name. This is consistent with the words of the prophets, as it is written: "After this I will return and I will raise up the tabernacle of David which has fallen; I will raise up its ruins, and I will set it up so that the rest of men may seek the Lord, all the gentiles, upon whom my name is invoked, says the Lord, who does these things" [Amos 9:11–12]. (Acts 15:13–17)

Acts quotes this passage of the prophet Amos according to the Septuagint, which differs from the Masoretic version. Instead of "that other men may seek the Lord," the Masoretic text reads "so that they [i.e., those of the tabernacle of David] may possess the remnant of Edom." Recent exegetical research opens up the possibility that the Septuagint version quoted by Acts may be closer to the meaning of the original Hebrew.[9]

Whatever the precise meaning of the text quoted from Amos, it is clear that in this speech James appears as the apostle who ensures that the reception of the gentiles into the Church comes about according to the fulfillment of the promises to Israel, that is, "according to the Scriptures." His concerns contrast with the attitude of Peter, who in his speech emphasizes two very different points. First, Peter insists upon the impossibility of perfectly observing the Law: "Why do you tempt God now by trying to impose upon these disciples [the gentiles] a yoke which neither our fathers nor we ourselves have had the strength to bear?" (Acts 15:10). This is exactly the same reasoning that Paul will use (see Gal 3:10; 6:13). Then, at the end of his discourse, Peter advances still another Pauline argument: "Indeed, it is through the grace of the Lord Jesus that we believe in order to be saved, just like them" (Acts 15:11; see Gal 2:15–16).

What is most significant in the apostolic interaction displayed in the Council of Jerusalem is that Peter, Paul, and James finally agree on three essential points concerning the reception of the gentiles into the Church:

1. It is by grace and faith in Jesus the Messiah, and not by the observance of the Law, that both Jews and gentiles are saved.

2. The conversion of the gentiles to Christ is the work of the Lord, who broadens the notion of what it means to belong to the people of God, a people which, according to the promises of the prophets, has now reached its messianic phase. Nevertheless, this broadening is accomplished through the integration of the gentiles, and it in no way implies

---

9. Cf. Michael A. Braun, "James' Use of Amos at the Jerusalem Council: Steps toward a Possible Solution of the Textual and Theological Problems." *Journal of the Evangelical Theological Society* 20.2 (1977) 113–21.

a separation of Christ's disciples from the people of Israel, to whom the Jewish believers in Christ still belong.

3. It does not mean that the distinction between Jew and gentile is abolished by faith in Christ. The gentiles remain gentiles; they do not become Jews, as did proselytes, and so they are not required to observe the Mosaic Law. This implies, in turn, that the Jews who believe in Jesus remain Jews, and are required as such to substantially fulfill the Law.

The first point, which will be of capital importance to Paul, is set forth by Peter, and it is not in any way contradicted by James. On the other hand, Peter and Paul symmetrically accept the way in which James shows how he sees the integration of gentiles into the people of Israel, maintaining the distinction between Jews and gentiles.

Who is this James, who guarantees that the apostolic Church belongs to the people of Israel that is now called to enter into the messianic age? He is certainly an "apostle" (Gal 1:19), in the broader sense of the term, but probably not one of the Twelve. At the same time, he is "the Lord's brother" (Gal 1:19), that is, a close relative of Jesus according to the flesh. The "brothers of Jesus" appear in the Gospels as an extended family group or clan. At the beginning of Jesus' public ministry, they deem that he had lost his mind (see Mark 3:21). Then, upon seeing the miracles he accomplished in Galilee, their behavior towards him tends to be more ambiguous:

> Now the Jewish feast of tents was near. So his brothers said to him: "Leave here and go to Judea, that your disciples may see the works that you are doing. For no man works in secret if he seeks to be known openly. If you do these things, show yourself to the world." Indeed, not even his brothers believed in him. (John 7:1–4)

What happened later on? Some became disciples of their relative. Scripture attests that the risen Lord Jesus appeared personally to James (1 Cor 15:7), and that the brothers of Jesus were present in the Upper Room at Pentecost. The Holy Spirit descended upon the witnesses of the entire life of Jesus: alongside the witnesses of Jesus' public ministry (see Acts 1:21–22), the twelve apostles and the holy women, we find the group of "his brothers," witnesses of his hidden life at Nazareth, with Mary, the Lord's mother (Acts 1:14), who serves as the link between the two groups.

As the "brother of the Lord," James is related to Jesus according to the flesh. This genealogical connection between James and Israel's Messiah, a connection reinforced by the Spirit of Pentecost, is a precious link binding the apostolic Church to the Jewish people, to whom Jesus came as the Messiah: "[son of God] from the seed of David according to the flesh" (Rom 1:3). By his very being James is a living reminder of the Jewishness of Jesus, as well as a living link with "Israel according to the flesh" (1 Cor 10:18), a nation that is still called to enter into the messianic fulfillment of the promises (see Rom 9:4–5). This fleshly and genealogical sacramentality, proper to the Jewish people, accounts for the fact that the Church of Jerusalem had as its first hierarchical leaders several "brothers of the Lord." According to Hegesippus, the choice of Simeon—another "brother of Jesus"—to succeed James, was decided by a council of the apostles and relatives of the Savior.

James connects the apostolic Church to the people of Israel, not only through his flesh, but also through his deep spiritual continuity with the tradition of Jewish wisdom. James is surrounded (Gal 2:12) by "members of the party of the Pharisees who had become believers" (Acts 15:5). These are the same people who ask Peter for an explanation, upon his return from the home of Cornelius: "Why have you joined the uncircumcised, and why did you eat with them?" (Acts 11:3). Later these men will enjoin the brothers who have come from the gentiles "to be circumcised and to keep the Law of Moses" (Acts 15:1, 5). On his last journey to Jerusalem, Paul went "to see James, with whom the elders were assembled" (Acts 21:18). It is now James alone, assisted by the presbyters, who governs the Church of Jerusalem. Those who are assembled on this occasion say to Paul: "You see, brother, how many thousands of Jews have embraced the faith and they are all zealous partisans of the Law!" (Acts 21:20). Hegesippus reports that James was revered as Jacob the Just by the Jews of Jerusalem, believers and non-believers in Christ alike, until he was put to death upon the order of the high priest in AD 62. It is even possible that our James is identical to a Jacob of that same period, echoes of whose wisdom are found in the *Talmud*.

Of course, the Epistle of James is also attributed to him. In this letter, the apostle addresses himself to the "twelve tribes in the Diaspora" (Jas 1:1), that is, to the Jewish Christ-believers scattered throughout the pagan nations. The letter reflects the best of the spirituality of the Pharisees, insisting on the importance of good works, without which faith is dead. It seems implicitly to engage in a discussion with the letter of Paul to the Galatians, commenting on the same biblical texts concerning Abraham, and the relation between faith and works. This letter of James could well be inserted between the letters of Paul to the Galatians and to the Romans, since in the second of these Paul expresses his ideas with greater nuance. The apparent opposition between James and Paul is more terminological than real. We need to remember that when Paul speaks of "works," he is spontaneously thinking of "dead works," those accomplished without love, and which therefore serve no purpose. And when he speaks of faith, he has in mind "living faith" or "faith working through love" (Gal 5:6). By contrast, when James speaks of faith, he spontaneously thinks of "dead faith," which is that of the demons; and when he speaks of works, he always has in mind "living works," which proceed from the grace of God through charity.

The final meeting in Jerusalem between Paul and James enables us to grasp the essence of their apostolic interaction, as we have sought to describe it. As Paul declared before a Jewish audience, he never denied his Jewishness, nor did he forgo any of the Mosaic observances, as long as these did not interfere with his mission to the gentiles. One demonstration of this is the Nazirite vow that he made (or perhaps completed) at Cenchreae (Acts 18:18). James knows that Paul "has also behaved as an observer of the law" (Acts 21:24). To cut short the reproaches of those who accuse him of "teaching the Jews who live among the gentiles to forsake Moses" (Acts 21:21), James advises Paul to accomplish his vow of purification publicly, in the temple, alongside four Jewish believers in Christ who are also under a vow (see Acts 21:23-24). And Paul does as he is told by James.

To understand this docility of Paul towards James, we need to recall the motive behind Paul's last visit to Jerusalem: the collection for "the saints" which he took up among the gentiles whom he had converted to the Lord. The faithful in Jerusalem are "saints" in a very special sense of the term: they have put all their property in common, and share everything according to individual needs (see Acts 2:43-45). This was a way of showing their abandonment to providence and, in fact, very soon, they fell "into poverty" (Rom 15:26) and needed to be rescued (see Acts 11:29-30). During his earlier visit with Peter, John, and James in Jerusalem, Paul had been asked to "remember the poor" of Jerusalem (Gal 2:10). And, he informs the Galatians, "that is precisely what I have been eager to do."

More profoundly, this collection indicates that the gentile Churches are connected to the Mother Church of Jerusalem and, through her, to the people of Israel. When he defends himself before the governor Felix and the high priest Ananias, who has come to accuse him, Paul expresses this idea in terms that are borrowed from the vocabulary of Jewish ritual: "I came to bring alms to my nation and to present offerings. As I was doing this, they found me purified in the temple" (Acts 24:17-18). The same priestly vocabulary is found in the letters of Paul when he explains the reason for the collection: "I am going to Jerusalem to minister to the saints. . . . [The gentiles] owe this to them: for if they have participated in their spiritual blessings, they must in turn serve them with their worldly goods" (Rom 15:25-27). In Paul's eyes, this is not only a debt of charity on the part of gentile believers towards the Church of Jerusalem; it is also for the gentiles a religious duty. "Because the rendering of this service not only supplies the needs of the saints, it is also a rich source of abundant thanksgiving to God. This service proves to them who you really are, so that they may glorify God for your obedience in the profession of the gospel of Christ and for the generosity of your communion with them and everyone" (2 Cor 9:12–13). Through the offering that he brings to James and to the Mother Church of Jerusalem, Paul intends to signify the spiritual connection of the gentiles to the people of Israel, from whom (in the person of Christ) and by whom (in the persons of the apostles) their salvation has come.

The carnal and genealogical ties that linked James to Christ were not transmitted beyond the first Jewish bishops of the Church of Jerusalem. On the other hand, the apostolic succession continued to be transmitted sacramentally through the bishops (for the most part gentiles) upon the seats of the apostles, to whom Jesus had promised: "Behold, I am with you all the days, unto the end of the age" (Matt 28:20). However, the apostles are, and remain forever, Jews, called by Christ to "judge the twelve tribes of Israel." Furthermore, the fundamental genealogical succession, which belongs to the Jewish people, continues to thrive on the basis of a divine election that is "irrevocable" (Rom 11:29), in the same way that the sacramental transmission of apostolic succession is based on a gift of God that is irrevocable. Any future encounter (in whatever form) reuniting these two distinctive types of succession in the Church must necessarily reflect the interaction among the apostles that we have attempted to point out in the pages of the New Testament. The universal primacy represented by Peter (in a Church confronted more and more by "the gates of hell [which, however,] will not prevail against her" [Matt 16:18]) can exercise its *charisma* in an entirely fruitful manner only if it is supported by the *charismata* of the two other apostolic pillars: that of Paul, for the universality of the mission, but also that of James, which guarantees the roots of the Church in the Jewish people. Indeed, when Peter inaugurated the mission to the gentiles, a mission Paul would later develop, he did so from his Jewish roots as "apostle to the circumcised" (Gal 2:8), roots for which James and the Mother Church of Jerusalem continue to serve as the guarantee. The *charisma* of James, acting through the Jews who believe in Christ while maintaining their Jewish identity, is a physical and spiritual reminder that the Church originally came from Jerusalem and from Israel through Jewish apostles. It also reminds the Church that she is and always will be based on the apostles and is eschatologically pointed by them towards the earthly Jerusalem, where Jesus "will come in the same way as he went" (Acts 1:11).

APPENDIX 3

Conclusion

Paul stands for the pilgrim Church sojourning in this world with her universal mission to all nations. To Peter was entrusted the ministry of receiving (see John 20:17) these "other sheep [i.e., gentiles] that are not of this fold" (John 10:16) into the catholic fullness of the "one flock" (John 10:16), whose unique shepherd is Christ. It is Peter in his role as "apostle to the circumcised" (Gal 2:8), who gathers this one flock inasmuch as it constitutes the messianic fullness of Israel in its "remnant" (Rom 11:5), which has now truly become "the light for the nations" (Isa 42:6; 49:6; Acts 13:47). In doing this, he illustrates that these two missions (to Israel on the one hand, and to the nations on the other) are not identical, even if they lead all people to the same salvation through Christ. In the case of the gentiles, reception of the good news implies renunciation of idolatry and entry into the covenant. In the case of the Jews, on the other hand, the good news represents God's fulfillment in his Son of his promises to Israel. This is why the ministry of Peter, which brings about the messianic and eschatological renewal to which the Jews are called, is inseparable from the continuity and stability of the election of Israel embodied by James, as well as from the universal mission to the nations of Paul.

The Jewish identity of the Twelve is central to their apostolic role as those who "judge the twelve tribes of Israel." The Jewish identity of Peter, as head of the Twelve, is integral to his particular role as "apostle to the circumcised." The Jewish identity of James, kinsman of Jesus, is especially noteworthy, as he stands guard over the relationship of the messianic *kahal* to the Jewish people as a whole and to the Jewish tradition. The Jewish identity of Paul is crucial to his apostolic mission as he represents Israel's vocation to be a "light to the nations." These reflections on the theological significance of the Jewishness of the apostles are supported by Paul's teaching, considered at the beginning of this essay, that suggests a structurally significant ecclesiological role of Jewish believers in Christ.

While quite striking in their potential implications, all of these fruits of exegesis would remain highly theoretical if it were not for the re-emergence of an explicitly Jewish corporate expression of faith in Christ in our own day. It is now conceivable that the Jewish structural dimension of the Church could once again find explicit visible expression. How and when this will occur is uncertain, but faith in the God who chose Israel, raised Jesus from the dead, and poured out the Spirit at Pentecost leads us to expect the unexpected and to imagine the unimaginable. As Paul states after reflecting on similar themes, "O the depth of the riches and wisdom and knowledge of God! How unsearchable are his judgments and how inscrutable his ways! . . .

For from him and to him and for him are all things. To him be glory forever. Amen" (Rom 11:33, 36).

APPENDIX 4

Finding our Way through Nicaea:
The Deity of Jesus, Bilateral Ecclesiology, and Redemptive Encounter with the Living God[1]

Mark S. Kinzer

In *Searching Her Own Mystery* I focus on Israel-Christology, and thus on the Jewish *humanity* of Jesus. In the paper that follows I address my fellow Messianic Jews about the centrality of our confession of Jesus' *divinity*. I also attempt to elucidate the orientation Messianic Jews should adopt toward the Jewish and Christian theological traditions. Both of these topics deserve sustained attention as Messianic Jews and Catholics engage one another in theological conversation.

The Question and Its Importance

A few years ago a controversy erupted in the Israeli Messianic Jewish movement over the question, "Is Jesus God?" Some leaders had publicly answered the question with a definitive "No!" Their refusal to call Jesus "God" ignited a firestorm. In the eyes of many, these dissenting leaders had denied the basic tenet of Messianic Jewish faith.

1. This paper was originally presented in February 2010 at the Hashivenu Forum in Los Angeles, California. (The Hashivenu Forum is an annual theological conference for leaders in the Messianic Jewish movement.) The paper was published later the same year in *Kesher*, a Messianic Jewish theological journal: *Kesher* 24 (2010) 29–52. In 2012 the article was translated into Italian and appeared in the Jesuit theological journal *Rassegna Di Teologia* ("Nicea e la divinità di Yeshua," 601–24).

Though common in Christian parlance, the wording of this question has problematic features, which we will examine later in this paper. Nevertheless, the passionate responses evoked on both sides showed that the question touched on a matter of grave concern to all.

The main reasons for this concern are threefold. First, the message of the good news challenges all of its hearers to answer Jesus' own question to Peter, "Who do you say that I am?" (Mark 8:29). The mystery of Jesus' identity underlies the narrative of all four Gospels, and constitutes the core proclamation of the apostles. The exalted character of Jesus is the central theme of the Johannine writings, which present him as the enfleshed divine Logos through whom all things were made, the bearer of the divine name who is one with the Father and who shared the Father's glory before the foundation of the world. While couched in a different idiom, this theme likewise permeates the Synoptic Gospels and the apostolic letters. "Who then is this, that even wind and sea obey him?" cry the stunned disciples after Jesus exercised authority over the elements (Mark 4:41). As the early Jesus-movement grew, its basic confession of faith became the affirmation, "Jesus is Lord!" (Rom 10:9; 1 Cor 12:3; Phil 2:11). The good news itself makes the question of Jesus' transcendent identity a matter of fundamental importance.

Second, discussion of this question dominated the first four centuries of the Jesus-movement, and resulted in the creedal definitions that gave shape to the Christian theological consensus of the past sixteen centuries. For most of those who identify themselves as "Christians" and as members of the historical community known as the Christian Church, the results of these councils define the substance of their faith, even if they have never heard of Nicaea or Chalcedon, and even if they consider the Bible their only doctrinal authority. Affirmation of the deity of Jesus—and, for many, acknowledgement of the doctrine of the Trinity—constitutes both the center of their confession and the boundary that demarcates its unique character.

As Jewish disciples of Jesus, we may identify as members of the revived *ecclesia ex circumcisione* rather than "the Christian Church"—which we see as the *ecclesia ex gentibus* (i.e., the Church of the gentiles), legitimate but incomplete without its Jewish partner. Nevertheless, we cannot ignore the reality of the historical Christian community as the primary enduring witness to Jesus in the world. If we embrace bilateral ecclesiology, then we must seek unity with the Christian Church even as we maintain our own distinctive identity. Once again, the question of Jesus' transcendent identity—now embodied in explicit and official doctrinal formulations—becomes a matter of fundamental importance.

APPENDIX 4

Third and finally, the denial of Jesus' deity has been almost as significant for classic forms of Judaism as its affirmation has been for the Christian faith. Until the Middle Ages, acknowledgement of Jesus' deity and worship of the trinitarian God were considered by Jewish authorities to be *avodah zara* (i.e., idolatry). Eventually this assessment changed in regard to gentile Christians, but not in regard to Jews who believe in Jesus. According to traditional Jewish sources, for a Jew to believe in Jesus as the divine Son of God—and not just as the human Messiah—is to violate the *Shema*, the central Jewish confession that undergirds all Jewish faith.

Jews and Christians thus have agreed on the central importance of the doctrine of Jesus' deity. The doctrine functioned for many centuries of Jews and Christians as a mutually accepted litmus test for distinguishing authentic Judaism from authentic Christianity. It provided a doctrinal correlate to the practical issue of Torah observance, drawing an unambiguous theological line between the two feuding religious communities, just as the Jewish observance (or Christian denigration) of circumcision, Shabbat, holidays, and *kashrut* established a clear boundary on the level of praxis. For the Jewish people, the chief community-defining positive commandment was "You shall observe the Torah" and the chief negative commandment was "You shall not believe that Jesus is the Son of God." For the Christian Church, the chief community-defining positive commandment was "You shall believe that Jesus is the Son of God" and the chief negative commandment was "You shall not observe the Torah."

The classical Jewish view of the deity of Jesus becomes especially troubling for Jewish disciples of Jesus who are convinced of the truth of bilateral ecclesiology, and who consequently see themselves as members of the Jewish religious community and heirs of its tradition, as well as partners with the Christian Church within the twofold Body of Messiah. Just as we are pressed from the Christian side to give up or dilute our conviction that Torah observance is incumbent on every Jew, so we are pressed from the Jewish side to give up or dilute our conviction that Jesus is more than a man. It would be far easier to deny bilateral ecclesiology, and to live either as Jewish Christians who affirm the deity of Jesus in classical Christian terms and treat Torah observance as a mere cultural option, or as conventional Torah-observant Jews who respect Jesus as a rabbi, prophet, or even Messiah but refuse to honor him as divine or to seek any organic connection to the Christian Church.

Thus, wherever we turn, we face this burning question, raised for us by the Jewish community in which we claim membership, by the Christian community with which we seek partnership, and by the good news itself, which has laid hold of our lives and claimed our unrestricted allegiance. As

Jews steeped in *Tanakh*, formed by a religious tradition centered on confession of the unity of God and ever-sensitive to the dangers of idolatry, how do we understand and articulate the transcendent identity of Jesus our Messiah, as presented to us in the good news? And how do we assess the Christian doctrinal tradition and its articulation of his identity?

The Way of Approach

We have now formulated our question. How shall we best proceed in addressing it? It would seem natural to begin by studying the relevant biblical teaching, and then continue by examining and critiquing the classic Christian creedal formulas on the basis of that teaching. This approach appears logical and cogent, since it reflects both the unique authority of Scripture within the tradition of the community of Jesus' disciples, and the historical progression whereby later theological developments build upon earlier ones. It also conforms to the standard methodology of evangelical scholarship, which has shaped the theological education of most leaders in the Messianic Jewish world.

I will propose and model here a different approach to the question. Instead of beginning with Scripture, I will begin with the consensus confession of the Christian world, the Nicene Creed, and consider it alongside and in light of Scripture and within a Jewish frame of reference. I will not assume that the Nicene formulation is the best available or the most appropriate for us as Messianic Jews, but I will look for points of continuity between that formulation and the biblical teaching, and will give it the benefit of the doubt when it is under scrutiny.

What is the value of such an approach?

First of all, it expresses an ecclesiological commitment that is controversial among Messianic Jews, but which I consider crucial. To grasp the nature of this commitment, we must ponder the meaning and implications of bilateral ecclesiology. This view perceives the *ecclesia* to be a single yet twofold reality: the one community of the Messiah takes both Jewish and multi-national forms. The two forms are distinct, but inseparable. The Messianic Jewish community has its own distinct identity, but it also has an intimate partnership with the Christian Church.

The history of the Christian Church features an abundance of figures, events, practices, decisions, and ideas that trouble us as Messianic Jews. Fortunately, many of them also trouble our Christian friends. The Christian tradition, like the Jewish tradition, has proved itself to be dynamic, reflective, and self-correcting. We have witnessed remarkable self-correction in the past sixty years in the Church's teaching regarding Judaism and the Jewish people, and the continuing nature of this process inspires hope for the Church's future. It also opens the door to the bilateral partnership required by a common life in Messiah.

For some Messianic Jews, one of the troubling elements of Christian history is Nicene orthodoxy. However, unlike supersessionism, antinomianism, the inquisition, and the blood-libel, it is inappropriate for us to ask our Christian partners to repent of the Nicene Creed. The Nicene consensus on Christology has endured over more than sixteen centuries, and continues to define the basic contours of Christian faith. In those settings where commitment to Nicene orthodoxy wanes, the Christian Church loses its grip on the good news as a whole, and weakens in its faith and spiritual vitality.

The Christian Church, which is our partner, is a Nicene Church. Bilateral ecclesiology calls us to a corporate commitment to this Church. If this is the case, then we cannot dismiss the Nicene Creed in a cavalier fashion. We cannot treat it in a neutral way, as though it were one of many equally viable doctrinal proposals on the table. This Creed summarizes the essential and enduring teaching of our ecclesiological partner, and as a consequence we must take it seriously and treat it with respect. The Creed need not remain immune to all criticism, but it should always be given the benefit of the doubt. This is sufficient reason to begin our study with the Creed, viewed alongside Scripture and in light of Jewish thought.

A second reason for this approach is hermeneutical. Once Nicene orthodoxy prevailed, it became the lens through which all read the biblical text. Even those who oppose the Nicene consensus read Scripture looking for evidence to support their anti-Nicene position, demonstrating that they also fail to escape the new interpretative horizon established by the Creed.

There is value in historical scholarship that attempts to bracket off ways of reading the Bible that have pervaded Christian civilization for more than a millennium and a half. However, as soon as we move from historical reconstruction to theological analysis and assertion, we should reckon with our inability to abstract ourselves from the flow of history. We should not pretend that we can construct a normative theological system directly from Scripture, uninfluenced by the later theological consensus, and can then evaluate and critique that later consensus objectively on the basis of the system we have constructed. Of course, we can attempt to follow such an approach, and many do. But we should then be unsurprised if many of our readers fail to see a resemblance between the method we purport to follow and the process we actually practice.

I am far from suggesting that a later theological consensus should automatically determine how we read the biblical text. That would be an untenable position for a Messianic Jewish theologian who must continually challenge conventional Christian and Jewish assumptions. I am only arguing that we need to keep both the later Christian theological consensus and the biblical material in sight, and seek to read each in light of the other—and also in light of additional relevant factors, such as the Jewish theological tradition. Scripture has logical and theological, but not methodological, priority.

In effect, I am proposing a theological and hermeneutical approach in which we as Messianic Jews take our place as part of the Jewish community with its tradition of interpretation, and as a partner to the Christian community with its tradition of interpretation, and from that place listen and respond to the Bible's witness to the God of Israel and the Messiah of Israel. From this place of communal connection, we learn to hear what Jews and Christians have heard before. However, because we are connected to *both* communities and traditions, we also hear new things that these communities' mutual and unnatural isolation prevent them from hearing.

We can describe this as a hermeneutic of *dialectical ecclesial continuity*. In this context, I am using the term "ecclesial" to refer to both the Jewish and Christian communities as historical realities. When we read as those covenantally bound to both of these communities, we read and listen expecting to discover continuity between the message of Scripture and the consensus interpretations it has received in the communal tradition. This expectation may not always be realized, but it nevertheless directs our reading and listening.

Of course, these two communities have disagreed with one another on fundamental matters. This is why our hermeneutic must be *dialectical* as well as *ecclesial*. We view these two communal traditions as one ruptured whole, the broken fragments of a schism that should never have occurred. To read and hear dialectically is to seek to gather up the fragments, to perform a *tikkun*—a repair of what has been broken. We expect each tradition to offer correction and healing to the other.

With our question defined and our approach to it explained, we are now ready to plunge into the deep theological waters that lie before us.

The Nicene Problems

The Problem with the Council

The Council of Nicaea, which convened in 325 C.E., gave its name to a creed that is still sung as part of the weekly liturgy in many Christian churches. As such, the name carries a positive resonance in the ears of most Christians.

APPENDIX 4

This is not so for Messianic Jews. At best, our visceral reaction to Nicaea is ambivalent—and for understandable reasons. First among them is the role played by the Emperor Constantine. The Emperor initiated the Council, and influenced its results. He desired a united Church to promote a united Empire. Thus began the long history of church-state entanglement that has had such dire consequences for the Jewish people.

A second concern arises from the lack of representation at Nicaea of the *ecclesia ex circumcisione*. Granted, at this time the community of Jewish disciples of Jesus who continued to identify and live as Jews was small and marginalized. But it did still exist, as Epiphanius and Jerome later attest. We do not know whether Nazarene bishops were deliberately excluded from the Council, or whether they chose to stay away, or whether they were so marginalized that the question of attendance never arose on either side. In any case, it is difficult for Messianic Jews to view Nicaea as a truly "ecumenical" council, since it was unilateral rather than bilateral in composition. It was a council of the *ecclesia ex gentibus*, the Church of the nations.

The most serious problem with Nicaea from a Messianic Jewish perspective is the explicitly anti-Jewish tenor of its conclusions regarding the celebration of Easter. An official synodal letter from the Council rejected any reckoning of the date of Easter in relation to the Jewish calendar:

> We further proclaim to you the good news of the agreement concerning the holy Easter . . . that all our brethren in the East who formerly *followed the custom of the Jews* are henceforth to celebrate the most sacred feast of Easter at the same time with the Romans and yourselves and all those who have observed Easter from the beginning.[2]

The concern of the Nicene Council was to end a situation where Christians followed "the custom of the Jews." The bishops rejected any sign that the Church was dependent on the Jewish people for its faith or way of life. This intent becomes even clearer in the letter written by the Emperor Constantine announcing the results of the Council:

> It was declared to be particularly unworthy for this, the holiest of all festivals, to follow the custom [the calculation] of the Jews, who had soiled their hands with the most fearful of crimes, and whose minds were blinded. . . . We ought not, therefore, to have anything in common with the Jews . . . and consequently, in unanimously adopting this mode, we desire, dearest brethren, to separate ourselves from the detestable company of the Jews,

---

2. Schaff and Wace, *Seven Ecumenical Councils*, 54. Emphasis added.

> for it is truly shameful for us to hear them boast that without their direction we could not keep the feast . . .³

Nicaea thus represents a definitive moment in the history of Christian supersessionism, when the Christian Church in alliance with the Roman Emperor formally renounced its bilateral constitution.

As a result of these three factors, Nicaea evokes a different visceral response from Messianic Jews than it does from most Christians. The Council as a whole symbolizes for us the Church's conscious and decisive *turning away* from the Jewish people and *turning to* the Roman Empire. We must acknowledge this inner reaction, and learn how to explain it to our Christian friends. But it need not determine our judgment of the Nicene Creed.

When Christians honor the Council of Nicaea, they are not paying homage to a Constantinian synthesis of church and state that most no longer see as valid, and that even the Catholic Church now finds lacking. They are not denying a vision of a bilateral Church of Jews and gentiles, which most have never even conceived as a possibility. They are not making the supersessionist claim that the Christian Church lacks any organic connection to or dependence upon Judaism and the Jewish people; in fact, it is theologians loyal to Nicene orthodoxy who have taken the lead over the last forty years in combating supersessionism. When Christians honor the Council of Nicaea, they are doing one thing and one thing only: they are paying homage to Jesus, and glorifying him as the divine Son who is "the reflection of God's glory and the exact imprint of God's very being" (Heb 1:3).

The Nicene Creed is thus analogous to the Church's celebration of Christmas, which is the Creed's ritual correlate. The latter traces its origins to a pagan festival. The former derives from a political process influenced at times by unsavory motives and interests. Neither the holiday nor the Creed should be judged by the purity of its sources or the circumstances of its adoption, but instead by the way it has been understood and practiced by Christians through the centuries.

The Problem with the Creed

These preliminary considerations concerning the Nicene Council clear the way for us to examine the Nicene Creed, and to assess it on its own terms. Before we look at what it says, however, we must raise a significant problem that Messianic Jews have with the Creed itself. The problem we see is not with what the Creed says, but with what it fails to say.

---

3. Ibid., 54.

APPENDIX 4

I refer to what Kendall Soulen calls structural supersessionism. Unlike punitive and economic forms of supersessionism, structural supersessionism involves a sin of omission rather than commission.[4] It summarizes the basic narrative of God's dealings with the world in a manner that ignores the central role played by the Jewish people. It tells the story in a way that moves directly from the creation and fall of human beings, to the incarnation, death, and resurrection of the Son of God. The people of Israel appear solely as background to the main plot. This supersessionist Christian narrative takes an authoritative form in the Nicene Creed. Like all major Christian confessional statements before and after, the Nicene Creed omits any reference to the people of Israel and its crucial role in the story of God's dealings with the world.[5]

Structural supersessionism constitutes both the most difficult form of supersessionism to overcome, and the easiest. It is most difficult because the Church must do more than merely reassess particular doctrinal positions, such as the enduring validity of Israel's election; the Church must reconstruct its entire theological framework in a manner that gives Israel its proper place in addressing every theological topic. But it is also the easiest form of supersessionsim to address, because it does not require the repudiation of any authoritative doctrinal positions from the Church's theological tradition. Instead, it calls for a doctrinal development that *adds to*, rather than subtracts from, the Church's confession of faith. To overcome structural supersessionism, the Church must only recontextualize its historically transmitted deposit of faith within the framework of God's dealings with Israel and the nations.

Thus, the structural supersessionism of the Nicene Creed need pose no problem for us here. We are not evaluating the adequacy of the Creed as an embodiment of the ecclesial canonical narrative. If we did, we would certainly find it lacking. It requires the addition of material dealing with the people of Israel, material that would provide the necessary context for the affirmations it makes about the person of Jesus. However, our purpose here is only to assess those affirmations. We are concerned with what the Creed says, not with what it fails to say.

Having examined the problems with Nicaea from a Messianic Jewish perspective, we are now ready to examine what the Creed teaches about Jesus.

---

4. For definitions of these terms, see Soulen, *God of Israel*, 29–31.

5. "This omission is reflected in virtually every historic confession of Christian faith from the Creeds of Nicaea and Constantinople to the Augsburg Confession and beyond" (ibid., 32).

FINDING OUR WAY THROUGH NICAEA:

The Nicene Creed

What the Creed Denies

To know what to expect from the Nicene Creed and the right questions to ask concerning it, we must understand the nature of explicit and official doctrine in the history of the Christian Church. George Lindbeck provides a helpful introduction.

> [C]ontroversy is the normal means whereby implicit doctrines become explicit, and operational ones official. For the most part, only when disputes arise about what it is permissible to teach or practice does a community make up its collective mind and formally make a doctrinal decision. . . . In any case, insofar as official doctrines are the products of conflict . . . they must be understood in terms of what they oppose (it is usually much easier to specify what they deny than what they affirm). . .[6]

This runs counter to our usual assumptions about official doctrine. We normally conceive of Church doctrine as though it were analogous to scientific theory, offering propositional affirmations about reality formulated in technical terms coined for their clarity and precision. Church doctrine does involve affirmations about reality, but they are rarely unambiguous in nature, as demonstrated by the debates concerning their interpretation that invariably follow the establishment of explicit and official doctrine. As Lindbeck points out, what is affirmed may be ambiguous, but what is denied must be clear.

In light of this perspective, let us begin our study of the Nicene Creed by looking at the doctrinal positions that the original Creed of Nicaea anathematized:

> But as for those who say, There was when He was not, and, Before being born He was not, and that He came into existence out of nothing, or who assert that the Son of God is from a different (*ex heteras*) hypostasis or substance (*ousia*) [from the Father], or is created, or subject to alteration or change—these the Catholic Church anathematizes.[7]

Nicene orthodoxy arises as a response to and rejection of Arianism. The Arians believed that the Son of God was a creature. They accepted the biblical teaching that he existed before becoming incarnate and that the world

---

6. Lindbeck, *Nature of Doctrine*, 75.
7. Kelly, *Early Christian Doctrines*, 232. Bracketed material added.

was made through him, but they held that "there was [a time] when He [i.e., the Son of God] was not." If all reality may be classified as either eternal and uncreated or temporal (i.e., with a beginning in time) and created, the Arians place the pre-incarnate Son of God in the "temporal and created" category. He is the first created entity, the highest of the angels, the most exalted being in all creation. But he is not eternal, and he is not truly divine.

The Arian position reflected the Hellenistic philosophical assumptions dominant in the period. According to those assumptions, the eternal realm of divinity was absolutely transcendent, and could have no direct point of contact with the temporal and material world. Such a system of thought excluded divine incarnation in principle. But its implications went far beyond the exclusion of incarnation. In effect, it suggested that the transcendent God was ultimately unknowable, and could not be truly present within the created order. *Such a system of thought excluded in principle the living God of Scripture, the self-revealing one who enters into an intimate covenantal relationship with the people of Israel.* In rejecting Arianism, the Nicene Creed took a stand *against* the common philosophical notions of the day, and *for* the biblical portrayal of the God of Israel

What the Creed Affirms

Now that we have a clear idea of what the Nicene Council sought to deny with its Creed, we are ready to consider what it affirmed.[8] For our purposes, it will be sufficient to look at the opening section of the Creed.

> We believe in one God, the Father Almighty,
> maker of heaven and earth and of all things visible and invisible.
> And in one Lord, Jesus Christ,
> the only begotten (*monogenē*) Son of God,
> begotten (*gennethenta*) of his Father before all worlds,
> Light from (*ek*) Light, true God from (*ek*) true God,
> begotten (*gennethenta*), not made,
> having the same *ousia* (*homoousion*) as the Father,
> through (*dia*) whom all things were made.

The basic framework of this confession of faith derives from Paul's teaching in 1 Corinthians 8:5-6:

---

[8]. We will be examining the form of the Nicene Creed adopted at the Council of Constantinople in 381 C.E., which has become its standard version. This Creed does not differ in Christological teaching from the one adopted at Nicaea.

Indeed, even though there may be so-called gods in heaven and on earth—as in fact there are many gods and many lords—yet for us there is one God (*Theos*), the Father, from (*ek*) whom are all things and for whom we exist, and one Lord (*Kyrios*), Jesus Christ, through (*dia*) whom are all things and through (*dia*) whom we exist.

Paul likely uses the term *Kyrios* here as a Greek substitute for both the tetragrammeton (i.e., the "four-letters" which spell the proper name of God in Hebrew) and the Hebrew word *Adonai* ("My lord"), which in Jewish practice acts as a surrogate for the tetragrammeton. In this way Paul builds upon the most fundamental biblical confession of faith, the *Shema*, highlighting the two primary divine names (*Theos/Elohim* and *Kyrios/Adonai*) and the word "one."[9] Paul thus expands the *Shema* to include Jesus within a differentiated but singular deity.[10] The Nicene Creed adopts Paul's language ("one God, the Father . . . one Lord, Jesus Christ . . ."), and thereby affirms its own continuity with the *Shema*. Paul's short confession is a messianic interpretation of the *Shema*, and the Nicene Creed is an expanded interpretation of Paul's confession.

Drawing upon Second-Temple Jewish traditions that see the creation of the world as occurring through the mediation of a hypostatic Wisdom or spoken Word, Paul presents "God" as the one "*from (ek) whom* are all things," and the "Lord" as the one "*through (dia) whom* are all things." The Nicene Creed likewise draws upon Paul's terminology here, describing God the Father as "the maker of heaven and earth and of all things" and Jesus the Lord as the one "*through (dia)* whom all things were made" (i.e., by God the Father). It thereby preserves both (1) the Pauline *distinction* between God the Father and the Lord Jesus by designating each of them with a different divine name (*Theos* and *Kyrios*) and by employing the characteristic Pauline preposition *dia* for the role of Jesus in the work of creation; and (2) the Pauline *identification* of God and Jesus through ascription to them of the two primary biblical names for Israel's singular deity; through reference to their joint activity as the source of all created things; and through reiteration of the word "one." Once again, Paul offers a messianic interpretation of existing Jewish tradition in light of the incarnation, and the Nicene Creed offers an expanded interpretation of Paul's teaching.

The Nicene Creed elaborates on this Pauline (and Jewish) framework by adding explanatory language drawn from elsewhere in Scripture. The

---

9. See Hurtado, *Lord Jesus Christ*, 114.

10. As the context makes clear, Paul's expanded messianic *Shema* is aimed, like its traditional Jewish model, at the rejection of pagan idolatry and polytheism.

APPENDIX 4

one Lord, Jesus the Messiah, is also "the only-begotten (*monogenous*) Son of God" (John 1:14, 18; 3:16, 18; 1 John 4:9). In John this word may or may not carry the connotation of "begetting"—it may simply mean "only (Son)."[11] The Nicene Creed, however, exploits the word's range of verbal associations by adding two references to the Son's "begetting": "begotten (*gennethenta*) of his Father before all worlds," and "begotten, not made." The Creed thus brings together the Johannine *monogenēs* with Psalm 2:7 ("You are my Son, today I have begotten you"; see Acts 13:33; Heb 1:5), and interprets John's *monogenēs* in light of Psalm 2 as "only-begotten Son."

But the Creed also interprets Psalm 2 in light of John. What is the meaning of the "today" in which the Son of Psalm 2 is begotten? Is this a reference to Miriam's conception of Jesus? To Jesus' birth? To his immersion in the Jordan at the hands of John?[12] To his resurrection from the dead?[13] For John the evangelist, the existence of the Son of God antedates all these events in the earthly life of Jesus, and precedes even the creation of the world (John 1:1-5; 18; 6:46; 17:5). Therefore the "today" of Psalm 2:7 must be eternal, rather than temporal. The Creed's exegetical juxtaposition of John and Psalm 2 thus yields the completely appropriate phrase, "begotten of his Father before all worlds."[14]

The Creed draws two conclusions from its fundamental proposition that the Son is "begotten of his Father before all worlds." These two conclusions are conveyed in the phrases, "Light from (*ek*) Light, true God from (*ek*) true God."[15] First of all, the Son draws his being from (*ek*) the Father. Their relationship has a *taxis*, a structure or form, in which the Father is the ultimate source of the Son's existence and nature. That structure is eternal rather than temporal; as a star never exists without emitting light, so the Father never exists without the Son. Secondly, the Son shares the Father's nature. As the Father is "Light," so the Son is "Light"; as the Father is "true God," so the Son is "true God." Though the Son is ordered after and in relationship to the Father, he is not a demigod, a secondary divinity at a lower level of being from the Father.

These two affirmations about the Father and the Son always belong together. They produce the ambiguity that has always characterized

11. Arndt and Gingrich, *Lexicon*, 527.
12. As implied by variant readings of Luke 3:22.
13. As implied by Acts 13:33.
14. Oskar Skarsaune argues that this phrase also "is an encapsulated version of Proverbs 8:22-31" and thus reflects the Wisdom Christology that is a central motif of the Nicene Creed. See *Shadow of the Temple*, 333.
15. The phrase "Light from Light" alludes to Wis 7:26 and Heb 1:3, again expressing Wisdom Christology (Skarsaune, *Shadow of the Temple*, 333).

discussion of the Son's "subordination" to the Father. The Son is subordinate to the Father in the sense that he derives his existence from the Father, and serves the Father in the fulfillment of the Father's purposes. But the Son is not subordinate to the Father in the sense of possessing a secondary level of divinity, as though occupying a lower rung in a Neoplatonic hierarchy of being.

The Son is "begotten, not made." This contrast between begetting and making is crucial for the teaching of the Creed. The Son is not like a painting or a sculpture that springs from the genius of an artist but remains fundamentally different in kind from the artist himself. Just as offspring in the temporal created order are of the same kind as those who generate them, so in the eternal uncreated order the Son is as much divine as is the Father from whom he derives his being.

The contrast between "begetting" and "making" helps explain the most famous phrase of the Creed, "having the same *ousia* (*homoousion*) as the Father." In this context *ousia* appears to mean the kind of entity that something is.[16] Thus, the *homousion* does not add anything new to what has already been presented in the Creed. It does not provide an explanation or theory for how this could all be so. Instead, it expresses through one technical Greek term what the Creed states elsewhere in more allusive biblical language.

The Nicene Creed thus offers a highly plausible rendering of the apostolic teaching on the divinity of Jesus, in light of controversies that had emerged in the early centuries of the Jesus-movement. Though it spoke in the language of its own time and place, it did not conform to the philosophical theories that were currently in fashion. Instead, the Creed upheld a commitment to an authentic encounter with the living God who acts in a revelatory and redemptive manner within the world. It maintained the Jewish and biblical witness to the qualitative difference between the transcendent creator and that which is created, the particular personal character of the creator as the God of Israel, and the reality of this God's activity within

---

16. For this view of the *homoousion*, see Skarsaune, *Shadow of the Temple*, 333-35. J. N. D. Kelly likewise thinks that the original intent of this term at Nicaea was to mean "of the same nature" (Kelly, *Early Christian Doctrines*, 234-37). Over time the term took on the additional meaning of "numerical identity," i.e., that the Father and Son (and Spirit) are together one being (ibid., 245-47), while the related term *hypostasis* expressed the distinct identities of the Father, Son, and Spirit. (As the creedal anathemas demonstrate, at Nicaea *hypostasis* and *ousia* are treated as synonyms.) Nevertheless, no true theological consensus emerged on the precise meaning of the terms *ousia* and *hypostasis*. All agreed only that the former expressed the unity of Father, Son, and Spirit, and the latter expressed their distinction.

the created order. It affirmed that God can be known and encountered in the person of Jesus the Messiah.

The Nicene Creed does this as an expansion of a Pauline confession of faith, which was itself an expansion of the *Shema*. In this way, it implicitly points us back to the basics of Jewish monotheism, and presents Jesus as the one who realizes in this world the revelatory and redemptive purposes of *Adonai*, God of Israel and Creator of all.

Medieval Jewish Parallels to the Arian Controversy

Jewish history provides us with a surprising parallel to the Arian controversy and the Nicene response. The similarity supports our contention that what is at stake at Nicaea is not merely an orthodox Christology, but the authenticity of human encounter with the redemptively self-revealing God of Israel.

Rabbinic texts treat the biblical accounts of God's self-revealing presence in a realistic fashion. The Sages are not embarrassed by biblical anthropomorphism. They assume that the figure who appeared to Moses, Isaiah, Ezekiel, and Daniel, and to all of Israel at the Sea and at Sinai, was none other than *Adonai*, the God of Israel. In fact, rabbinic tradition sometimes makes the anthropomorphism of the biblical theophanies look restrained. God is there portrayed as wearing *tefillin* (i.e., phylacteries), praying, and arguing about the Torah with the angels. In recent decades, scholars have even employed the language of incarnation to describe this dimension of the rabbinic imagination.[17]

The ninth-century Karaites, influenced by Greek philosophical currents absorbed into Islamic thought, attacked the anthropomorphism of the rabbinic texts. To ward off these attacks, Saadia Gaon drew upon the same philosophy that guided the Karaites. He reinterpreted rabbinic thought in a way that eliminated all anthropomorphism, even from the biblical theophanies. His formulation had tremendous consequences for later Jewish thought, and is worth citing at length:

> Peradventure however, someone, attacking our view, will ask: "But how is it possible to put such constructions on these anthropomorphic expressions and on what is related to them, when Scripture itself explicitly mentions a form like that of human beings that was seen by the prophets and spoke to them ... let alone the description by it of God's being seated on a throne, and His being borne by the angels on top of a firmament (Ezekiel

17. For example, see Neusner, *The Incarnation of God*.

1:26)." ... Our answer to this objection is that this form was something [specially] created. ... It is a form nobler even that [that of] the angels, magnificent in character, resplendent with light, which is called *the glory of the Lord*. It is this form, too, that one of the prophets described as follows: *I beheld till thrones were placed, and one that was ancient of days did sit* (Daniel 7:9), and that the sages characterized as *Shekhinah*. Sometimes, however, this specially created being consists of light without the form of a person. It was, therefore, an honor that God had conferred on His prophet by allowing him to hear the oracle from the mouth of a majestic form created out of fire that was called *the glory of the Lord*, as we have explained.[18]

On the one hand, Saadia treats realistically the biblical theophanies. He does not doubt that Ezekiel, Isaiah, and Daniel truly saw an enthroned human figure, referred to in the text as *Adonai*. He also does not doubt that such a figure possessed objective existence beyond the imagination of the prophet. On the other hand, his philosophical commitment to absolute divine transcendence—which he understands as a necessary corollary of the divine unity—excludes the possibility that this enthroned human figure can in fact be the eternal uncreated one. Therefore, he concludes that the form seen by the prophets—the *Kavod* (Glory) or *Shekhinah*—must be a created entity, more exalted than the angels, but not divine.

As Gershom Scholem notes, Saadia's interpretation became "a basic tenet of the [Jewish] philosophical exegesis of the Bible." We find it in such classic writers as Yehudah Halevi and Maimonides. Scholem also points out its radical novelty.

> These respected authors could hardly have ignored the fact that this conception of the *Shekhinah* as a being completely separate from God was entirely alien to the talmudic texts, and could only be made compatible with them by means of extremely forced interpretation of these texts. Nevertheless, these philosophers preferred "cutting the Gordian knot" in this way rather than endanger the purity of monotheistic belief by recognizing an uncreated hypostasis.[19]

The parallel here to the Arian interpretation of the *Logos* should be evident. The underlying concerns are identical: a desire to guard the purity of divine transcendence and unity understood in terms of Greek philosophical conceptions. The problems encountered as a result of this concern are likewise

---

18. Saadia Gaon, *Beliefs and Opinions*, II:10, 121.
19. Scholem, *Mystical Shape of the Godhead*, 154–55.

APPENDIX 4

identical: the realistic biblical presentation of God's self-revelation to Israel. Finally, the strategies adopted to overcome the problems are the same: the thesis that the one who is called by the divine name and who apparently manifests the divine Presence is a created entity, distinct from God and at a lower level in the hierarchy of being.

Just as the Jewish philosophical reinterpretation of the *Kavod/Shekhinah* parallels the Arian reinterpretation of the *Logos*, so the kabbalistic response to the Jewish philosophers parallels the Nicene response to the Arians. Like the Nicene fathers, those who championed the tradition of the *Zohar* agreed with their opponents on the ineffable and transcendent nature of God. These Jewish mystics employed the term *Eyn Sof* (i.e., the Infinite One) to refer to this aspect of the divine reality. However, also like the Nicene fathers, the kabbalists viewed the self-revelation of God (the biblical *Kavod*, whom they referred to as the *sefirot*) as *both* distinct from *and* one with *Eyn Sof*. The infinite and transcendent nature of God required the distinction, but the objective reality and truthfulness of divine revelation required the unity. If the *Kavod* revealed to Israel is not truly and fully divine, then God remains unknown to the world, and Israel's claim to a covenant with a redemptively self-revealing God is rendered fraudulent.

Even the language used by the kabbalists to express the relationship between the *sefirot* and *Eyn Sof* resembles the language employed within the stream of Nicene orthodoxy. "The kabbalists insisted that Ein Sof and the sefirot formed a unity 'like a flame joined to a coal.' 'It is they and they are It.'"[20] This language distinguishes both *kabbalah* and Nicene orthodoxy from Neoplatonic thought, in which each stage of emanation involves a gradation in the hierarchy of being, and in which everything below the ineffable "One" occupies a lower ontological status in that hierarchy. "The hidden God in the aspect of *Ein-Sof* and the God manifested in the emanation of *Sefirot* are one and the same, viewed from two different angles. There is therefore a clear distinction between the stages of emanation in the neoplatonic systems, which are not conceived as processes within the Godhead, and the kabbalistic approach."[21] Thus, while kabbalistic thought in some ways resembles Neoplatonism, and was influenced by it, on this fundamental point the two systems diverge. *Kabbalah* here has more in common with Basil of Caesarea than with Plotinus.

This commonality derives less from direct influence than from similar issues and concerns. For both the Christian and the Jewish traditions, Greek philosophy challenged the biblical presentation of the God of Israel and the

---

20. Matt, *Zohar*, 33.
21. Scholem, *Kabbalah*, 98.

living faith of the communities who worshipped that God. Nicene orthodoxy and Jewish mysticism responded by drawing insights and terminology from the challenging philosophical systems and employing them within a new framework provided by Scripture and the tradition of the worshipping community. The philosophical terminology of *ousia* and emanation now served faithful testimony to the infinite transcendent God who acts within the world to establish a covenant relationship with a people, a relationship in which this God is genuinely and redemptively known.

Post-Nicene Christology in Messianic Jewish Perspective

We have examined the teaching of the Nicene Creed concerning the deity of Jesus in light of Scripture and Jewish tradition, employing the hermeneutic of *dialectical ecclesial continuity*. This examination has exposed nothing objectionable in the teaching of the Creed, but instead has confirmed it as a faithful witness to Israel's God and Messiah by the Church of the nations in the particular circumstances of the fourth-century Greco-Roman world.

However, affirmation of the Nicene Creed need not imply uncritical reception of the normative Christian piety and theological expression that it generated. Here, we must stress the *dialectical* component in our hermeneutic. At this point our Jewish sensibility comes to the forefront, and raises pressing questions.

First, many Messianic Jews question whether Christian thought and practice have dealt adequately with the differentiation of the Father and the Son. As noted above, the Creed rules out any inequality of ontological status between the Father and Son, at the same time as it recognizes that the Son derives his being from the Father and is thus ordered after and towards the Father. It rules out the one type of "subordination," while implying the other.

However, in the history of Christian spirituality this delicate balance became increasingly precarious, as the equal divinity of the Son was stressed at the expense of the distinction between the Father and the Son. Especially in the Western Church, this exaltation of the Son threatened the unique position of the Father as the source and goal of all things. Consequently, many Christians have a diminished sense of the inner order and differentiation within the divine life, an order that was expressed in the early Jesus-community by its normal mode of worshipping the Father, through the Son, in the Spirit.[22]

---

22. Many Christian theologians of the twentieth and twenty-first centuries have recognized the need to recapture the structure or *taxis* of differentiation between the Father and the Son. For example, John Zizioulas writes: "In making the Father the

APPENDIX 4

Though the Messianic Jewish movement possesses few universal characteristics, a reasonable candidate for this designation is the custom of addressing formal congregational worship to God the Father rather than to Jesus the Son. This almost instinctive pattern of Messianic Jewish prayer arises, I suggest, as a result of a Jewish sensibility that sees Jesus as the one who brings us to the Father, who mediates a relationship with the Father by revealing rather than replacing the Father. He can only do this because he is fully divine. But he must do this because the Father is the source and goal of his own existence.[23]

Secondly, the continuation of the second article of the Nicene Creed affirms unambiguously the historical humanity of Jesus, who was born of Mary and suffered under Pontius Pilate. Nevertheless, the challenge posed by Arianism led the Christian Church to stress Jesus' divine rather than human nature. Just as the delicate balance between the equality and differentiation of the Father and the Son was threatened, so also was the balance between Jesus' divinity and humanity. Christians found it increasingly difficult to accept at face value the biblical texts that point to Jesus' ignorance of future happenings, growth in knowledge, need for companionship, fear of death, and learning of obedience amid temptation.

The Creed's lack of reference to Israel rendered it vulnerable to this imbalance. If the person and work of Jesus had been properly situated in

---

'ground' of God's being—or the ultimate reason for existence—theology accepted a kind of subordination of the Son to the Father without being obliged to downgrade the *Logos* into something created. But this was possible only because the Son's otherness was founded on the *same substance*" (*Being as Communion*, 89). Similarly, Colin Gunton: "There is, in the biblical representation of the way in which the acts of God take shape in time, some support for Zizioulas' giving of priority to the Father. It is often said that when the New Testament writers use the word 'God' *simpliciter*, they are referring to God the Father, so that Irenaeus is true to Scripture in speaking of the Son and Spirit as the two hands of God, the two agencies by which the work of God the Father is done in the world.... Such talk of the divine economy has indeed implications for what we may say about the being of God eternally, and would seem to suggest a subordination of *taxis*—of ordering within the divine life—but not one of deity or regard.... The Spirit is the giver of faith, not in himself, nor even, strictly speaking, in Christ, but in the Father through Christ. In that respect, we return to the theme that God *simpliciter* is God the Father, the fount and goal of our being. But we neither receive our being in the first place apart from Christ, the mediator of creation and salvation, nor are directed to our goal apart from the Spirit, the perfecting cause." (*Promise of Trinitarian Theology*, 197, 199). Finally, from Thomas F. Torrance: "All the revealing and saving acts of God come to us from the Father, through the Son and in the Holy Spirit, and all our corresponding relations to God in faith, love and knowledge are effected in the Spirit through the Son and to the Father." (*Christian Doctrine of God*, 147).

23. A concern about the role of God the Father as the primary addressee of prayer appears in the two most seminal texts of the early Messianic Jewish movement: Dan Juster's *Jewish Roots*, 241, and David Stern's *Messianic Jewish Manifesto*, 94.

relation to his own people, it would have been more difficult to swallow up his humanity in his divinity. If the Creed had mentioned not only his birth but also his circumcision, it would have buttressed its affirmation of his concrete and particular human identity. Instead, the reverse happened: the accentuation of Jesus' divinity at the expense of his humanity made it more difficult for the Christian Church to grasp the significance of Israel or to recognize the implications of the fact that it had been incorporated into the body of a resurrected Jew.

Once again, a concern about this historical imbalance tends to characterize the Messianic Jewish movement as a whole. Our Jewish sensibility attunes us to the importance of bodily realities. Our convictions about the enduring significance of our own Jewish identity are connected to our confession of the enduring significance of Jesus' Jewish identity—for us, but also for the nations of the world, and for all creation.

These two reservations about the outworking of Nicene Christology in the life of the Christian Church reveal the problematic nature of the question with which we began our paper: "Is Jesus God?"[24] This three-word question seems simple and straightforward, yet it contains at least two ambiguities that render any answer similarly ambiguous. These two ambiguities correspond to our two reservations stated above. First, the question could mean, "Is Jesus the fullness of divinity, so that there is no Father distinct from the Son, from whom the Son receives his existence and to whom that existence is eternally oriented?" The answer to that question, according to Nicaea, is a resounding "no." Secondly, the question could mean, "Is the flesh and blood of the man Jesus divine, so that it is uncreated, eternal, and thus unlike our own flesh and blood that is created and comes into being at a particular time?" Once again, the answer to that question, according to Nicaea, is a resounding "no."

One might say, "Nobody who asks this question means it in either of these ways!" This may be the case. However, in light of the two historical imbalances in Christian spirituality and thought described above, we have good grounds for assuming that many of those who ask the question fail to consider with sufficient care exactly what they do mean when they ask it. Moreover, as Messianic Jews we must also consider what our fellow

---

24. Referring to Jesus as "God" is rare in the apostolic writings, but becomes extremely common in the early centuries of the Christian Church. It is a reflection of a Christian linguistic convention known as the sharing of attributes (*communicatio idiomatum*), in which verbal expressions specifically appropriate to Jesus' divine or human nature are applied also to his integrated divine-human person (see Kelly, *Early Christian Doctrines*, 143; 296–301). This ancient practice is not illegitimate, as it is also attested (albeit infrequently) in Scripture (e.g., John 20:28). However, our Jewish sensibility alerts us to its potential for misunderstanding and abuse.

Jews understand when they hear such a question, and when they hear it answered in the affirmative. What they hear and understand is usually as far beyond the limits of normative Christian faith as it is of Jewish orthodoxy.

Our hermeneutic of *dialectical ecclesial continuity* thus enables us to receive appreciatively from our Christian ecclesial partner, but also to offer proposals for rebalancing and repair that derive from our participation in the ongoing stream of Jewish ecclesial tradition. We can affirm the Nicene Creed, and then add our voice to the continuing argument as to how it should best be interpreted and practiced.

Conclusion

The primary contention of this paper finds expression in the parallel discovered between Arius and Saadia, Nicaea and *kabbalah*. In accordance with the clear teaching of Scripture, we see Jesus not only as the Messiah but also as *Chochmah* (Wisdom), the *Logos*, and the *Kavod*, the mediator of all God's work in creation, revelation, and redemption. Obviously, mainstream *kabbalah* does not accept this view, but it does affirm a distinct hypostatic reality, represented by the *sefirot*, which fulfills an analogous role. Both Nicene orthodoxy and *kabbalah* accept the philosophical acknowledgement of God as infinite, transcendent, invisible, and incomprehensible. But they also reject philosophical interpretations that negate the reality of God's involvement with and in the world, and which so separate God from creation as to render God utterly unknowable. They both accomplish this correction of the philosophical currents in their own religious traditions by distinguishing between God the Father and God the Son, or between *Eyn Sof* and the *sefirot*, while simultaneously asserting their inseparable unity.

Thus, what is at stake here is not an articulation of doctrinal truth that lacks any direct bearing on our lives. We are not debating the number of angels that can dance on the head of a pin. Instead, we are seeking to bear verbal witness to the reality of a redemptive encounter with the living God in a way that does justice to the authenticity of that encounter and which effectively invites others to share in it. This is what it means for us to confess the deity of Jesus.

A promising answer to an important question always raises several new questions. Our answer to the question of Jesus' deity immediately provokes a host of new queries, three of which deserve note and comment as we conclude this initial stage of the journey.

First, affirmation of the deity of Jesus leads inevitably to the question of the hypostatic identity of the Spirit, and from there into discussion of the triunity of God. Thus, the Council of Nicaea (325 C.E.), which addressed the issue of Jesus' deity, was followed by the Council of Constantinople (381 C.E.), which addressed the deity and distinct identity of the Holy Spirit. We cannot adequately appreciate the significance of the deity of Jesus for our life until we have taken this further stage of the journey. According to Scripture, the Spirit joins us to Jesus, who bring us to God the Father. Not only are we encountering God in Jesus; in union with him, we are being ushered into God's mysterious inner life. Once again, *kabbalah* offers suggestive parallels. But that is a discussion for another day.

Second, affirmation of the deity of Jesus leads to the question of how this truth should function in the definition of our identity as a Messianic Jewish community. As noted earlier, the Christian Church has treated this doctrine both as its theological center and as its external line of demarcation. In many contexts denial of the deity of Jesus places one outside the Church's communal boundary. While we might question whether this should be so, we can also appreciate the rationale for such an exclusionary practice. For gentiles, union with Jesus opens up for the first time participation in the covenant that God made with the patriarchs and matriarchs. Rejection of Jesus' role as divine mediator of God's creative, revelatory, and redemptive purposes puts the covenant status of these gentiles in jeopardy.

However, the Messianic Jewish community finds itself in a different situation. Our position in the bilateral *ecclesia* involves partnership with the Christian Church and also membership in the Jewish people. Messianic Jews are born into the covenant with the patriarchs and matriarchs, and then discover its full meaning and power in Jesus. When someone in our world rejects the deity of Jesus, they are putting in jeopardy the full realization of their covenantal identity, but *not* their covenantal identity itself. They are usually motivated, at least in part, by pressures exerted from the wider Jewish community. In effect, they are choosing a closer social connection to the covenant community of Israel at the expense of a connection to the Church. They are accepting the negative doctrinal boundary marker asserted by the wider Jewish community.

As part of the bilateral *ecclesia*, we refuse to accept the Jewish community's negative doctrinal boundary marker, just as we refuse to accept the Christian community's negative boundary marker dealing with our covenantal practice of the Torah. (Once again, we realize the significance of our hermeneutic of *dialectical* ecclesial continuity.) But should we exclude from our midst those Messianic Jews who adhere to these negative boundary markers, i.e., who deny the deity of Jesus, or who deny the covenantal obligation of Torah? I am not convinced that we should. Affirmation of the deity of Jesus and affirmation of the covenantal obligation of Torah observance

APPENDIX 4

for Jews are the two central principles of our communal existence, and we can rightly require that our leaders uphold them. They are our center, but they need not constitute our outer boundary.

Third, as we have just seen, affirmation of the deity of Jesus brings us into conflict with the wider Jewish community that we call our own. Is it viable on a long-term basis for us to identify so wholeheartedly with a community that has erected a social and cultural boundary that consists of a denial of what we so centrally affirm? I would answer: probably not. In the same way, bilateral ecclesiology lacks long-term viability if the Christian Church maintains its negative boundary concerning the covenantal obligation of Torah.[25] These two negative boundary definitions provided the Church and the Jewish community with a comfortable, unambiguous, mutually accepted border, fenced and well patrolled. They also supported the illusion that these two social bodies represented two religions, each of which made total sense apart from the other. Our existence as a corporate Messianic Jewish presence bears witness to the arbitrary and unsustainable nature of this border, and of the religious illusion it perpetuates.

We exist as a movement in part to protest this negative border. Such a protest constitutes a crucial element in our prophetic calling. Moreover, our long-term viability depends on the success of that protest. We already see significant changes in the Church's attitude towards its negative boundary. While the Messianic Jewish view on the Torah has not yet carried the day, the contrary view is no longer a universal presupposition. We can and should hope and pray for the same changes in the Jewish community's attitude towards its negative boundary.

But this will never happen if we surrender our affirmation of the deity of Jesus, or lose sight of its true significance, or yield to pressure and hide it from public view. It will also never happen if this affirmation becomes for us an abstract proposition, prominently displayed as a mark of doctrinal orthodoxy, but divorced from the revelatory and redemptive power to which it is meant to bear witness.

It is especially appropriate that this message be spoken and heard in the context of the Hashivenu Forum. The name "Hashivenu" has become emblematic in the Messianic Jewish world for the stream of Jewish disciples

---

25. Of course, our movement does recognize a sense in which full-orbed observance of the Torah should function as a boundary—not between the *ecclesia* and the Jewish people, but between the *ecclesia ex circumcisione* and the *ecclesia ex gentibus*. This boundary distinguishes but does not divide—it is not a fortified border between two feuding countries, but a line marking out the territory of two provinces within the same nation. And it is not a negative boundary (except in the limited sense that it does not bind Christians), for the Christian Church should honor the Torah and endorse its full-orbed observance by all Jews.

of Jesus who uphold Torah observance, Jewish tradition, and the importance of integration within the wider Jewish world. As such, those who identify with the name are also those exposed to the greatest temptation to deny or minimize the deity of Jesus.

It is my hope that future generations will identify the name Hashivenu with a bilateral ecclesiology that transcends both the Christian and the Jewish negative boundaries—or, in more fitting positive terms, a form of Messianic Judaism that exalts the Torah as the covenantal constitution of the Jewish people, while joyfully confessing the deity of Jesus, light for revelation to the gentiles and the glory of his people Israel.

Bibliography

Aquinas, Thomas. *Summa Theologica, Volume 2*. Westminster, MD: Christian Classics, 1981.

———. *Summa Theologica, Volume 4*. Westminster, MD: Christian Classics, 1981.

Arndt, William F., and F. Wilbur Gingrich. *A Greek-English Lexicon of the New Testament*. Chicago: University of Chicago, 1979.

Bader-Saye, Scott. *Church and Israel After Christendom: The Politics of Election*. Eugene, OR: Wipf and Stock, 1999.

———. "Post-Holocaust Hermeneutics: Scripture, Sacrament, and the Jewish Body of Christ." *Cross Currents* 50.4 (2000) 458–74.

Bagatti, Bellarmino, O.F.M. *The Church from the Circumcision: History and Archaeology of the Judaeo-Christians*. Jerusalem: Franciscan, 1971.

Bailey, Sarah Pulliam. "Yes, We Have a Witness: Historian Vinson Synan Reflects Personally on the Pentecostal Movement." *Christianity Today*, 21 April 2010. Online: http://www.christianitytoday.com/ct/2010/april/26.67.html.

Barth, Karl. *Church Dogmatics* IV/1. Translated and edited by G. W. Bromiley. Edinburgh: T. & T. Clark, 1956.

———. *Church Dogmatics* IV/4., *Study Edition*. Translated by G. W. Bromiley. Edinburgh: T. & T. Clark, 2010.

Barth, Markus. *Ephesians 1–3*. Anchor Bible Commentary 34. Garden City, NY: Doubleday, 1974.

———. *Israel and the Church: Contribution to a Dialogue for Peace*. Eugene, OR: Wipf & Stock, 1969.

Bauckham, Richard. *Jude and the Relatives of Jesus in the Early Church*. Edinburgh: T. & T. Clark, 1990,

Beasley-Murray, G. R. *Baptism in the New Testament*. Grand Rapids: Eerdmans, 1973.

Benedict XVI, Pope (Joseph Cardinal Ratzinger). *Jesus of Nazareth, Part One—From the Baptism in the Jordan to the Transfiguration*. New York: Doubleday, 2007.

———. *Jesus of Nazareth, Part Two—Holy Week: From the Entrance into Jerusalem to the Resurrection*. San Francisco: Ignatius, 2011.

———. *Many Religions–One Covenant*. San Francisco: Ignatius, 1999.

Birnbaum, Philip. *The Birnbaum Haggadah*. New York: Hebrew, 1976.

Bouyer, Louis. *Eucharist: Theology and Spirituality of the Eucharistic Prayer*. Translated by Charles Underhill Quinn. South Bend, IN: University of Notre Dame Press, 1968.

Boyarin, Daniel. *Border Lines: The Partition of Judaeo-Christianity*. Philadelphia: University of Pennsylvania Press, 2004.

———. *The Jewish Gospels: The Story of the Jewish Christ*. New York: New Press, 2012.

Buber, Martin. *Hasidism*. New York: Philosophical Library, 1948.
Connelly, John. *From Enemy to Brother: The Revolution in Catholic Teaching on the Jews 1933-1965*. Cambridge: Harvard University Press, 2012.
Cunningham, Philip A., and Didier Pollefyt. "The Triune One, the Incarnate Logos, and Israel's Covenantal Life." In *Christ Jesus and the Jewish People Today: New Explorations of Theological Interrelationships*, edited by Philip A. Cunningham et al., 183-201. Grand Rapids: Eerdmans, 2011.
Dan, Joseph. *Jewish Mysticism and Jewish Ethics*. Northvale, NJ: Aronson, 1986.
Daniélou, Jean Cardinal. *The Theology of Jewish Christianity*. Translated by John A. Baker. London: Darton, Longman & Todd, 1964.
Dunn, James D. G. "Jesus, Table-Fellowship, and Qumran." In *Jesus and the Dead Sea Scrolls*, edited by James H. Charlesworth, 254-72. New York: Doubleday, 1992.
Eisenbaum, Pamela. *Paul Was Not a Christian: The Original Message of a Misunderstood Apostle*. New York: HarperOne, 2009.
Etz Hayim. New York: Jewish Publication Society, 2001.
Eusebius. *Ecclesiastical History* 2:23, 4-6. Translated by Kirsopp Lake. Cambridge: Harvard University Press, 1926.
Evans, Craig A. "Jesus and the Continuing Exile of Israel." In *Jesus and the Restoration of Israel*, edited by Carey C. Newman, 77-100. Downers Grove, IL: IVP Academic, 1999.
Ferguson, Everett. *Baptism in the Early Church: History, Theology, and Liturgy in the First Five Centuries*. Grand Rapids: Eerdmans, 2009.
Falk, Daniel K. "Jewish Prayer Literature and the Jerusalem Church in Acts." In *The Book of Acts in its First Century Setting, Volume 4: Palestinian Setting*, edited by Richard Bauckham, 267-301. Grand Rapids: Eerdmans, 1995,
Fowl, Stephen E. *Ephesians*. The New Testament Library. Louisville: Westminster John Knox, 2012.
Fredriksen, Paula. *Sin: The Early History of an Idea*. Princeton: Princeton University Press, 2012.
Friedman, Elias. *Jewish Identity*. New York: Miriam, 1987.
Garrigues, Jean-Miguel. *Le people de la première Alliance*. Paris: Cerf, 2011.
———. *L'unique Israël De Dieu*. Limoges: Criterion, 1987.
Greenberg, Irving. *For the Sake of Heaven and Earth: The New Encounter between Judaism and Christianity*. Philadelphia: Jewish Publication Society, 2004.
Gregerman, Adam. "A Jewish Response to Elizabeth Groppe, Philip A. Cunningham and Dieder Pollefyt, and Gregor Maria Hoff." In *Christ Jesus and the Jewish People Today New Explorations of Theological Interrelationships*, edited by Philip A. Cunningham et al., 221-28. Grand Rapids: Eerdmans, 2011.
Groppe, Elizabeth. "The Tri-Unity of God and the Fractures of Human History." In *Christ Jesus and the Jewish People Today New Explorations of Theological Interrelationships*, edited by Philip A. Cunningham et al., 164-82. Grand Rapids: Eerdmans, 2011.
Gunton, Colin E. *The Christian Faith*. Oxford: Blackwell, 2002.
———. *The Promise of Trinitarian Theology*. London: T. & T. Clark, 1991.
Harrington, Daniel J., S.J. *The Gospel of Matthew*. Sacra Pagina 1. Collegeville, MN: Liturgical, 1991.
Hart, David Bentley. *The Beauty of the Infinite*. Grand Rapids: Eerdmans, 2003.

Henrix, Hans Hermann. "The Son of God became Human as a Jew: Implications of the Jewishness of Jesus for Christology." In *Christ Jesus and the Jewish People Today: New Explorations of Theological Interrelationships*, edited by Philip A. Cunningham et al., 114–43. Grand Rapids: Eerdmans, 2011.

Herberg, Will. "A Jew Looks at Jesus." In *Jewish Perspectives on Christianity*, edited by Fritz A. Rothschild, 256–63. New York: Continuum, 1996.

———. "Judaism and Christianity: Their Unity and Difference." In *Jewish Perspectives on Christianity*, edited by Fritz A. Rothschild, 240–55. New York: Continuum, 1996.

Heschel, Abraham Joshua. *God in Search of Man*. New York: Noonday, 1955.

———. *Moral Grandeur and Spiritual Audacity*. New York: Noonday, 1996.

Hocken, Peter. *The Challenges of the Pentecostal, Charismatic and Messianic Jewish Movements: The Tensions of the Spirit*. Farnham, UK: Ashgate, 2009.

———. *The Glory and the Shame: Reflections on the 20th Century Outpouring of the Holy Spirit*. Guildford, UK: Eagle, 1994.

Hoffman, Rabbi Lawrence A., ed. *My People's Prayer Book: Traditional Prayers, Modern Commentaries, Vol. 2: The Amidah*. Woodstock, VT: Jewish Lights, 1998.

Hurtado, Larry W. *Lord Jesus Christ*. Grand Rapids: Eerdmans, 2003.

Jeremias, Joachim. *The Eucharistic Words of Jesus*. Translated by Norman Perrin. Philadelphia: Fortress, 1966.

John Paul II, Pope. *Spiritual Pilgrimage*. Edited by Eugene J. Fischer and Leon Klenicki. New York: Crossroad, 1995.

Johnson, Luke Timothy. *The Writings of the New Testament: An Interpretation*. Minneapolis: Fortress, 1999.

Juster, Daniel. *Jewish Roots: Understanding Your Jewish Faith*. Shippensburg, PA: Destiny Image, 2013.

Kadushin, Max. *The Rabbinic Mind*. New York: Blaisdell, 1965.

———. *Worship and Ethics: A Study in Rabbinic Judaism*. New York: Bloch, 1963.

Kasper, Walter Cardinal. "Foreword." In *Christ Jesus and the Jewish People Today: New Explorations of Theological Interrelationships*, edited by Philip A. Cunningham et al., x–xviii. Grand Rapids: Eerdmans, 2011.

Kellner, Menachem. *Maimonides' Confrontation with Mysticism*. Portland: Littman Library of Jewish Civilization, 2006.

Kelly, J. N. D. *Early Christian Doctrines*. New York: Harper & Row, 1978.

Kinzer, Mark S. "'All Things under His Feet': Psalm 8 in the New Testament and in Other Jewish Literature of Late Antiquity." PhD diss., University of Michigan, 1995. Online: http://deepblue.lib.umich.edu/bitstream/handle/2027.42/90885/Kinzer-All_Things_Under_His%20Feet-Dissertation.pdf?sequence=1

———. "Finding our Way through Nicaea." *Kesher* 24 (2010) 29–52.

———. *Israel's Messiah and the People of God: A Vision for Messianic Jewish Covenant Fidelity*. Eugene, OR: Cascade, 2011.

———. "The Messianic Fulfillment of the Jewish Faith." In *The Witness of the Jews to God*, edited by David W. Torrance, 115–25. Edinburgh: Handsel, 1982. (Also found in *Israel's Messiah and the People of God*, 3–13.)

———. "Messianic Gentiles and Messianic Jews." *First Things* 189 (January 2009) 43–47.

———. "Nicea e la divnità di Yeshua." *Rassegna Di Teologia* Anno LIII (2012) 601–24.

———. *Postmissionary Messianic Judaism: Redefining Christian Engagement with the Jewish People*. Grand Rapids: Brazos 2005.
Klawans, Jonathan. *Purity, Sacrifice, and the Temple: Symbolism and Supersessionism in the Study of Ancient Judaism*. Oxford: Oxford University Press, 2006.
Levering, Matthew. *Christ's Fulfillment of Torah and Temple*. South Bend, IN: University of Notre Dame Press, 2002.
———. *Sacrifice and Community: Jewish Offering and Christian Eucharist*. Oxford: Blackwell, 2005.
Leithart, Peter J. "Old Covenant and New in Sacramental Theology New and Old." *Pro Ecclesia* XIV.2 (2005) 174–90.
Levine, Baruch A. *The JPS Torah Commentary: Leviticus*. Philadelphia: The Jewish Publication Society, 1989.
Levenson, Jon. *The Death and Resurrection of the Beloved Son*. New Haven: Yale University Press, 1993.
———. *Sinai and Zion*. New York: Harper and Row, 1985.
Lincoln, Andrew T. *Ephesians*. Word Biblical Commentary 42. Dallas: Word, 1990.
Lindbeck, George A. *The Nature of Doctrine*. Philadelphia: Westminster, 1984.
Lohfink, Norbert. *The Covenant Never Revoked*. Translated by John J. Scullion, S.J. New York: Paulist, 1991.
Lustiger, Jean-Marie Cardinal. *Cardinal Jean-Marie Lustiger On Christians and Jews*. Edited by Jean Duchesne. New York: Paulist, 2010.
———. *The Promise*. Translated by Rebecca Howell Balinski et al. Grand Rapids: Eerdmans, 2007.
Marshall, Bruce D. "Elder Brothers: John Paul II's Teaching on the Jewish People as a Question to the Church." In *John Paul II and the Jewish People*, edited by David G. Dalin and Matthew Levering, 113–29. New York: Sheed and Ward, 2008.
Matt, Daniel. *Zohar*. Ramsey, NJ: Paulist, 1983.
McRay, John. *Paul: His Life and Teaching*. Grand Rapids: Baker, 2003.
Mendes-Flohr, Paul. "Law and Sacrament: Ritual Observance in Twentieth-Century Jewish Thought." In *Jewish Spirituality from the Sixteenth Century Revival to the Present*, edited by Arthur Green, 317–45. New York: Crossroad, 1997.
Meyer, Lester V. "Remnant." In *Anchor Bible Dictionary, Volume 5*, edited by David Noel Freedman, 669–71. New York: Doubleday, 1992.
Milgron, Jacob. *Leviticus 17–22*. Anchor Bible Commentary. New York: Doubleday, 2000.
Mussner, Franz. *Tractate on the Jews: The Significance of Judaism for Christian Faith*. Translated by Leonard Swidler. Philadelphia: Fortress, 1984.
Neuhaus, Richard John. "Salvation is from the Jews." In *Jews and Christians: People of God*, edited by Carl E. Braaten and Robert W. Jenson, 65–77. Grand Rapids: Eerdmans, 2003.
Neusner, Jacob. *The Incarnation of God*. Atlanta: Scholars, 1992.
———. *The Mishnah: A New Translation*. New Haven: Yale University Press, 1988.
———. *A Short History of Judaism: Three Meals, Three Epochs*. Minneapolis: Fortress, 1992.
Norris, Thomas J. "The Jewish People at Vatican II: The Drama of a Development in Ecclesiology and Its Subsequent Reception in Ireland and Britain." In *Christ Jesus and the Jewish People Today: New Explorations of Theological Interrelationships*, edited by Philip A. Cunningham et al., 251–67. Grand Rapids: Eerdmans, 2011.

O'Donaghue, Neil Xavier. "The Shape of the History of the Eucharist." *New Blackfriars* 92.1037 (2011) 71–83.
Painter, John. *Just James*. Minneapolis: Fortress, 1999.
Pannenberg, Wolfhart. *Systematic Theology, Volume 3*. Translated by Geoffrey W. Bromiley. Grand Rapids: Eerdmans, 1998.
Pitre, Brant. *Jesus and the Jewish Roots of the Eucharist: Unlocking the Secrets of the Last Supper*. New York: Doubleday, 2011.
Rashi (Rabbi Shlomo ben Yitzchak). *Rashi: Shemos/Exodus*. Translated by Rabbi Israel Isser Zvi Herczeg. Brooklyn: Mesorah, 1995.
Riegner, Gerhart M. "Preface." In *Church and Jewish People: New Considerations*, by Johannes Cardinal Willebrands, ix–xvi. New York: Paulist, 1992.
Rudolph, David, and Joel Willitts, eds. *Introduction to Messianic Judaism: Its Ecclesial Context and Biblical Foundations*. Grand Rapids: Zondervan, 2013.
Rutishauser, Christian, S.J."'The Old Unrevoked Covenant' and 'Salvation for All Nations in Christ': Catholic Doctrines in Contradiction?" In *Christ Jesus and the Jewish People Today: New Explorations of Theological Interrelationships*, edited by Philip A. Cunningham et al., 229–50. Grand Rapids: Eerdmans, 2011.
Sacks, Jonathan. *The Koren Siddur*. Jerusalem: Koren, 2009.
Saadia Gaon. *Book of Beliefs and Opinions*. Translated by Samuel Rosenblatt. New Haven: Yale University Press, 1948.
Schaff, Philip, and Henry Wace, eds. *The Seven Ecumenical Councils. Nicene and Post-Nicene Fathers of the Christian Church, Second Series, Volume XIV*. Reprint. Grand Rapids: Eerdmans, 1983.
Skarsaune, Oskar. *In the Shadow of the Temple*. Downers Grove, IL: IVP Academic, 2002.
Schoeman, Roy H. *Salvation is from the Jews*. San Francisco: Ignatius, 2003.
Scholem, Gershom. *Kabbalah*. Jerusalem: Keter, 1974.
———. *On the Kabbalah and Its Symbolism*. New York: Schocken, 1965.
———. *On the Mystical Shape of the Godhead*. New York: Schocken,1991.
Schönborn, Christoph Cardinal. "Judaism's Way to Salvation." *The Tablet*, March 29, 2008. Online: http://archive.thetablet.co.uk/article/29th-march-2008/8/judaisms-way-to-salvation.
Sforno, Ovadia. *Sforno: Commentary on the Torah*. Translated by Rabbi Raphael Pelcovitz. Brooklyn: Mesorah, 1997.
Slater, Thomas. Review of *Ephesians: A Commentary* by Stephen E. Fowl. *Review of Biblical Literature* (July 2014). Online: http://www.bookreviews.org/pdf/8910_9815.pdf.
Smith, Dennis E. "Meals." In *The Eerdmans Dictionary of Early Judaism*, edited by John J. Collins and Daniel C. Harlow, 924–26. Grand Rapids: Eerdmans, 2010.
Soulen, R. Kendall. *The God of Israel and Christian Theology*. Minneapolis: Fortress, 1996.
Stern, David H. *Jewish New Testament*. Jerusalem: Jewish New Testament, 1989.
———. *The Jewish New Testament Commentary*. Jerusalem: Jewish New Testament, 1992.
———. *Messianic Jewish Manifesto*. Jerusalem: Jewish New Testament, 1991.
Symposium on Jewish-Christians and the Torah. *Modern Theology* 11.2 (1995).
Tomson, Peter J. *Paul and the Jewish Law*. Minneapolis: Fortress, 1990.

Torrance, Thomas F. *The Christian Doctrine of God: One Being Three Persons*. Edinburgh: T. & T. Clark, 1996.

———. *The Mediation of Christ*. Colorado Springs: Helmers and Howard, 1992.

———. *Theology in Reconciliation*. Reprint. Eugene, OR: Wipf & Stock, 1996.

Vall, Gregory. "'Man Is the Land': The Sacramentality of the Land of Israel." In *John Paul II and the Jewish People*, edited by David G. Dalin and Matthew Levering, 131–67. New York: Rowman and Littlefield, 2008.

Van de Sandt, Huub, and David Flusser. *The Didache: Its Jewish Sources and its Place in Early Judaism and Christianity*. Compedia Rerum Iudaicarum ad Novum Testamentum. Minneapolis: Fortress, 2002.

"The Vatican: The Pope's Powerful No. 2." *Time*, March 14, 1969. Online: http://content.time.com/time/magazine/article/0,9171,839846,00.html#ixzz2sSW2dVEN)

Willebrands, Johannes Cardinal. *Church and Jewish People: New Considerations*. New York: Paulist, 1992.

Williamson, Peter, and Kevin Perrotta, eds. *Christianity Confronts Modernity: A Theological and Pastoral Inquiry by Protestant Evangelicals and Roman Catholics*. Ann Arbor, MI: Servant, 1981.

Wilken, Robert Louis. *The Spirit of Early Christian Thought: Seeking the Face of God*. New Haven: Yale University Press, 2003.

Wright, N.T. *The Climax of the Covenant*. Minneapolis: Fortress, 1991.

———. *Jesus and the Victory of God*. London: SPCK, 1996.

———. *The New Testament and the People of God*. London: SPCK, 1992.

Wyschogrod, Michael. *Abraham's Promise: Judaism and Jewish-Christian Relations*. Grand Rapids: Eerdmans, 2004.

———. *The Body of Faith*. Northvale, NJ: Aronson, 1996.

Yee, Tet-Lim N. *Jews, Gentiles and Ethnic Reconciliation: Paul's Jewish Identity and Ephesians*. Cambridge: Cambridge University Press, 2005.

Yoder, John Howard. *The Jewish-Christian Schism Revisited*. Grand Rapids: Eerdmans, 2003.

Yoder Neufeld, Thomas R. *Ephesians*. Believers Church Bible Commentary. Scottdale, PA: Herald, 2002.

Zizioulas, John. *Being as Communion*. Crestwood, NY: St. Vladimir's Seminary Press, 1985.

Name Index

A

Aaron, 64, 113, 188
Abraham, 13, 49, 53, 63, 72, 89, 97, 126, 148, 154, 156, 156n19, 186, 211
Adam, 81
Adam, Karl, 2
Amos, 209, 209n9
Ananias, High Priest, 212
Andronicus, the Apostle, 202
Aquinas, Thomas, 28, 53n16, 122, 122n23, 151, 151n8, 152, 179n11
Arius, 236
Arndt, William F., 228n11
Augustine, 122

B

Bader-Saye, Scott, 121, 121n20, 122, 122n21–23, 123n24
Bailey, Sarah Pulliam, 33n8
Baker, John A., 201n2
Barnabas, 202, 206, 208
Barth, Karl, 66n9, 67, 67n10, 72n18, 74n22, 91n6, 121–22, 122n21
Bauckham, Richard, 85, 85n32–33
Baum, Gregory, 17
Beasley-Murray, G. R., 97n11
Benedict XVI, Pope, 11, 11n23–24, 12, 13, 114n9, 116, 117n12, 118–19, 119n14–15, 138n18, 163n36, 165, 181n16

Benelli, Giovanni Cardinal, 25–26, 26n1, 27, 31
Birnbaum, Philip, 136n14
Bloch, Renee, 17
Bouyer, Louis, 31, 107n1, 138, 138n16–18, 139, 143, 145n25, 201n2
Braun, Michael A., 209n9
Brotman, Manny, 34n10
Buber, Martin, 150n3

C

Caligula, 207
Cavnar, Jim, 29
Cephas, 206
Chalcedon, 217
Charlemagne, 205
Chernoff, David, 34n10
Christ Jesus. *see* Jesus Christ
Clark, Steve, 26, 29, 30, 31, 33–34, 35
Connelly, John, 1n1, 2n3–4, 16, 17, 17n38, 22n49
Constantine, 222
Cornelius, 134, 135, 205, 206, 211
Cottier, Georges Cardinal, 36, 36n14, 37, 177
Cunningham, Philip, 165, 165n42, 166, 187
Cyril of Alexandria, 91

D

Dan, Joseph, 162n34

247

NAME INDEX

Daniel, 133–34, 230, 231
Daniélou, Jean Cardinal, 31, 201n2
David, King, 13, 64, 64n5, 65, 87, 115
Demaan, Paul, 17
Di Sante, Carmine, 201n2
Dunn, James D. G., 142n22

E

Eisenbaum, Pamela, 151n7
Elijah, 92, 95
Epiphanius, 222
Eusebius, 86, 86n34
Evans, Mike, 34n10
Ezekiel, 79, 93, 94, 94n8–9, 102–3, 230, 231

F

Felix, Governor, 212
Ferguson, Everett, 91n2–3
Fichtenbauer, Johannes, 32, 36, 37
Flusser, David, 138n17
Fowl, Stephen, 82n27
Francis of Assisi, 28
Fredriksen, Paula, 144, 144n24
Friedman, Elias, 173n1, 179–80n12, 180n15

G

Gannon, Ray, 34n10
Garrigues, Jean-Miguel, 37, 37n15, 88n36, 149n1, 198–215, 201n3
Goble, Phil, 34n10
God's Son. *see* Jesus Christ
Greenberg, Irving, 185n19
Gregerman, Adam, 188, 188n25
Gringrich, F. Wilbur, 228n11
Gunton, Colin, 54n17–19, 234n22

H

Halevi, Yehudah, 231
Harrington, Daniel J., 142n23

Hart, David Bentley, 112n5
Hegesippus, 85, 86, 211
Henrix, Hans Hermann, 11–13, 11n22, 12n25–26, 13n27, 165–166, 166n43
Herberg, Will, 23, 23n53–54
Herod, King, 13
Heschel, Abraham Joshua, 161, 161n31, 161n33, 162
Hildebrand, Dietrich von, 16
Hillel, 87
Hocken, Peter, 32, 32n6, 34, 36, 37
Hoffman, Lawrence, 132, 132n8–9
Hurtado, Larry W., 227n9
Hussar, Bruno, 17

I

Irenaeus of Lyons, 87, 207, 207n7–8, 234n22
Isaac, 53, 97, 148, 154, 156n20
Isaiah, 13–14, 79, 92, 96, 110, 118, 130, 230, 231

J

Jacob, 53, 55, 56, 103, 148, 154, 156n20, 211
James, Brother of Jesus, 48, 85–86, 202, 204, 205, 208–14, 209n9, 214
James, son of Zebedee, 110–12, 118, 123, 124
Jeremiah, 79, 94n9, 116
Jeremias, Joachim, 107n1, 114n10, 139, 139n19–20
Jerome, 222
Jesus Christ, 2–3, 8–9, 11–13, 15–24, 25–26, 28–29, 31–33, 38, 42–45, 46–60, 53n16, 63–67, 63n4, 64n5, 65n6, 69–73, 71n17, 75–92, 77n26, 91–92n7, 91n6, 95–101, 97n11, 98n13, 99n15, 102–125, 112n6, 112n8, 114n10, 128–29, 136–37, 139–51, 151n9, 158n23, 162–65, 165–71,

173–78, 181, 183–85, 187, 189, 191–92, 193–97, 198–204, 206–7, 209–11, 213–14, 216–19, 221, 223, 226–28, 228–30, 233–34n22, 233–35, 235n24, 236–39
Joel, 91
John, the Apostle, 11, 90, 110, 111, 112, 112n7, 118, 119, 123, 124, 134, 135, 204, 205, 208, 212, 228
John, the Baptist, 90, 91, 91–92n7, 92–96, 94n9, 99, 100, 110, 134, 189, 228
John Paul II, Pope, 1, 5–8, 5n12, 6n13–14, 7n17, 8n18–19, 9, 10–11, 13, 14, 24, 25, 36, 36n14, 38, 46n9, 49, 50, 50n13, 51, 57, 148n30, 157–58n23, 165, 172, 173–74, 173n2, 174n4, 176–77, 176n5, 177n6–7, 177n8, 179, 181n16, 189
Johnson, Luke Timothy, 66n9, 72n18, 73n21, 77n25
John XXIII, Pope, 1, 8, 24, 25, 27
Joseph, 97, 174
Joshua, 87, 157, 164
Journet, Charles, 173n1
Judah, 64
Jungmann, Josef Andreas, 138–39n18
Junias, 202
Juster, Daniel, 34–35
Juster, David, 36, 234n23

K

Kadushin, Max, 150n4–5, 151n6, 159, 159n28, 160, 160n29
Kasper, Walter Cardinal, 11n21, 180n13
Katz, Art, 34n10
Kellner, Menachem, 153n13
Kelly, J. N. D., 225n7, 229n16, 235n24

Kinzer, Mark S., 23, 23n51, 25–39, 28n2, 33n7, 35n13, 38n17, 40n1, 90n1, 148n30, 151n10, 166n44, 169, 182n18, 186n23, 198n1, 216–239
Klawans, Jonathan, 144n24
Kraus, Annie, 17

L

Leah, 53, 148, 154
Leihart, Peter J., 163–64n39
Levenson, Jon, 137–38, 138n15, 155–56, 155n16, 156n17
Levering, Matthew, 40n1, 53n16, 140, 141n21
Levi, Joshua ben, 137
Levine, Baruch A., 129n1
Levy, Antoine, 182, 182n18
Liberman, Paul, 34n10
Lincoln, Andrew T., 66n8
Lindbeck, George, 225, 225n6
Lohfink, Norbert, 50n13, 116, 116n11, 117, 117n13
Luke, 96, 109, 111, 114, 115, 124–25, 124n25, 204
Luria, Isaac, 162
Lustiger, Jean-Marie Cardinal, 12–16, 14n28–30, 15n32–34, 16–17, 16n35–37, 17, 19–20, 20n45–48, 23–24, 25, 38, 39, 39n18, 51, 52–53, 52n14–15, 57, 57n22, 91–92n7, 94n9, 97, 97n12, 98n13, 100, 100n16, 101n17, 163n37–38, 164, 166, 166n45, 167, 167n46–47, 167n48, 169n49, 174, 175, 181n16, 188, 189, 189n26

M

Maimonides, 231
Malachi, 94, 95
Maritain, Jacques, 173n1
Maritain, Raissa, 17

NAME INDEX

Mark, 109, 109n4, 111, 113, 118, 124, 206
Marshall, Bruce, 173, 173n1, 173n3
Martin, Francis, 32n4
Martin, Ralph, 29, 31, 33–34, 35
Mary, mother of Jesus, 2–3, 42, 43, 48, 55–56, 58, 69, 97, 189, 191, 210, 228, 234
Matt, Daniel, 232
Matthew, 24, 92, 93, 94, 96, 109, 109n4, 111, 113, 119, 120, 124, 125
Matthias, 205
McRay, John, 66n9, 67, 67n10, 68n12, 72, 72n19, 74n22, 84n30
Melchizedek, 63–64, 156
Mendes-Flohr, Paul, 161n31
Messiah. *see* Jesus Christ
Meyer, Lester V., 83n28
Milgrom, Jacob, 157, 157n21–22
Miriam. *see* Mary, mother of Jesus
Moses, 63, 87, 108, 113, 116, 131, 153, 155, 158, 191, 230
Mussner, Franz, 68–69, 68n15, 75

N

Nathanael, 103
Nero, 207
Neuhaus, David, 182
Neuhaus, Richard John, 6, 6n16, 47n9
Neusner, Jacob, 131n6, 145, 145n26, 146, 146n27–29, 146n29, 230n17
Nicodemus, 102–103
Nixon, Richard President, 26n1
Norris, Thomas J., 4n6, 40n2

O

O'Donaghue, Neil Xaier, 138n18
Oesterreicher, John, 4n9, 16, 17, 40

P

Painter, John, 86n35
Pannenberg, Wolfhart, 48–49, 49, 49n11, 120, 120n19
Paul, 3, 17, 22n49, 23, 24, 45, 48, 58, 70, 72, 73n21, 80, 81–82, 82n27, 83, 84, 85, 100, 112n7, 114, 115, 139, 143, 144, 167, 191, 198–200, 202, 204–7, 208–14, 227n10
Paul VI, Pope, 26n1, 31, 191n1
Perotta, Kevin, 32n5
Peter, 31, 48, 111, 134, 135, 202, 204–7, 208–14
Pitre, Brant, 107–8, 107n2–3
Plotinus, 232
Pollefyt, Dieder, 165, 165n42, 166, 187
Pontius Pilate, 234

Q

Quinn, Charles Underhill, 201n2

R

Rachel, 53, 148, 154
Rashi (Rabbi Shlomo ben Yitzchak), 63, 63n3, 70
Ratzinger, Joseph Cardinal, 114
Rauch, Gerry, 29
Rebecca, 53, 148, 154
Riegner, Gerhart, 22n49
Rosen, Moishe, 34n10
Rosenzweig, Franz, 161n31
Rudloff, Leo, 17
Rutishauser, Christian, S. J., 18–20, 18n40, 19n42–44, 180n13

S

Saadia Gaon, 231n18, 236
Sacks, Jonathan, 136n13, 156n18
Saint Ambrose, 55–56
Sarah, 53, 148, 154
Schaff, Philip, 222n2–3
Schism, 46–47n9

Schmidt, Wilhelm Father, 2n3
Schoeman, Roy H., 173n1
Scholem, Gershom, 158n27, 231, 231n19, 232n21
Schönborn, Christoph Cardinal, 36, 37, 72n18, 180–81, 180n14
Sforno, Ovadia, 62–63, 63n2
Shammai, 87
Silvanus, 206
Simeon, 85, 211
Skarsaune, Oskar, 228n14–16
Slater, Thomas, 66n7
Smith, Dennis E., 142n22
Solomon, 130, 133, 203
Son of Abraham. see Jesus Christ
Son of David. see Jesus Christ
Son of God. see Jesus Christ
Son of Mary. see Jesus Christ
Soulen, Kendall, 224, 224n4
Stern, David H., 34, 34n9, 34n11, 234n23
Stone, Haskell, 33
Suenens, Leo Joseph Cardinal, 30–31
Sullivan, Leo, 27
Synan, Vincent, 33

T

Theime, Karl, 17
Timothy, 202
Tomson, Peter J., 84n29
Torrance, Thomas, 22, 22n50, 40, 40n3, 41, 41n4, 44n8, 47, 91, 91n6, 98–99, 98n14, 99n15, 151n9, 234n22

V

Vall, Gregory, 158n23, 162–63, 163n35
Van de Sandt, Hubb, 138n17
Vermes, Geza, 17
Vetö, Miklos, 188, 189
Virgin, The. see Mary, mother of Jesus

W

Wace, Henry, 222n2–3
Waldman, Marty, 35, 36
Weinandy, Thomas, 32n4
Wilken, Robert Louis, 91n3
Willebrands, Johannes Cardinal, 4n10, 5n11, 9–10, 10n20, 18n40, 59, 59n23
Williamson, Peter, 32n5
Wojtyla, Karol Cardinal, 1–2
Wright, N. T., 14n31, 23, 23n52, 94n10, 119–120, 120n17–18
Wyschogrod, Michael, 154, 154n15, 185–86, 186n21–22

Y

Yee, Tet-Lim N., 66n9, 68n13, 73n20, 74n22, 77n24
Yeshua. see Jesus Christ
Yoder, John Howard, 46n9
Yoder Neufeld, Thomas R., 66n9, 67, 67n11, 72n18, 74n22, 76n23

Z

Zebedee, sons of, 109
Zechariah, 134
Zizioulas, John, 233–34n22

Scripture Index

TANAKH (HEBREW BIBLE)

Genesis

2	153
14	64
14:18	156
22:2	97
23:4	205
24:5–6	156n20
28:10–17	156n20
28:11–12	103
32:24–32	156n20
49:8–12	112n5

Exodus

3:5	153, 158n25
3:12	153
3:13–15	158n25
3:22	153
3:23	153
4:22	70
4:22–23	14, 97
13:2	153
15:13	156
15:17	156–57
15:17a	157n21
19:5–6	63
19:6	62, 151n7
19:22	71n16
20:11	156n19
21:1	76n23
22:30	161n30
23:12	156n19
24	124
24:5–8	113
24:7	116
24:9–11	113
24:18	63n2
24:40	113
25:8	154
25–31	63
28:1	62
28:29	113
29:8	75
29:38–42	131
29:39	137
31:12–17	155
31:13–14	155
31:18	63n2–3
32	63
32:29	62
33:16	154
35:1–3	155
40:12–15	75

Leviticus

2:1–16	135
9:8	75
9:22–24	129
9:24	134
10:5	75

17–18	177–78	8:48	130

Leviticus (*continued*)

18:24–30	157
20:3	158n24, 158n26
22:2	158n24, 158n26
22:32	158n24, 158n26
26:3	161

Numbers

3:11–13	62
6:22–27	129
6:24–26	132, 135
6:27	129
8:9–10	75
10:10	136
15:37–41	131
15:38–41	160
19	94n8
26:52–56	156n19
28:2–8	131
28:4	137
28–29	136

Deuteronomy

	94n9, 98
3:20	156n19
4:21	156n19
4:38	156n19
6:4–9	131, 131n2
7:6	69
11:13–21	131
12:5–7	141–42
12:10	156n19
12:11–12	141–42
12:18	141–42
16:18—18:22	54
25:19	156n19

1 Kings

4:7–8	203
8:10	135
8:22	130
8:28–30	130

2 Kings

1:8	92

Isaiah

	13
25:6–8	142
29:23	158n24
40:1–11	92
40–55	118
41:8	96
42:1	96
42:6	214
44:1–3	96
49:3	96
49:6	214
51:17	111
52:7	92
52–53	111
53	96, 97, 124
53:11–12	110, 118–19
56:7	130
57:19	75
59:21	48
65:17	47
66:22	47
66:23	192n8

Jeremiah

	94n9
31	114–17, 125
31:31–32	45, 48
31:31–34	114–15
31:33	117
31:34	119
31:35–37	115

Ezekiel

	94n9
1:1–5	154
1:26	230–31
10:18–22	154
11:22–25	154
36	96, 125
36:20–23	158n24, 158n26

36:24–28	93–94, 102
36:25	104
36–37	102–3, 104
37:14	102
39:7	158n24
43:7	158n24
43:7–9	158n26

Hosea 11:1 — 97

Joel

1:15—2:3	92
2:28	91

Amos

2:7	158n24
5:18–20	92
9:11–12	209
9:13–15	112n5

Zephaniah

1	92
3:9	192

Zechariah

9:16–17	112n5
14:8–9	152
14:20–21	152

Malachi

3	96
3:1–4	94
3:2–3	95
4:1	95
4:5–6	92, 95

Psalms

2:7	228
33:21	158n24
39:13	205
78:54	157n21
103:1	158n24
105:3	158n24
106:47	158n24
110:1	64–65
110:2	64
110:4	64
114:1–2	154
134:1	135
141:2	130
145:21	158n24

Proverbs 8:22–31 — 228n14

Daniel

6:10	130, 133, 134
7:9	203, 231
7:22	203
9:21	134n11

Ezra 9:5 — 134n11

1 Chronicles

15:16–22	129
16:4–5	129
16:10	158n24
16:35	158n24
22:9	155
29:16	158n24

2 Chronicles

5:11–14	129
7:4–6	129

DEUTEROCANONICAL BOOKS

Wisdom of Solomon 7:26 — 228n15

Judith 9:1 — 134n11

NEW TESTAMENT

Matthew

1:1	87
1:3, 5, 6	24
1:16	87
2	13–14
2:2	53
3	92, 100
3:1–6	92
3:7–10	92
3:10	93
3:11–12	93
3:12	93
3:13–15	95–96
3:16–17	96
3:17	14
4	97
4:5	166
5:17	195
5:17–19	166
5:35	166
10:2	202, 203
11:10	94
11:14	95
14:17	123
16:17	206
16:18	204, 213
16:21	140
19:16–30	125
19:28	81, 101–2, 123, 203
20:17–19	109
20:20–28	109, 123
22:1–14	143
22:30	87
23:23	166
23:34–39	112n8
23:39	168
24:20	166
26:20	123
26:20–30	109n4
26:28	119–20
26:29	111
26:42	111, 116
27:11	53
27:29	53
27:37	53
28:10	91n6
28:18–20	204
28:19	90
28:20	213

Mark

1:2	94
1:4	93
3:14	202
3:21	210
4:41	217
6:3	208
7:24–30	124n25
8:29	217
10	112
10:32–34	109
10:35–45	109, 110, 123
10:38–39	118
10:39	112
10:45	118
12:1–11	112n8
12:35–37	64n5
14:3–9	124n25
14:17–26	109n4
14:25	111
14:32–35	111
14:39	111
16:15	204

Luke

1:5	131n5
1:8	131n5
1:17	95
2:1	77n26
2:32	60
3:22	228n12
4:38–39	124n25
6:13	202
7:36–50	124n25

8:1–3	124n25	11:50–52	119
10:38–42	124n25	13:1–17	118
12:49–50	96	14:20	174
13:28	143	15:4–5	174
15:22–24	142	15:27	202
19:44	192n5	16:13	201
22:14	123	17:5	228
22:14–38	109n4	17:20–21	175
22:15–16	125	19:6	192n9
22:17–18	111	20:17	214
22:20	114	20:24–28	48
22:24–27	109, 118, 124	20:28	235
22:28–29	203	21:15–17	204
22:28–30	81, 125		
22:30	142	**Acts**	134–35
22:32	204	1:4	147–48
23:56	166	1:11	213
24:13–32	48	1:14	210
24:30–31	143	1:15	205
24:35	143	1:21–22	210
24:40	48	2:14	205
24:47	204	2:15	77n26, 135n12
		2:33	96
John		2:38	99
1:1	11	2:43–45	212
1:1–5	228	2:46	143, 145
1:14	228	3:1	134
1:18	228	3:11–12	205
1:47	103	3:19–21	58
1:49	103	4:7–13	205
1:51	103	4:36	202
2:1–11	112n5	5:27–32	205
3	102, 123	9:13	198
3:3	101, 102	10:3	134
3:3–5	90	10:4	136
3:5	101, 102	10:14	206n4
3:9	102	10:30	134n11
3:10	102	10:47	99–100
3:12	102	10:48	205
3:16	228	11:3	211
4:9	228	11:29–30	212
6:46	228	12:17	205, 208
7:1–4	210	13:31	202
10:16	214	13:33	228, 228n13

Acts (continued)

13:47	214
15	167, 177
15:1	211
15:5	208, 211
15:7–11	206
15:7–29	208
15:10	209
15:11	209
15:13–17	209
15:19	208
15:28–29	206
17:7	77n26
18:18	212
19:21	206
20:7	143, 144–45
20:11	143
21:18	211
21:20	166, 211
21:20–24	166
21:21	212
21:23–24	212
21:24	212
23	206–7
23:1–5	48
23:11	207
24:11	166
24:17–18	212
26:17–18	199

Romans 17, 23, 62, 82–86, 87

1	74
1:1	202
1:3	24, 85–86, 211
1–3	73
1:3–4	65
1:17—3:20	73n21
1:18	73n21
2:2	73n21
2:3	73n21
3:22–24	200
6:1–11	90
6:3–4	99
8:5	24
8:11	96
8:17	112n7
9:4	70
9:4–5	85, 191, 211
9–11	18, 83
10:9	217
10:12	200
11: 28–29	3, 46
11	83
11:1	83
11:5	214
11:5–7	83
11:11–32	192n8
11:12	58
11:13	200
11:14	199
11:15	58, 83, 201
11:16	83, 84, 167, 207
11:17–24	148, 191n3, 198
11:18	201
11:20–26	58
11:25	58
11:25–27	167
11:28	192n6
11:28–29	167, 192n7
11:29	180, 195, 213
11:33	214–15
11:36	214–15
15:8	199
15:9	199
15:15–16	84, 85
15:20	206
15:24	206
15:25–26	84
15:25–27	84–85, 212
15:26	198, 212
16:7	202

1 Corinthians

7:18	166
8:5–6	226–28, 230
9:1	202
10:1	200

10:4	68, 164
10:14–21	143–44
10:18	24, 45, 211
11	144–45
11:20–22	143
11:23–25	109n4, 139
11:23–26	143
11:25	114
11:26	139, 203
11:33–34	143
12:3	217
12:13	99–100
15:3	202
15:5	202
15:6	202
15:7	202, 210
15:8	205
15:9	205
15:28	58, 203
16:1	84

2 Corinthians

1:5	112n7
4:10–11	112n7
8:4	84
9:1	84
9:12–13	213
10:15–16	206
12	84

Galatians

1:1	202
1:15–16	205–6
1:16	202, 206
1:17	206
1:18	202
1:18–19	208
1:18–21	206
1:19	85, 202, 208, 210
2:7–9	205
2:8	205, 206, 213, 214
2:9	208
2:10	212
2:11	205, 206
2:12	206, 208, 211
2:13	206
2:14	206
2:15–16	209
3:7	191n2
3:26–28	200
5:6	212

Ephesians

	62, 87
1:3	78
1–3	65–66, 66n9, 67, 68, 69–73, 74, 81–82
1:3–8a	69
1:3–14	67, 72, 75
1:4	72, 73, 79
1:5	70, 71, 72
1:6	72
1:8	73
1:10	72, 80
1:11–12	71
1:11–13	200
1:11–14	72, 72n18
1:12	72, 73, 75
1:13	72, 72–73
1:13–14	71
1:15	79
1:15–23	67, 72
1:17	73
1:18	73
1:20	78
1:20–23	73
2	73–79, 80
2:1–2	73, 73n21
2:1–3	74
2:1–10	67
2:1–11	73
2:3	73, 75
2:4–6	74
2:5	74
2:6	74, 78
2:7	71
2:7–8a	70

Ephesians (continued)

2:8b–10	70–71
2:11	200
2:11–12	74, 79
2:11–13	67
2:11–22	66–69, 70, 72, 74, 80
2:12	67, 68, 71, 74–75, 167, 199
2:13	70, 74, 75, 77, 78
2:14	67, 77
2:14–16	74, 75–76, 76n23, 78, 191n4
2:14–17	18
2:15	78, 81, 200
2:16	70, 200
2:17	67, 69, 70, 75
2:17–18	77–78
2:18	67, 70, 78, 200
2:19	67, 68, 199
2:19–22	67, 74, 78
2:20	79
2:21–22	67
3	79–81
3:1	67
3:1–6	80
3:1–13	67
3:5	79
3:5–6	66
3:6	80, 199
3:12	78
3:14–19	67, 81
3:20–21	67
4:4–6	175–176
4:11	79
4:13	58, 176
4:24	48

Philippians

2:11	217
3:10	112n7

Colossians

1:12	199
1:24	112n7
2:12	99
3:10	48

1 Timothy

4:14	202

2 Timothy

1:6	202

Titus

3:5	99–100, 101

Hebrews

	62, 87
1:3	223, 228n15
1:5	228
1:13	65
7:4–10	63
7:13–14	63, 64
7:15–16	64
7:16	63–64
10:12–14	65
11:1—12:2	112n8

James

1:1	211
1:18	84

1 Peter

1:1	205
2:11	205
4:16	205
5:12–13	206
5:13	205, 207

Revelation

6:9–11	112n7
7:4	203
7:9	203
11:7–8	112n7
12:10–11	112n7
17–18	207
20:4	203

21:1	47
21:9–27	152
21:12	203
21:14	203

DEAD SEA SCROLLS

1 QS 6.4–5	142n23
1 QSa 2.17–22	142, 142n23
Berachot	
26b	135
27b	137
Pirke Avot 1	87

RABBINIC LITERATURE

m. Taanit 4:2	133
m. Tamid 4:1–2	131
m. Tamid 4:3	131
m. Tamid 5:1	131
m. Avot 1	87
b. Berachot 26b	135
b. Berachot 27b	137
Leviticus Rabbah 35:3	161
Saadia Gaon	230–31

GREEK AND LATIN WORKS

Augustine	122
Clement	
Letter to the Corinthians 5:3–5	
	207n6
Didache	138n17
Eusebius	
Ecclesiastical History	18, 86
Ignatius of Antioch	
Ephesians 18:2	90n2
Iranaeus	
Adversus haereses, III,3,2	207n7–8

Thomas Aquinas	
Summa Theologica Vol. 2	151, 152
Summa Theologica Vol. 4	53n16, 122, 122n23

AUTHORITATIVE CATHOLIC DOCUMENTS

Catechism of the Catholic Church

63	49, 57
528	50–51
612	112n6
674	58
748–975	51
753	52
774	151
774–75	150
839	49n12, 50
840	50
1090	152
1130	152
1131	150
1213	89
1374	121
1377	121
1536	65
1536–53	61
1541	63n4
1544	63n4
1544–45	61
1547	62
1552–3	62
1575	204n4
1577	204n4

Gaudiun et spes (Pastoral Constitution of the Church in the Modern World)

22	52, 52n15

Lumen Gentium (The Dogmatic Constitution of the Church)

1	157–158n23
2	43
2–4	42–43
3	4n7
7	41
8	42n5
9	7, 44, 45–47, 57, 58–59
9–17	10, 42, 43
10–11	42n6
10–13	42
10–16	53–54
12	42n6
13–16	42n6
16	3, 10, 46, 50, 59, 104
18–29	43
19–21	43n7
21	42, 42n6
22	43n7
25–27	42, 42n6
34–36	42, 42n6
48	41
52–69	43
53	55
55	56
63	55
65	56

Nostra Aetate (Declaration on the Relation of the Church to Non-Christian Religions)

1	6
2	6
3	6
4	1–9, 10–11, 14, 16, 18, 21–22, 23, 38, 39, 41, 50, 51, 57, 59, 172–73

www.ingramcontent.com/pod-product-compliance
Lightning Source LLC
Chambersburg PA
CBHW030613230426
43661CB00053B/1970